DEFIANT CHIEFS

THE AMERICAN STORY

DEFIANT CHIEFS

by the Editors of Time-Life Books, Alexandria, Virginia

CONTENTS

THE ROOTS OF DEFIANCE

Tecumseh, chief of the Shawnees, arrived with 80 followers on August 15, 1810, to confer with Governor William Henry Harrison of the Indiana Territory at his spacious Grouseland Estate, along the Wabash River. Harrison's residence, with its columned portico for councils, had an air of permanence that Tecumseh must have found unsettling. For until recently, this part of Indiana had been just what the territory's name implied—Indian country, reserved for the Shawnees and other tribes by treaty in 1795.

Harrison had since undermined that accord by purchasing 70 million acres of land west of the state of Ohio for the American government from chiefs who represented only a small part of the native population living there, prompting Tecumseh to form an alliance of tribes to oppose the land deals. The chief came to Grouseland in peace, but he was not about to entrust his safety to the federal troops guarding the site. In the heat of summer his followers wore blankets, under which they harbored knives, clubs, and tomahawks.

Harrison planned to receive the visitors on the portico, but Tecumseh, a tall, imposing man in his early forties, refused to set foot there. "I do not care to talk with a roof above us," he declared. So Harrison agreed to meet with him on the lawn, assuring him that it was the wish "of your great father in Washington that you be shown every courtesy."

"My father?" Tecumseh responded, refusing to recognize that term for the president. He gestured to the sky and said, "The sun is my father; the earth is my mother, who nourishes me, and on her bosom I will recline." Exuding conviction, Tecumseh spoke eloquently of the ties that bound tribes to the land. No chief had a right to sell territory, he insisted: "Sell a country! Why not sell the air, the clouds, and the great sea, as well?"

After two days of fruitless talks, Harrison ventured to the chief's camp, outside the estate, for one last parley. Tecumseh promised to make peace if President James Madison would agree to give up the disputed land and make no more treaties "without the consent of all the tribes." Harrison offered to relay those terms, but warned that the president would never accept them. Tecumseh could only hope that the Great Spirit would put some sense in the head of the "great white chief" in Washington, who was perhaps too far away to feel the consequences. "He may sit in town and drink his wine," Tecumseh told Harrison, "while you and I will have to fight it out."

Those words proved to be sadly prophetic. The 37-year-old Harrison, an accomplished army officer before he became governor, soon embarked on a devastating campaign against the chief and his allies that cost Tecumseh his life in 1813. Afterward, the dejected Shawnee people were driven west across the Mississippi River and had to compete with other exiled tribes for a homeland. Harrison, for his part, won renown as an Indian fighter and served the nation briefly as president before his death in 1841.

Tecumseh's defeat did not bode well for other tribal leaders devoted to their homelands. Whites now far outnumbered Indians, and warriors who attacked land-hungry settlers risked fierce reprisals by the army. Nor were tribes spared assaults if they cooperated with the intruders. In the eastern woodlands groups like the Cherokees had long been in contact with whites and had adopted many of their customs, but even they came under relentless pressure to abandon homelands guaranteed them by treaty.

Besieged by white settlers and troops, tribal leaders faced an agonizing choice—submit to the intruders and try to salvage something in the way of territory, or defy them and risk losing everything. Some chiefs who cherished their homeland, like Major Ridge of the Cherokees, relinquished their territory under duress and accepted removal to a strange and distant country, thus antagonizing fellow tribesmen who held their ground to the bitter end. Other leaders, like Quanah Parker of the Comanches, fought desperately until their followers faced annihilation, at which point they surrendered and helped reconcile their people to reservation life. Elsewhere, chiefs of legendary resolve, like Sitting Bull of the Lakota Sioux and Geronimo of the Apaches, opposed white authorities with such tenacity that they remained symbols of resistance even in defeat.

Whatever path they chose, these leaders sought to uphold the traditions of their people. Like Tecumseh they owed allegiance not to the Great Father in Washington but to the Great Spirit above and to other ancestral powers, who brought their people blessings and infused them with a deep devotion to their homeland *(pages 8-15)*. In time these defiant bands would become part of the nation that subjugated them. Yet as Native Americans and as members of distinct tribal communities, they retained a powerful sense of sovereignty, reinforced by compelling stories of past chiefs and their unyielding determination.

IN PRAISE OF THE HOMELANDS

SHORES OF LAKE SUPERIOR, HOME OF THE OJIBWA ▶
OJIBWA WARRIOR ▼

"Father, do you ask how we possess this land? It is well known that
4,000 years have passed since the creator first placed us here...from the time
that our ancestors thus obtained it, it has been truly deemed ours.
This land where lie the bones of our ancestors is ours. We have never sold it, nor
has it been taken from us by conquest, or by any other means."

PEAU DE CHAT

"The Hopi Tusqua is our love and will always be, and it is the land upon which our leader
fixes and tells the dates for our religious life. Our land, our religion, and our life are one....It is from
the land that each true Hopi gathers the rocks, the plants, the different woods, roots, and his life,
and each in the authority of his rightful obligations brings our ceremony proof of our ties to
this land. Our footprints mark well the trail to these sacred places."

ELDERS OF SHONGOPOVI

"Look at me and look at the earth. Which is the oldest, do you think? The earth, and I was born on it....
It does not belong to us alone; it was our fathers' and should be our children's after us.
When I received it, it was all in one piece, and so I hold it. If the white men take my country, where can I go?
I have nowhere to go. I cannot spare it, and I love it very much. Let us alone."

CHIEF SITTING BULL

"*We had hoped the white men would not be willing to travel beyond the mountains;*
now that hope is gone. They have passed the mountains, and have settled upon Cherokee land....
Finally, the whole country, which the Cherokees and their fathers have so long occupied, will be demanded
and the remnant of the Ani Yunweya, the Real People, once so great and formidable
will be compelled to seek refuge in some distant wilderness."

DRAGGING CANOE

ᏣᎳᎩ ᏧᎴᎯᏌᏅᎯ.

CHEROKEE PHOENIX.

VOL. I. NEW ECHOTA, THURSDAY FEBRUARY 21, 1828. **NO. 1.**

EDITED BY ELIAS BOUDINOTT.

PRINTED WEEKLY BY

ISAAC H. HARRIS,
FOR THE CHEROKEE NATION.

At $2 50 if paid in advance, $3 in six months, or $3 50 if paid at the end of the year.

To subscribers who can read only the Cherokee language the price will be $2,00 in advance, or $2,50 to be paid within the year.

Every subscription will be considered as continued unless subscribers give notice to the contrary before the commencement of a new year.

The Phoenix will be printed on a Super Royal sheet, with type entirely new procured for the purpose. Any person procuring six subscribers, and becoming responsible for the payment, shall receive a seventh gratis.

Advertisements will be inserted at seventy-five cents per square for the first insertion, and thirty-seven and a half cents for each continuance; longer ones in proportion.

☞ All letters addressed to the Editor, post paid, will receive due attention.

A GOOD CONSCIENCE.

WHAT is there, in all the pomp of the world, the enjoyments of luxury, the gratification of ambition, comparable to the tranquil delight of a good conscience? It is the health of the mind. It is a sweet perfume, that diffuses its fragrance over every thing near it without exhausting its store. Unaccompanied with this, the gay pleasures of the world are like brilliants to a diseased eye, music to a deaf ear, wine in an ardent fever, or dainties in the languor of an ague. To lie down on the pillow, after a day spent in temperance in beneficence, and piety, how sweet is it! How different from the state of him, who reclines, at an unnatural hour, with his blood inflamed, his head throbbing with wine and gluttony, his heart aching with rancorous malice, his thoughts totally estranged from Him who has protected him in the day, and will watch over him, ungrateful as he is, in the night season! A good conscience is, indeed, the peace of God.

Christian Philosophy.

Flattery.—Few things are more universally condemned than flattery; yet there are few men, who are above its influence, and still fewer, who have courage sufficient to repel it with a faithful rebuke. The following anecdote is recommended, as affording a specimen of a good answer to flatterers. A certain clergyman in New England, eminent both for talents and humility, was one day accosted by a parishioner, who highly commended some of his performances, of which the clergyman himself had a very low opinion. After patiently hearing him a few moments, the clergyman replied; "My Friend, if that you say gives me no better opinion of myself than I had before, but gives me a worse opinion of you."

CONSTITUTION OF THE CHEROKEE NATION,

Formed by a Convention of Delegates from the several Districts, at New Echota, July 1827.

WE, THE REPRESENTATIVES of the people of the CHEROKEE NATION in Convention assembled, in order to establish justice, ensure tranquility, promote our common welfare, and secure to ourselves and our posterity the blessings of liberty; acknowledging with humility and gratitude the goodness of the sovereign Ruler of the Universe, in offering us an opportunity so favorable to the design, and imploring his aid and direction in its accomplishment, do ordain and establish this Constitution for the Government of the Cherokee Nation.

ARTICLE I.

Sec. 1. THE BOUNDARIES of this nation, embracing the lands solemnly guaranteed and reserved forever to the Cherokee Nation by the Treaties concluded with the United States, are as follows; and shall forever hereafter remain unalterably the same—to wit—Beginning on the North Bank of Tennessee River at the upper part of the Chickasaw old fields; thence along the main channel of said river, including all the islands therein, to the mouth of the Hiwassee river, thence up the main channel of said river, including Islands, to the first hill which closes in on said river, about two miles above Hiwassee old Town; thence along the ridge which divides the waters of the Hiwassee and little Telico, to the Tennessee river at Tallassee; thence along the main channel, including Islands, to the junction of the Cowee and Nanteyalee; thence along the ridge in the fork of said river, to the top of the blue ridge; thence along the blue ridge to the Unicoy Turnpike road; thence by a straight line to the main source of the Chestatee; thence along its main channel, including Islands, to the Chattahoochy; and thence down the same to the Creek boundary at Buzzard Roost; thence along the boundary line which separates this and the Creek Nation, to a point on the Coosa river opposite the mouth of Wills Creek; thence down along the South bank of the same to a point opposite to Fort Strother; thence up the river to the mouth of Wills Creek; thence up along the East bank of said creek, to the West branch thereof, and up the same to its source; and thence along the ridge which separates the Tombecbee and Tennessee waters, to a point on the North top of said ridge; thence due North to Camp Coffee on Tennessee river, which is opposite the Chickasaw Island; and thence to the place of beginning.

Sec. 2. The Sovereignty and Jurisdiction of this Government shall extend over the Country within the boundaries above described, and the lands therein are, and shall remain, the common property of the Nation; but the improvements made thereon, and in the possession of the citizens of the Nation, are the exclusive and indefeasible property of the citizens respectively who made, or may rightfully be in possession of them; *Provided,* That the citizens of the Nation, possessing exclusive and indefeasible right to their respective improvements, as expressed in this article, shall possess no right nor power to dispose of their improvements in any manner whatever to the United States, individual States, nor to individual citizens thereof; and that, whenever any such citizen or citizens shall remove with their effects out of the limits of this Nation, and become citizens of any other Government, all their rights and privileges as citizens of this Nation shall cease; *Provided nevertheless,* That the Legislature shall have power to re-admit by law to all the rights of citizenship, any such person or persons, who may at any time desire to return to the Nation on their memorializing the General Council for such

---

readmission. *Moreover,* the Legislature shall have power to adopt such laws and regulations, as its wisdom may deem expedient and proper, to prevent the citizens from monopolizing improvements with the view of speculation.

ARTICLE II.

Sec. 1. THE POWER of this Government shall be divided into three distinct departments;—the Legislative, the Executive, and the Judicial.

Sec. 2. No person or persons, belonging to one of these Departments, shall exercise any of the powers properly belonging to either of the others, except in the cases hereinafter expressly directed or permitted.

ARTICLE III.

Sec. 1. THE LEGISLATIVE POWER shall be vested in two distinct branches; a Committee, and a Council; each to have a negative on the other, and both to be styled, the General Council of the Cherokee Nation; and the style of their acts and laws shall be,

"Resolved by the Committee and Council in General Council convened."

Sec. 2. The Cherokee Nation, as laid off into eight Districts, shall so remain.

Sec. 3. The Committee shall consist of two members from each District, and the Council shall consist of three members from each District, to be chosen by the qualified electors of their respective Districts for two years; and the elections to be held in every District on the first Monday in August for the year 1828, and every succeeding two years thereafter; and the General Council shall be held once a year, to be convened on the second Monday of October in each year, at New Echota.

Sec. 4. No person shall be eligible to a seat in the General Council, but a free Cherokee Male citizen, who shall have attained to the age of twenty-five years. The descendants of Cherokee men by all free women, except the African race, whose parents may be or have been living together as man and wife, according to the customs and laws of this Nation, shall be entitled to all the rights and privileges of this Nation, as well as the posterity of Cherokee women by all free men. No person who is of negro or mulatto parentage, either by the father or mother side, shall be eligible to hold any office of profit, honor or trust, under this Government.

Sec. 5. The Electors, and members of the the General Council shall, in all cases except those of treason, felony, or breach of the peace, be privileged from arrest during their attendance at election, and at the General Council, and in going to, and returning from, the same.

Sec. 6. In all elections by the people, the electors shall vote *viva voce.* Electors for members to the General Council for 1828, shall be held at the places of holding the several courts, and at the other two precincts in each District which are designated by the law under which the members of this Convention were elected; and the District Judges shall superintend the elections within the precincts of their respective Court Houses, and the Marshals & Sheriffs shall superintend within the precincts which may be assigned them by the Circuit Judges of their respective Districts, together with one other person, who shall be appointed by the Circuit Judges for each precinct within their respective Districts; and the Circuit Judges shall also appoint a clerk to each precinct.—The superintendents and clerks shall, on the Wednesday morning succeeding the election, assemble at their respective Court Houses and proceed to examine and ascertain the true state of the polls, and shall issue to each member, duly elected, a certificate; and also make an official return of the state of the polls of election to the principal Chief, and it shall be the du-

CHAPTER 1

TRIALS OF THE CHEROKEE NATION

"You can live on your lands in Georgia if you choose, but I cannot interfere with the laws of that state to protect you."

PRESIDENT ANDREW JACKSON TO A CHEROKEE DELEGATION, 1831

Three elegantly dressed men strode purposefully up Pennsylvania Avenue in Washington, D.C., on a sultry July day in 1831 and presented themselves at the White House for an interview with President Andrew Jackson. Two of the callers, John Ridge and William Coodey, were eager youths in their twenties; the third, Richard Taylor, was a solemn-faced older gentleman carrying a slender silver pipe. With their stylish apparel and rich southern accents, they bore a passing resemblance to the eager office seekers from Jackson's native Tennessee who had paid court to the president since his inauguration two years before. But these men were southerners of a different breed—Cherokees whose tribal ancestors had lived in and around the Great Smoky Mountains for centuries before the first white traders arrived there in the early 1700s and intermingled with them. Proud citizens of their own Indian nation, they wanted nothing more from Jackson than what had already been promised to them by federal treaty: the right to occupy the remnants of their southeastern homeland without further interference or intrusions.

The Cherokees were not the first Indian delegation to appear at the White House. Jackson's predecessors had often invited tribal chiefs to Washington,

hoping that they would be duly impressed by the cavernous buildings and the crowds in the streets and would recognize the futility of defying the powerful Americans. But the Cherokees differed from many earlier Indian visitors to the capital in that they were partly of white ancestry and understood Anglo-American terms. The delegates knew what to expect in the capital and were not overawed. John Ridge in particular was well prepared to serve as an ambassador to Washington. A leading member of the Cherokee ruling council at the age of 27, schooled by missionaries and fluent in English, he was poised, perceptive, and eloquent. When he and his colleagues walked into the White House and confronted Andrew Jackson, they held their heads high.

The 64-year-old president, with his gaunt frame, shock of silver hair, and blazing blue eyes, made an imposing figure. Never short of confidence, he was all the more assured on this occasion because he had the Cherokees at a disadvantage. That very morning, John Marshall, chief justice of the United States, had dismissed a case brought by lawyers for the Cherokees against the state of Georgia, which had summarily asserted its authority over much of the Cherokee homeland in 1828, shortly after Jackson was elected president. Although sympathetic to the Cherokees, Justice Marshall ruled that, contrary to their claim, they did not constitute a foreign nation as defined in the Constitution and thus had no legal basis for challenging Georgia's authority in the Supreme Court. Marshall's decision pleased Jackson, who favored the removal of the Cherokees and other eastern Indians from their fertile homelands—long coveted by white settlers—to less desirable territory west of the Mississippi River.

Jackson, with a bluntness characteristic of his frontier heritage, made no attempt to smooth over his differences with the visiting Cherokees. "I'm particularly glad to see you at this time," he declared. "I knew that your claims before the Supreme Court would not be supported. The Court has sustained my views in regard to your nation." Then he chided his visitors for trusting in lawyers, who never missed a chance to prolong a case. "I have been a lawyer myself long enough," he confided with a gruff attempt at humor, "to know how lawyers will talk to obtain their clients' money."

John Ridge was not amused by the sally. Shorter than Jackson and slender of build, he was a handsome man with light brown skin, close-cropped, curling black hair, and dark eyes that sparkled with determination. "We don't believe you would blame the Cherokees for their efforts to maintain their rights before the proper tribunals," he remarked intently to the president.

"Oh, no," replied Jackson, "I don't blame you for that. I only blame you for suffering the lawyers to fleece you." During his celebrated career as a general, he added, Cherokees had fought bravely alongside him: "How could I be otherwise than their friend?"

Ridge then took issue with the Supreme Court ruling, but Jackson promptly veered onto another topic, reminiscing about the Catawbas, a southeastern tribe who had once been so powerful that they had inflicted more than a few defeats on their hard-fighting Cherokee rivals in earlier times. Since then, prolonged contact with whites had rendered the Catawbas "poor and miserable and reduced in num-

A leading proponent of his people's rights, Major Ridge *(below)* combined the attributes of a southern planter and a traditional Cherokee warrior.

"Let us hold fast to the country which we yet retain. Let us direct our efforts to agriculture, and to the increase of wealth, and to the promotion of knowledge."

MAJOR RIDGE

bers," Jackson observed, "and such will be the condition of the Cherokees if they remain surrounded by the white people."

The moral of Jackson's brief history lesson was clear: The Cherokees should bow to pressure and exchange their cherished homeland in the Southeast for territory in the West, where they would presumably be free of white people and their baneful influences. John Ridge had heard such arguments for removal before, but like most of his fellow Cherokees, he remained skeptical of the idea. If the country beyond the Mississippi was worth having, he wondered, why did land-hungry American settlers not desire it for themselves?

Before Ridge could voice any such objection to Jackson, however, a congressional representative from Georgia was announced. The visitors rose rapidly to their feet. There was no one they wished less to see at the moment than a Georgia politician.

Jackson shook the hand of each Cherokee delegate politely in parting. Yet his closing words to them were chilling: "You can live on your lands in Georgia if you choose, but I cannot interfere with the laws of that state to protect you."

Jackson's refusal to intervene in the dispute was disheartening to many Cherokees, but it came as a particular affront to John Ridge. For no Cherokee had done more to help Jackson win renown in battle than John Ridge's own father, known to Cherokees as Kah-hung-da-cla-geh, or the Man Who Walks on the Mountaintop. Referred to in English simply as the Ridge, he took the name Major Ridge after he earned that rank for supporting then-General Jackson against hostile Indians during the War of 1812. Major Ridge was a firm friend of the Americans in peacetime as well. A prosperous planter with a passion for education, he and his son John tirelessly promoted democracy and the rule of law among their people, trusting that the United States would in turn respect the Cherokee Nation and honor its sovereignty.

Whites had long been encroaching on the Cherokee homeland when Ridge was born in 1771 to a woman of mixed Cherokee and Scottish parentage and her full-blooded Cherokee husband. They made their home in the tribal village of Hiwassee, situated in what is now Polk County, Tennessee, west of the Great Smokies near the Georgia border. One of Ridge's earliest memories was of being hurried into a dugout canoe one morning when he was five years old and paddling down the chill waters of the Hiwassee River. Behind him white troops burned the village to the ground. The year was 1776 and the soldiers were Americans, retaliating for raids that summer by Cherokee warriors allied with the British against the rebellious colonists. The Cherokees had hoped to drive out the Americans, who were intruding on their settlements and hunting grounds. But the colonists struck back with a fury, destroying more than 50 Cherokee villages in all.

Young Ridge and his kin found refuge to the west, away from the hostile settlers. There he enjoyed a childhood not unlike that of his Cherokee ancestors. Game remained plentiful in the back-woods and clearings of Tennessee, and the boy joined his father and other male elders on fishing expeditions and on hunts for wild turkey, deer, bear, and the occasional buffalo, still to be found in small numbers between the crest of the Appalachians and the banks of the Mississippi.

His mother was vital to the boy's upbringing as well. From her he inherited membership in the Deer Clan, one of seven Cherokee clans that were organized matrilineally, meaning that both sons and daughters joined their mother's group. A similar clan system prevailed among the Iroquois of New York, to whom the Cherokees were distantly related in culture and language. Traditionally Cherokee women not only figured prominently in clan affairs but also advised the men serving as village chiefs and helped sustain the community by cultivating corn and other crops, which made up much of the diet. Thanks to abundant harvests, Cherokees did not have to move from place to place in search of game. Long before they encountered Europeans they were living a settled life in villages of thatch-covered lodges, grouped by clan around a broad plaza that

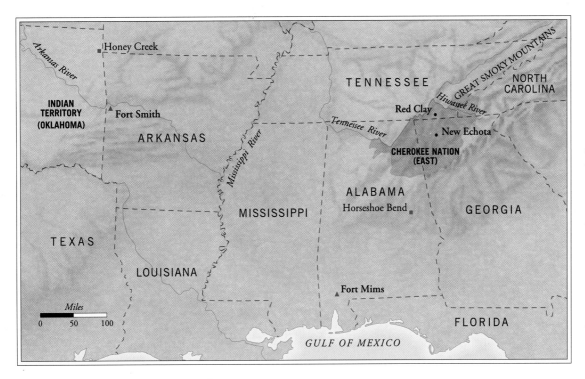

By the 1820s the Cherokee homeland had been reduced to the area shown on the map at left. Much of that area was claimed by the state of Georgia. To satisfy the demands of land-hungry settlers from Georgia and other states, American officials pressured Cherokees and neighboring tribal groups like the Creeks to emigrate to the Indian Territory *(far left)*.

served the community for meetings, dances, and other rousing ceremonies.

The Cherokee homeland in the early days of European contact encompassed much of what is now Kentucky and Tennessee, the western reaches of Virginia and the Carolinas, and northern Georgia and Alabama. Villagers farmed the lush valleys of the western Appalachian foothills, fished the clear rivers that tumbled down from the heights, and hunted avidly in the dense deciduous forest, afire in autumn with reds and golds. Originally each Cherokee village was largely independent, but during the 18th century chiefs of the various settlements began meeting in council to coordinate their policies in relation to the British and to neighboring tribes such as the Creeks, who occupied much of lower Alabama and Georgia. Cherokees came to think of themselves collectively as a nation and impressed

Located about halfway between the White House and the Capitol, Jesse Brown's Indian Queen Hotel *(center)* housed Cherokee delegates and other tribal representatives on their many missions to Washington. Jesse Brown, touted as the "prince of landlords," greeted his arriving guests at curbside. He charged $1.25 per day for room and board.

visitors with their statesmanship. American naturalist William Bartram, who traveled among them in the late 1700s, described them as "grave and steady; dignified and circumspect in their deportment . . . tenacious of their liberties and natural rights of men; . . . deliberate and determined in their councils; honest, just and liberal."

By the time of the American Revolution, years of contact with Europeans had brought about significant changes in the traditional Cherokee way of life. Whites like Ridge's Scottish grandfather had provided the villagers with firearms to augment the bow and arrow, metal pots to replace clay vessels, and shirts and dresses of cotton and wool to supplement traditional garments of tanned hide and fur. Already some Cherokees were emulating white settlers by building log cabins, cultivating wheat and fruit trees as well as corn, and raising pigs and other livestock. Most

Cherokees traded readily with whites, and more than a few intermarried with them, acquiring family names such as Vann, Lowrey, and Ross. But whatever their appearance or way of life, all those who claimed any Cherokee ancestry were accepted as Cherokees and were prepared to support and defend their tribal homeland. Young men who were partly white identified wholeheartedly with the Cherokee cause and did not hesitate to make war on the intruding colonists.

Although the Americans achieved victory over the British in 1783, it took them much longer to stifle resistance among the Cherokees and other defiant Indians along the Appalachian frontier. In 1788, at the age of 17, Ridge painted his face for battle and joined a band of warriors who were challenging American settlers and troops. He was already tall,

for his stirring oratory. Not long after peace was restored he was chosen to represent his village at the Cherokee Council. There he spoke out against the so-called Blood Law, an ancient tribal custom that called for any killing, whether deliberate or accidental, to be avenged by a kinsman of the deceased, who could claim the life of one of the murderer's relatives if the culprit himself fled. Ridge was not against wreaking vengeance on guilty parties, but he deplored the killing of innocents and the feuding that resulted. Through his persuasion, the Blood Law was repealed in council.

Ridge owed much to his wife Sehoya, later known by her English name of Susanna. Described by an acquaintance as a "handsome and sensible girl," she was steeped in Cherokee traditions but

"The Cherokees in their disposition and manner are grave and steady; dignified and circumspect in their deportment;...deliberate and determined in their councils; honest, just and liberal, and are ready always to sacrifice every pleasure and gratification, even their blood, and life itself, to defend their territory and maintain their rights."

NATURALIST WILLIAM BARTRAM, VISITING THE CHEROKEES IN THE LATE 1700S

broad-shouldered, and impressive, and in the years to come he proved himself as an *outacite*, or "man-killer," a term of honor among Cherokees for those who claimed enemy lives.

Finally, in 1794, devastating American attacks on Cherokee villages forced the warriors to lay down their arms and accept the terms of a treaty negotiated earlier between Cherokee leaders and President George Washington. The pact reduced their territory but solemnly guaranteed the sanctity of their remaining homeland "for all time." One chief expressed the fervent hopes of his people at the close of hostilities: "Our tears are wiped away, and we rejoice in the prospect of our future welfare, under the protection of Congress." Ridge returned home, convinced that Cherokees must henceforth remain at peace with the powerful Americans.

In the years that followed he won recognition among Cherokees both for his sound judgment and

proved receptive to new ideas. Sometime after their marriage the young couple left the small Cherokee community of Pine Log and settled along the fertile banks of the Oostanaula River, near present-day Rome, Georgia. Susanna cultivated cotton as well as corn and learned to spin and weave while her husband, forsaking the pursuit of game that was growing increasingly scarce as white settlers intruded, raised horses, hogs, and cattle.

They soon prospered and acquired black slaves, as did other wealthy Cherokees of the day. With the help of their slaves, the couple built up an impressive estate. Their original log cabin was superseded by an elegant two-story house with four brick fireplaces and verandas in front and back looking out over apple and peach orchards that expanded to contain more than 1,500 trees. Susanna bore four surviving children, including John, who was born in 1803. Among the Cherokees who joined Ridge and Susanna in the lush valley was Ridge's brother, Oowatie, who took to using Watie as a European-style surname for himself and his family.

The success of the Cherokees made their domain all the more attractive to white settlers, and American agents stopped at nothing to induce Cherokee chiefs to cede territory. An intemperate leader named Doublehead, who served as speaker of the Cherokee Council, infuriated many of his people by signing away large tracts of their land in exchange for special considerations that amounted to bribes. In 1807 chiefs met in his absence and condemned Doublehead to death for his transgressions. Ridge was among three men chosen to carry out the deed. More than willing to do away with a chief he deemed a traitor, he confronted Doublehead in a tavern in Tennessee, shot him through the jaw, and left him for dead, only to discover afterward that the chief had survived the attack and was being cared for at the tavernkeeper's house. A short time later Ridge and a fellow executioner forced their way into Doublehead's room. They grappled with the wounded chief, who resisted mightily until Ridge's confederate buried a battle-ax deep in his skull.

The execution of Doublehead did not bring an end to the dubious land deals. Federal authorities now had a fresh inducement for Cherokees inclined to surrender their holdings—the promise of a new home in what would become known as the Indian Territory, part of that vast area west of the Mississippi River obtained in 1803 from France through the Louisiana Purchase. In 1808 Indian agent Return Jonathan Meigs quietly traveled through Cherokee lands, offering the more susceptible Cherokee chiefs money and guns in exchange for their pledge to move west. He even managed to win over the principal chief, Black Fox, who dictated a message to be delivered by Cherokee emissaries to President Thomas Jefferson: "Tell our Great Father, the President, that our game has disappeared, and we wish to follow it to the West. We are his friends, and we hope he will grant our petition, which is to remove our people towards the setting sun. But we shall give up a fine country, fertile in soil, abounding in watercourses, and well adapted for the residence of white people. For all this we must have a good price."

When Black Fox presented this message to the Cherokee Council and asked the delegates to endorse it, Ridge rose to his feet in anger. "My friends," he declared, "you have heard the talk of the principal chief. He points to the region of the setting sun as the future habitation of this people. As a man he has a right to give his opinion, but the opinion he has given as the chief of this nation is not binding; it was not formed in council in the light of day, but was made up in a corner—to drag this people, without their consent, from their own country, to the dark land of the setting sun." Ridge challenged his fellow chiefs at the council, which operated by consensus, to assert their will and preserve their land: "What are your heads placed on your bodies for, but to think, and if to think, why should you not be consulted? I scorn this movement of a few men to unsettle the nation and trifle with our attachment to the land of our forefathers!"

Ridge's forceful words swayed the council and thwarted Black Fox. To the chief's disgrace, the council declined to endorse his prepared message and instead sent an uncommitted delegation to Washington to meet with President Jefferson. Ridge was among the party that rode the red-clay roads to the capital. There they thanked the author of the Declaration of Independence through an interpreter for "his protecting and fostering hand, under which they progressed in agriculture and domestic manufactures much beyond their own expectations or the expectations of their white Brethren of the United States." Between whites and Cherokees, they added, "the great Spirit has made no difference, except in the tint of their skins."

Such words echoed Jefferson's public declarations that Indians had the innate capacity to live peaceful and productive lives and should be encouraged to do so. Privately Jefferson saw little future in the populous East for even the Cherokee Nation or any of the other Indian groups that whites considered to be civi-

A COSTLY COUP FOR THE RED STICKS

On August 30, 1813, 1,000 militant Creeks known as Red Sticks attacked an ill-defended stockade in present-day Alabama called Fort Mims, where rival Creeks with close ties to the Americans had taken refuge with some white troops and settlers and their black slaves. The massacre, portrayed above by 19th-century artist Alonzo Chappel, sent shock waves across the South and drew Major Ridge and other Cherokees into a retaliatory campaign.

The roots of the conflict went back to 1811, when the Shawnee chief Tecumseh visited the Creeks and encouraged them to defend their native land and traditions against white incursions. Tecumseh's gospel soon spread to Cherokees, alarming Major Ridge, who favored cooperation with the Americans. "My friends, the talk you have heard is not good," he warned Cherokees in 1812. "It would lead us to war with the United States, and we should suffer."

Such a fate befell the Red Sticks, named for their painted war clubs. They were opposed by the White Sticks, Creeks who backed the United States. By the summer of 1813, White Sticks were allied with American settlers against the Red Sticks, who saw a chance to deal their twin foes a crushing blow at Fort Mims.

The American commander there dismissed warnings from two black slaves, who ventured out briefly on August 30 to round up some cattle and saw Indians creeping toward the fort through tall grass. At noon the Red Sticks raised their battle cry and poured through the open gate, overwhelming the troops. The attackers took many of the blacks captive but killed most of the settlers and White Sticks. After the massacre Ridge affirmed his commitment to the United States by joining with General Andrew Jackson against the Red Sticks, who would pay dearly for the attack on Fort Mims.

lized. The president hoped that Cherokees would soon accept removal to the Indian Territory, but he tactfully refrained from pressing the delegation on that point and instead encouraged the Cherokees to emulate the democratic institutions of the United States. It was advice that they would take to heart in the years to come. After the delegation returned home, a small group of Cherokees led by a brother-in-law of Doublehead chose to give up their land and move west to the Indian Territory, perhaps because they feared that their ties to Doublehead would make them the target of his executioners. But except for this handful of emigrants, the rest of the nation held firm.

With one crisis averted, Ridge resumed the tranquil life of a planter. Soon, however, a new threat arose on the Cherokee borders. As tensions increased between the United States and Britain on the eve of the War of 1812, many Indians along the frontier saw an opportunity to defy the distracted Americans and put an end to their incursions.

A number of tribes to the north joined the influential Shawnee chief Tecumseh in an alliance with the British against the United States. But even tribes to the south with few ties to the British harbored growing opposition to American settlers and their ways. After Tecumseh visited the Creeks in Georgia and Alabama, for example, prophets, or medicine men, inspired by his visit urged their followers to return to their ancestral traditions and spurn the whites. Some of the prophets declared that a great change was at hand, and when a comet streaked across the sky that fall, some took it as an omen confirming the prophecy. In December a tremendous earthquake centered on the lower Mississippi River convulsed the countryside for hundreds of miles around—yet another portent, people said, of the impending crisis.

In this time of upheaval, a rift opened among the Creeks between militant traditionalists, known as Red Sticks for their crimson war clubs, and an opposing faction, sometimes referred to as White Sticks, who favored accommodation with the Americans. After skirmishes between the two sides in 1813, the Red Sticks attacked White Sticks holed up with American settlers and troops at Fort Mims in Alabama and overran the stockade, slaughtering hundreds of men, women, and children. Afterward, the White Sticks appealed for help both to the United States and to the Cherokee Nation.

At the Cherokee Council that September, Ridge called for volunteers to join him against the Red Sticks. He warned that if Cherokees failed to take sides after the carnage at Fort Mims, angry Americans would recognize no distinctions among Indians. All of them, regardless of nation, tribe, or clan, would be punished for the hostile actions of a few. Ridge argued further that if the Red Sticks prevailed, everything that the Cherokees had done to achieve civilization on their own terms would be imperiled.

Hundreds of Cherokee warriors answered Ridge's call. Ridge and his recruits soon joined forces with General Andrew Jackson when he descended from Tennessee into Alabama with 5,000 troops and embarked on a bloody campaign against the Red Sticks that culminated explosively at a sharp curve in the Tallapoosa River called Horseshoe Bend.

The morning of March 27, 1814, amid the booming of field guns and the rattle of musketry, Major Ridge, recently granted that honorary rank by his American allies for his service against the Creeks, rode to the bank of the Tallapoosa at Horseshoe Bend with a contingent of Cherokee warriors looking for a chance to strike at the enemy. Across the water, 1,000 intransigent Creeks—men, women, and children from six Red Stick villages overrun in the recent fighting—had taken refuge on high ground within the bend. They were nearly encircled by the protective waters of the twisting Tallapoosa. Only by traversing a narrow neck of land on the far side of the encampment from where Ridge was stationed could attackers reach the Red Sticks without crossing the river in boats under sharp fire, and the Creeks had raised up stout breastworks of earth-covered logs across that neck.

The prospect was one that might have discouraged a less resourceful band of fighters than Ridge and his recruits; after all, they were not under orders to cross the river and challenge the well-armed Creeks. General Jackson had attached them to the command of his subordinate, General John Coffee, who was assigned to wait across from the encampment while Jackson's main force assaulted the breastworks on the far bank after a preliminary bombardment by artillery. The Cherokees and Coffee's American troops were there to deal with any Creeks who tried to flee across the water when Jackson's men breached the breastworks and overran the Red Stick stronghold.

Major Ridge was not hard to spot amid Coffee's forces. A big man, his wide shoulders thrown back, he wore two feathers in his headband with a deer tail hanging down behind—insignia meant to distin-

an advance guard that held their ground on the far shore until the entire force of several hundred Cherokees had paddled over, wave after wave.

To meet this new threat from across the river, the Creeks had to divert warriors from the breastworks, even as Jackson's main force stepped up the pressure from the other side. Finally, the weary defenders at the breastworks gave way, and American troops swarmed over the barricade, driving the desperate Creeks back toward the river. Some were scythed down by Ridge and his men, who wielded swords and knives at close quarters. Others eluded the Cherokees and swam across the river, only to be caught in murderous volleys unleashed by Coffee's waiting troops. In the bloody melee no distinction

> *"My friends, you have heard the talk of the principal chief. He points to the region of the setting sun as the future habitation of this people....What are your heads placed on your bodies for, but to think, and if to think, why should you not be consulted? I scorn this movement of a few men to unsettle the nation and trifle with our attachment to the land of our forefathers!"*
>
> MAJOR RIDGE ADDRESSING THE CHEROKEE COUNCIL, 1808

guish the Cherokees from hostile Indians in close fighting. By late morning Ridge and his men had grown weary of waiting for the Creeks to come to them. For two hours the American field guns had pounded the breastworks to little effect, and Jackson's infantry had failed to break through. The Creeks, inspired by the songs and prayers of their prophets, were determined not to surrender. But the Cherokees saw an opportunity to attack the Creeks from the rear. Ridge and his men had no boats of their own in which to cross the river, but they could see the empty canoes of the Red Sticks beached on the far bank, just asking to be taken.

Three of Ridge's strongest men plunged into the cold water and swam across under protective fire. One of them, a stout Cherokee called Whale, was wounded on the far shore and returned empty-handed, but his two companions each made it back to the near bank with a canoe. Those canoes were used to retrieve more, and Ridge then crossed with

was made between warriors and their wives or children. By Jackson's tally fewer than 100 of the 1,000 Creeks escaped alive that day—a toll that dwarfed even the slaughter at Fort Mims.

Major Ridge had waged many hard battles, but this was something new and sobering for him. In the past, Cherokees had sometimes been attacked in their villages by whites or by rival Indians and had assaulted enemy settlements in return. Ridge had never witnessed a massacre like this, however; it was a stark demonstration of the tremendous armed might the Americans could unleash against any Indians who chose to oppose them.

He also had to reckon with the fact that his Cherokees had paid a high price for the victory compared with the much larger American force, accounting for 18 of 55 men killed on Jackson's side and 36 of 146 wounded. "The Cherokee warriors have fought and bled freely," Indian agent Meigs wrote in his report on the battle, "and according to

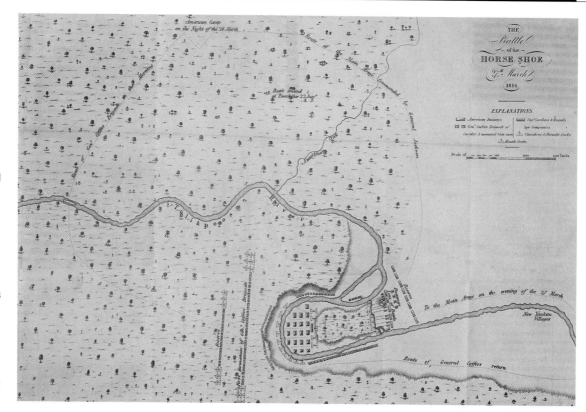

This map of Horseshoe Bend on Alabama's Tallapoosa River, drawn after the March 1814 battle there, shows the Red Stick encampment inside the bend. When General Jackson's main force *(dotted line at right)* stalled at the breastworks the Red Sticks had built across the bend's neck, Cherokee warriors on the far side of the river with General John Coffee's forces *(parallel lines at center)* crossed in canoes seized from the Red Sticks and mounted an attack that helped Jackson break through.

their numbers have lost more men than any part of the Army." But the glory went to Jackson and the white frontiersmen who had signed up to fight under him, including two young men who would make their mark as politicians in Tennessee, Sam Houston and Davy Crockett.

The Cherokees felt that they had earned the gratitude of the Americans. Yet on their weary way home from the battle, they encountered bitter evidence to the contrary: White volunteers from Tennessee returning home after their enlistment terms expired had ravaged Cherokee farms along the way, killing livestock and stealing food, supplies, and clothing from the residents. Ridge and his colleagues sought compensation from General Jackson. But despite corroboration from such independent witnesses as Davy Crockett, Jackson maintained that the Cherokee claims of looting were a "complete tissue of groundless falsehood."

Major Ridge and his people faced even deeper disappointments in the years to come. Buoyed by

General Jackson's defeat of the British at New Orleans in 1815 and his subsequent campaign against defiant Seminole Indians in Florida that had helped to wrest that territory from Spanish control, the Americans embarked on a fresh round of treaty making in the Southeast aimed at securing more Indian land for white settlers. The devastated Creeks were forced to make major concessions. And even the Cherokees, who had shed blood on behalf of the United States, were pressured anew to cede territory and move west.

Cherokee chiefs managed to avoid removal, but only by submitting in 1819 to a new federal treaty that stripped them of close to 6,000 square miles—nearly one-fourth of their territory. What remained to them lay largely within boundaries claimed by the state of Georgia under an agreement it had made with the federal government in 1802. In the agreement the federal government had promised that it would eventually extinguish all Indian title to land in the state of Georgia. That dubious promise, made without the knowledge or consent of the Cherokees, had not been fulfilled by the federal government, and Georgia's supposed claim on Cherokee land had languished. The Treaty of 1819 contained no mention of such a claim. To the contrary, it reconfirmed the territorial rights of the Cherokees and guaranteed their homeland permanently against intrusions. At the same time, no steps were taken to invalidate the 1802 compact.

Despite the loss of Cherokee land under the treaty and the threat that Georgia might take action on the old compact some day, Major Ridge remained optimistic about the future. He was determined that the Cherokees would not cede any more territory, and he believed that education would give them the capacity to hold their own against the expansion-minded Americans. He had high expectations for his children—in particular, his son John, whom he envisioned as a new kind of leader for his people. To be sure, Major Ridge was an intelligent, articulate man who commanded the respect of the Cherokee Nation. And yet on one score he felt inadequate: He had not mastered the white man's language. His English was halting, and he used a translator when speaking to whites. And, like many other Cherokees, he could not read. His illiteracy forced him to rely on others when he was negotiating the written terms of a treaty.

Major Ridge had already taken steps to ensure that John would labor under no such handicaps. In 1817, despite the misgivings of his wife, who wanted to keep her children close to home, he had enrolled John and his sister Nancy as boarders at the Brainerd School in Tennessee, where missionaries instructed young Cherokees in reading, writing, and other fundamentals. John was such a gifted student that he soon learned all that Brainerd had to teach him. So in 1818, when he was barely 15, his father sent him off to a more rigorous academy—the Foreign Mission School in Cornwall, Connecticut. It accepted students from around the world and offered them an education that combined religious and vocational instruction with classes in history, literature, and the sciences. There John would live and study with his cousin, Buck Watie, and a few other Cherokee students. It was a demanding and fateful venture, one that shaped John's destiny in ways that his proud father could scarcely have foreseen.

Many hopes rested on the slim shoulders of young Ridge. Physically he would never be as strong as his father. A chronic inflammation of the hip made it difficult for him to walk without crutches. Although no one would have mistaken him for a warrior in the traditional mold, his journey to Cornwall was not unlike those undertaken by Cherokee youths in the past, who went off to prove themselves in battle. Like them, John Ridge had to demonstrate courage and composure in alien surroundings.

After several weeks on the road, traveling on horseback and stopping in crowded taverns and hostelries, John and his companions arrived at Cornwall in November. Back in their homeland, autumn lingered graciously, but here in New England it had already come and gone. Gusty winds drove fallen leaves across the village green, which was lined with neat frame houses. To young Ridge the trim town with its bright, sharp edges must have seemed at once impressive and forbidding.

At first the pious teachers at the school had some trouble with the strong-minded boy. He larked about with the other students, including his fellow Cherokees, two Choctaws from the lower Mississippi region, an Abenaki from northern New England, and several Polynesians. Although he read the Bible with interest and honored the Great Spirit, he declined to convert to Christianity, frustrating the hopes of teachers that he might one day serve among Cherokees as a missionary. But no one could complain of his devotion to learning. He was a diligent pupil, as was his cousin Buck, who had acquired a new name. When they had passed through New Jersey on their way to Cornwall, the youths had been introduced to Elias Boudinot, who had served as the president of the Continental Congress and was now head of the American Bible Society. Boudinot had taken a special interest in Buck and, at the elderly man's suggestion, the young Cherokee adopted Boudinot's name as his own.

In four years at the school John learned more than some college students of the day. He read classical literature, recited the orations of Cicero, and composed elegant verse. By the age of 18 he had triumphed in his adopted setting. He was cultivated, well spoken, and passionate—all of which made a profound impression on the daughter of the school's steward, young Sarah Northrup, an auburn-haired girl four years his junior who brought John his meals when his hip was acting up. By the fall of 1821 she and Ridge were so taken with each other that people at the school were beginning to talk. Sarah's mother

bolster John's position as a leader among his people. When he made it clear that his heart was set on marrying Sarah, however, his mother reluctantly gave her consent. Finally the Northrups agreed to the match as well, but only if John went off for a year or two and improved enough in his health that he could walk without crutches.

In December 1823 John Ridge returned to Cornwall in a fine carriage driven by a liveried servant, having tossed away his crutches. His wedding to Sarah at the Northrup home the following month caused an uproar. An editorial in a local paper denounced the "unnatural connection," claiming that Sarah "has thus made herself a *squaw*." As the young couple left the wedding in their coach, they were hounded and jeered. Only when they reached

"An Indian is almost considered accursed. He is frowned upon by the meanest peasant, and the scum of the earth are considered sacred in comparison to the son of nature.... The most stupid and illiterate white man will disdain and triumph over this worthy individual. It is disgusting to enter the house of a white man and be stared full in face with inquisitive ignorance."

JOHN RIDGE IN THE *CHRISTIAN HERALD,* 1823

questioned them both and learned to her dismay that the youngsters were in love. Mrs. Northrup could not deny that John was, as she put it, a "noble youth, beautiful in appearance, very graceful, a perfect gentleman." But she feared for her daughter if the relationship led to marriage. Many white men had taken native wives among the Cherokees and other tribes, but it was considered scandalous for a white woman to marry an Indian.

Sarah was packed off to relatives living in New Haven, to be introduced there to other young suitors who, her family hoped, would make her forget John. But she pined away and lost so much weight that her parents brought her back to Cornwall and allowed her to see John again. He wrote home for permission to marry Sarah, only to discover that his parents had their own misgivings about the proposed match. They wanted him to wed a Cherokee girl, preferably the daughter of a chief, who would

Major Ridge's home in the Cherokee Nation were they safe from the "hatred and slander of thousands who bear the Christian name," as one missionary put it sadly. A few years later Cornwall witnessed a fresh outburst of intolerance when Elias Boudinot married Harriet Gold, the daughter of a man associated with the Foreign Mission School. Townspeople burned the bride in effigy, and letters to the press threatened her husband's life. Although Harriet Boudinot hoped to serve one day as a missionary among the Cherokees, the marriage drew heated protests from professed Christians, prompting an indignant Major Ridge to ask a clergyman if he knew of anything in the Bible that made it a sin for an Indian man to wed a white woman.

John Ridge, who admired the egalitarian principles of American society, was struck by how far from those ideals whites fell in their dealings with Indians. "An Indian is almost considered accursed," he

wrote. "He is frowned upon by the meanest peasant, and the scum of the earth are considered sacred in comparison to the son of nature." No matter how polite or well educated an Indian might be, John added, "the most stupid and illiterate white man will disdain and triumph over this worthy individual. It is disgusting to enter the house of a white man and be stared full in face with inquisitive ignorance."

He was glad to be back among his own people. After living for a while with his parents, he and Sarah settled several miles away beside the Oostanaula River in a two-story house called Running Waters, surrounded by oaks and hickories and an expansive orchard. Already the lovely, flowering slopes along the river were known as Ridge's Valley. Even Cherokees who were far less fortunate admired the Ridges and what they had accomplished. Yet more than ever the family was identified with the Americans and their ways. By marriage and education John Ridge embodied the hope that Cherokees would benefit by embracing the best whites had to offer them. He could only pray that his faith in the American system was well founded.

While John Ridge was away in Connecticut completing his education, a lame Cherokee silversmith named Sequoya was devising a system that would enable thousands of his people to read and write without going away to school or learning English. Like the Ridges Sequoya believed in the power of books and learning, but he was determined to harness that power on Cherokee terms, without the help of outsiders. Although his father was a white man Sequoya was raised separately by his Cherokee mother and never mastered English. Instead, when he set out to capture spoken Cherokee symbolically—a project he likened to "catching a wild animal and taming it"—he drew inspiration from the ancient Indian

Sequoya, shown wearing a medal awarded to him by grateful Cherokees in 1824, devised a Cherokee script so that his people could read without learning English, which he called "the language of deceit." Nevertheless, he drew on English script when he devised the 86 symbols of his alphabet. By 1835 nearly 40 percent of the Cherokees had learned to read.

art of communicating through pictographs representing objects or ideas. He identified 86 distinct sounds, or syllables, in his native language and devised a symbol for each, writing on bark with ink derived from the juice of pokeberries. Introduced in the early 1820s, his syllabary was so clear and comprehensible that hitherto illiterate Cherokees mastered it within days.

Sequoya's invention was a great step forward for the Cherokee Nation. By 1824, wrote one missionary, it was "spreading through the nation like fire among the leaves." The phenomenal growth in literacy set the stage for another significant innovation—a Cherokee newspaper. In 1828 Elias Boudinot became the first editor of the *Cherokee Phoenix,* a four-page weekly printed partly in English and partly in Cherokee. Subscribers ranged as far afield as Europe, and the paper had tremendous influence over Cherokee affairs.

The inaugural edition of the *Phoenix* carried the text of the Cherokee constitution, which had been adopted in 1827 by a special council that convened at the fledgling Cherokee capital of New Echota, a crossroads situated in the area claimed by Georgia. The constitution was closely modeled on that of the United States. "We, the Representatives of the people of the Cherokee Nation," it began, "in Convention assembled, in order to establish justice, ensure tranquillity, promote our common welfare, and secure to ourselves and our posterity the blessings of liberty . . . do ordain and establish this Constitution for the Government of the Cherokee Nation." The document called for the direct election of representatives to the Cherokee Council, which in turn would appoint the principal chief and his advisers. In the government that was formed under this constitution, John Ridge was named to the position of clerk of the council and Major Ridge assumed the important advisory role of counselor to

Well versed in the writings of the country's founding fathers, John Ridge, spokesman for the Cherokees, declared that the future of his nation depended on the "faith and honor" of the United States.

the new principal chief—an unwavering patriot with the name of John Ross.

Known as Tsan Usdi, or Little John, because of his small stature, Ross seemed at first glance to be an unlikely choice for chief. By ancestry, he was seven-eighths white; English was his first language, and he spoke Cherokee haltingly. He looked like a florid, bristle-browed Scotsman. Yet he was a true Cherokee at heart, utterly devoted to the cause of his people. As a youngster, he had cast off the tailored suit his parents bought for him in favor of traditional buckskin after neighboring Cherokees taunted him as *unaka,* or "white man." He later endeared himself to his people by marrying an influential full-blooded Cherokee woman named Quatie. Ross admired and emulated Major Ridge, who was nearly 20 years his elder. He had served with the major against the Red Sticks and had since prospered as a planter and slaveholder on an estate replete with peacocks that was near Major Ridge's on the Oostanaula River.

When Ross became principal chief in 1828, he and the Ridges were united in opposition to any scheme that would separate Cherokees from their homeland. Yet late that year Andrew Jackson—their former ally, who had later emerged as a powerful advocate of Indian removal—was elected president of the United States. Major Ridge still hoped that Jackson might uphold the territorial rights of the Cherokees, to whom he owed no small debt. But Jackson's political instincts argued against such a concession. With the election of this man of the people, born in a log cabin, poor white settlers everywhere who wanted Indian land took heart. Georgians in particular interpreted Jackson's triumph as a sign that they could now freely assert their claim to Cherokee territory. Rumor had it that Jackson, in a meeting with Georgia officials, had remarked of the Cherokees: "Build a fire under them. When it gets hot enough they'll move." In Georgia a popular song made the rounds:

All I ask in this creation
Is a pretty little wife and a big plantation
Way up yonder
In the Cherokee Nation.

Barely a month after Jackson's election, the Georgia legislature passed a harsh set of laws to eradicate Cherokee sovereignty. The legislation prohibited the Cherokee Council from meeting within the boundaries claimed by the state, banned Cherokee courts there, and called for the arrest of Cherokees who advocated resistance to removal. Also, no Indian or descendant of an Indian could bear witness in a Georgia court against a white person; nor would any contract signed by an Indian be held valid unless witnessed by two white men. "Here is the secret," protested Elias Boudinot in the *Cherokee Phoenix*: "*Full license to our oppressors, and every avenue of justice closed against us.* Yes, this is the bitter cup prepared for us by a *republican* and religious government—we shall drink it to the very dregs."

The legislation was plainly designed to "build a fire" under the Cherokees and make things so hot for them that they would gladly emigrate. But the defiant leaders of the Cherokee Nation refused to be intimidated. They pledged to turn their backs to the west and "set our faces to the rising sun." They campaigned tirelessly against removal, traveling rutted roads and fording swollen creeks to urge their people to stand fast. When government agents sought out local chiefs and offered them cash to sign away land and emigrate, the Cherokee Council enacted a law drafted by John Ridge and strongly endorsed by his father that made it a crime punishable by death

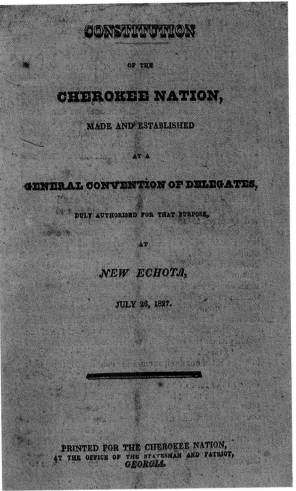

CONSTITUTION

OF THE

CHEROKEE NATION,

MADE AND ESTABLISHED

AT A

GENERAL CONVENTION OF DELEGATES,

DULY AUTHORISED FOR THAT PURPOSE,

AT

NEW ECHOTA,

JULY 26, 1827.

PRINTED FOR THE CHEROKEE NATION,
AT THE OFFICE OF THE STATESMAN AND PATRIOT,
GEORGIA.

BIRTH OF A NATION

The Cherokee constitution *(above)* was drafted by men of learning like John Ridge who modeled the document after that of the United States. Fittingly, they convened at New Echota, their nation's capital, on the Fourth of July, 1827, and formed a government made up of a legislative, an executive, and a judicial branch. At the same time, they sought to keep their country from being acquired by Americans by defining all Cherokee lands as "the common property of this Nation," not to be disposed of without the consent of the legislative council.

for anyone to sell or cede by treaty Cherokee land without the "consent of the legislative council of this nation." The law specified that offenders were to be tried in Cherokee court, but should they abscond, any Cherokee was entitled to execute them without being "held accountable for the same."

Meanwhile, Cherokees were struggling to protect their holdings from simple thievery. White prospectors infringing on Cherokee territory discovered gold there, and by the summer of 1829 the rush was on. "Men came from every state," one witness reported. "They came afoot, on horseback, and in wagons, acting more like crazy men than anything else." In fact, there wasn't much gold—just enough to be tantalizing, just enough to bring in more intruders who saw the prosperous lands of the Cherokees and wanted a piece. Some whites moved into homes that had been abandoned by the small number of Cherokees who had already emigrated west. Others formed so-called pony clubs, roving groups of bandits who stole the Cherokees' loosely guarded pigs and cows.

In late 1829 John Ross convened a meeting at his estate to discuss the crisis with the Ridges and General John Coffee, the former commander of the Cherokees at Horseshoe Bend who was serving now as an envoy from President Jackson. Major Ridge, speaking through his son, told the general of "many depredations committed in his nation by intruders and the frontier inhabitants of Georgia." Coffee could not promise action by the federal government and advised the Cherokee leaders to deal with the problem themselves. Perhaps he felt safe in making the suggestion because he thought nothing would come of it. The Cherokees had no army. But they did have a determined old war leader in the person of Major Ridge, and there was still some fight left in him.

A few dozen Cherokee volunteers gathered around Major Ridge at his plantation on the chill morning of January 4, 1830. Their faces and torsos were striped with black and crimson war paint, so heavily applied that most were unrecognizable. Ridge, still vigorous and muscular at 60 years of age, proudly lifted a buffalo headdress, an enduring symbol of strength and authority among many tribes west of the Appalachians, and pulled it over his gray hair.

His aim was to evict white families from homes abandoned by Cherokee emigrants near the Alabama border. Although Major Ridge and his men resembled a war party in every respect, they had no intention of claiming lives or seizing captives. Chief Ross, in authorizing the raid, had insisted that the offending settlers be shown "all possible lenience and humanity." That did not preclude destroying the homes the intruders had occupied and scaring them away for good. Major Ridge wanted the attack to be bloodless yet fearsome.

Raising a shrill battle cry and firing a pistol, he led his Cherokee warriors on horseback against the white squatters, who were taken completely by surprise and thought their time had come. Once the Cherokees had announced their presence, however, they pulled up their horses and gave the occupants time to pack up and leave. Then the warriors set the houses and other buildings on fire. They were Cherokee property, after all, and if left standing might soon be reoccupied by whites.

The sole casualty of the raid was a Cherokee. As the band returned home, several warriors doubled back to the settlement and celebrated with a keg of whiskey found in the smoking ruins, thus violating orders that all the men were to remain sober and orderly. A white sheriff later arrived on the scene with his deputies from the Georgia town of Carrollton and found the Cherokees hopelessly drunk. The Georgians beat their captives and led them off to Carrollton. One battered warrior named Chewoyee fell dead from his horse, and was left behind on the trail.

Although none of the white settlers suffered any harm, the Georgians branded the raid an act of war and called for retribution. Shots rang out along the contested borders of the Cherokee Nation. Ross and Major Ridge received death threats, and squads of supporters stood guard outside their houses. The Cherokee leaders were undeterred by such threats, but they recognized that the raid had only incited their foes, who were now looking for an excuse to drive the Indians out of their own territory. As Elias Boudinot editorialized in the *Phoenix:* "It has been the desire of our enemies that the Cherokees may be urged to some desperate act. . . . If our word will have any weight with our countrymen in this very trying time, we would say, *forbear, forbear.*"

Renouncing armed resistance did not mean giving up the fight. A legislative campaign to overturn the treaty rights of Indians was building in Washington, and Cherokee leaders prepared to resist legally and diplomatically. In the spring of 1830, Congress took up the Indian Removal Act, introduced by Andrew Jackson. The act expanded on earlier efforts to remove Indians by authorizing the president to offer as much land as he deemed necessary west of the Mississippi River to eastern tribes in

John Ross, seen here in a portrait he signed in English *(center)* and in Cherokee *(left),* served as principal chief of the Cherokees from 1828 until his death in 1866. Although only one-eighth Cherokee by birth, he faithfully represented the majority in his nation, who were largely of Cherokee ancestry and steadfastly opposed to removal. "It is I who serve under them," he wrote, "not them under me."

exchange for their present territory, even if that homeland was guaranteed by existing treaties. The act did not require tribes to accept such offers and move west, but it exposed them to a fresh round of bargaining, during which the president's agents could use federal funds, and the implied threat of federal troops, to break down the resistance of chiefs and secure their signatures on removal treaties.

Jackson piously defended the act by claiming that removing Indians west of the great river would help "preserve this much injured race" by distancing them from whites, who were fast reducing tribal hunting grounds and "destroying the resources of the savage." Cherokees answered that they were thriving in their homeland, despite the loss of game, and asked only that the federal government live up to its pledges. If treaties were to be renegotiated repeatedly at the convenience of the Americans, demanded Elias Boudinot, why should anyone believe them? "Who would trust his life and fortune to such a faithless nation?" he wrote. "No Cherokee *voluntarily* would."

Many congressional representatives in Washington agreed that the Indian Removal Act brought discredit on the United States and its treaty commitments. Congressman Davy Crockett of Tennessee, an ally of the Cherokees in the Creek War, spoke out against the bill, knowing that his stand might well cost him reelection to Congress, as in fact it did. After heated debate, both the House and the Senate passed the act by narrow margins. It led to the establishment of the Indian Territory, whose borders roughly corresponded to those of present-day Oklahoma.

President Jackson lost little time in pressuring the Cherokee Council to accept a removal treaty. The agent he dispatched that fall to New Echota, where the council continued to meet in defiance of Georgia's repressive edict, began his speech to the Cherokees diplomatically enough. He assured them that he was there to promote their "future peace and happiness" and offered them territory in the West and funds for transportation and resettlement if they agreed to relinquish their homeland. Having offered a carrot, the agent then brandished a stick, inform-

George Lowrey, who served as assistant principal chief under John Ross, sometimes wore native attire, as in this portrait, but he was no stranger to the ways of whites. He once poked fun during a Washington dinner party at a fellow guest—a Georgia congressman who had disparaged Cherokees as "savages subsisting upon roots"—by pointing to a bowl of sweet potatoes and asking loudly for some of those "roots" Cherokees were so fond of.

ing the council that Jackson would do nothing to prevent Georgia officials from carrying out their recently declared intention of surveying Cherokee country for the purpose of distributing lots there to whites. Once again, however, the Cherokee leadership refused to bow to threats. Speaking for the council, John Ross replied unequivocally: "The Cherokees have long since come to the conclusion never again to cede *another foot of land*."

Elias Boudinot, the first editor of the *Cherokee Phoenix*, worked with missionary zeal to promote a well-educated Cherokee society. "It is this which will ensure respect," he wrote. "It is this which will preserve us from the common burial place of Indians—oblivion in which many tribes are forgotten."

It was that case, entitled *Cherokee Nation* v. *State of Georgia,* that brought John Ridge and two other Cherokees—Richard Taylor and William Coodey, a nephew of John Ross—to Washington in the summer of 1831. There they looked on in dismay as Chief Justice Marshall ruled that the Cherokees were not citizens of a foreign nation and that the Supreme Court therefore lacked jurisdiction over their complaint. Their subsequent meeting with Andrew Jackson in the White House offered them no encouragement. Ridge and his companions did meet with some sympathetic listeners in Washington, however, including a reporter for the *New York Observer* who spoke with the Cherokees at length and found them well informed and persuasive. "They enforce respect and esteem," he wrote. "They actually know more of the institutions, laws, and government of the United States than a large fraction of those who occupy seats in the House of Representatives; and this may be said without dishonouring that body."

The deep regard of the Cherokees for the founding principles of the American Republic made it that much harder for them when authorities failed to live up to those ideals. At times, they were overcome by the sadness of it all. In Washington that year Ridge and Coodey attended a session of the House where the consequences of the Indian Removal Act were being debated. Sitting in the crowded gallery they listened intently to Massachusetts representative Edward Everett, a staunch opponent of removal whose bitter words echoed their own sentiments. "Here, at the center of the nation, beneath the portals of the Capitol, let us solemnly auspicate the new era of violated promises, and tarnished faith," declared Everett. "Let us kindle a grand council-fire, not of treaties made and ratified, but of treaties annulled and broken. Let us send to our archives for the worthless parchments, and burn them in the face of day. . . . They ought to be destroyed, as a warning to the Indians to make no more compacts with us."

Among those present as Everett spoke was the reporter for the *New York Observer,* who was listening from the gallery just below the two Cherokees when

With the political tide running strongly against them, Cherokees drew on the support of missionaries and other whites who were sympathetic and challenged the authority of Georgia in court. They began by appealing the conviction of a Cherokee who had been tried for murder and sentenced to death in a Georgia court. Before the appeal could even be heard by the U.S. Supreme Court, Georgia authorities hastily executed the condemned man. Cherokees then applied for an injunction from the Supreme Court barring Georgia from imposing its laws on their nation or otherwise violating their sovereignty, citing a constitutional provision that gave federal courts jurisdiction over disputes between a state and a foreign nation.

he heard "something like a drop of rain" fall on his cloak by his ear. "I looked up," he wrote, "and the head of one of these Cherokees had fallen upon his hand, and he was endeavoring to conceal his tears." The reporter did not identify the man by name, perhaps out of respect for his privacy in this time of heartbreak. "I knew him—had talked with him sympathetically," the reporter noted. "But *now* he asked no sympathy. He was overtaken in an unexpected moment. And he sought to hide his grief— and in that very effort his grief was betrayed."

While John Ridge, Richard Taylor, and William Coodey were off in Washington in July 1831, a detachment of Georgia Guards led by Sergeant Jacob Brooks approached the home of Samuel Worcester, a white missionary to the Cherokees who had helped Elias Boudinot start up the *Phoenix*. When Brooks informed Worcester that he was under arrest for offenses that included refusing to pledge allegiance to the state of Georgia, the missionary protested that his wife was ill and required his care. Nonetheless, Worcester was carted off to jail by the guards along with several other missionaries. On the way, Brooks pelted the prisoners with obscenities; one missionary, Elizur Butler, was collared and chained to the neck of a guardsman's horse. On July 10 they reached their place of detention, Camp Gilmer, which had been established near Cherokee territory to enforce state edicts. "This is where all the enemies of the state of Georgia will have to land," Brooks told his captives. "There and in hell."

The peculiar law that required whites living in Cherokee country to pledge allegiance to Georgia was aimed directly at missionaries like Worcester who not only were preaching and teaching among Cherokees but also were supporting them in their efforts to preserve their territory and sovereignty. Several of the missionaries who were rounded up and convicted subsequently took the pledge of allegiance and were pardoned. Worcester and Butler held out, however, and were sentenced to four years at the state penitentiary in Milledgeville. Their plight aroused national sympathy and gave Cherokees a fresh opening in their legal battle against the state. Unlike the many Cherokees languishing in Georgia jails, Worcester was a citizen of the United States, and the appeal he filed fell clearly within the jurisdiction of the Supreme Court.

Here as in the earlier case that reached the Supreme Court, the Cherokee cause was represented brilliantly by William Wirt, a former attorney general of the United States who took a dim view of Andrew Jackson's policies concerning the Indians and gladly volunteered his services. In Worcester's case, Wirt made a broad argument for Cherokee sovereignty. He contended that Worcester was a legal resident not of Georgia but of the Cherokee Nation, whose borders were guaranteed against intrusions by treaties with the United States.

Justice Marshall, no longer constrained by the matter of jurisdiction, listened sympathetically to Wirt and issued a strong ruling for the majority on the Court. Although he had earlier concluded that the Cherokees were not a foreign power but rather a "domestic, dependent nation," he accepted as binding their treaties with the United States. "The Cherokee Nation then is a distinct community," he ruled on February 28, 1832, "occupying its own territory." The laws of Georgia could have no bearing there, he added, without the assent of the Cherokees. Indeed, the laws in question were "in direct hostility with treaties, repeated in a succession of years, which mark out the boundary that separates the Cherokee country from Georgia; guaranty to them all the land within their boundary; solemnly pledge the faith of the United States to restrain their citizens from trespassing on it; and recognize the pre-existing power of the nation to govern itself." Marshall declared the legislation that had led to the conviction of the missionaries void and overturned their sentences.

It was a stunning victory for the Cherokees, and most were jubilant. "The question is forever settled as to who is right and who is wrong," Elias Boudinot wrote ecstatically to his brother Stand Watie. But John Ridge, off on a speaking tour in New England,

President Andrew Jackson, portrayed here in a political cartoon with a brood of childlike tribal delegates, epitomized the Great Father in his treatment of Indians. In 1816, as an envoy for President James Madison, he set the tone for his own future administration when he urged the Cherokees to sell part of their homeland to the government. "Receive the offering of your Beloved Father the President," he told them. "Give him proof that you return his love."

warned in a letter of his own to Stand Watie that "the contest is not over." He doubted that Andrew Jackson would antagonize his supporters in Georgia by enforcing the Supreme Court ruling. "The Chicken Snake General Jackson has time to crawl and hide in the luxuriant grass of his nefarious hypocracy," Ridge wrote. "We shall see how strong the links are to the chain that connect the states to the Federal Union."

Ridge was right to caution Watie against optimism. In a meeting with officials from Georgia, Jackson reportedly told them: "John Marshall has made his decision. Now let him enforce it." Confident that they could do as they pleased without having to worry about interference from the U.S. government, Georgians ignored the Supreme Court ruling and continued to tighten their grip on Cher-

harboring the same thoughts. Privately they began to talk of the need to negotiate a favorable removal treaty for Cherokees as soon as possible—a position that put them sharply at odds with John Ross.

Chief Ross realized that Cherokees would be hard pressed to preserve their homeland. He had met with Andrew Jackson himself in recent months to discuss the issue of removal. "If you cannot protect us in the East," he asked the president pointedly, "how can we believe that you will protect us in the West?" Given such uncertainties, Ross thought it better for Cherokees to hold out as long as they could and try to extract concessions from the United States; perhaps a deal could be struck that would allow them to remain in some part of their homeland as American citizens. He was supported in that stance by the

> *"The Chicken Snake General Jackson has time to crawl and hide in the luxuriant grass of his nefarious hypocracy.... We shall see how strong the links are to the chain that connect the states to the Federal Union."*
>
> JOHN RIDGE TO HIS COUSIN STAND WATIE, 1832

okee country. In spite of the fact that their convictions had been overturned, Worcester and Butler remained in prison until 1833, when the state's governor saw fit to release them.

For John Ridge, among others, Jackson's refusal to uphold Justice Marshall's decision dashed any lingering hope that Cherokees could retain their homeland. With a heavy heart he ventured once more to the White House and asked the president directly if he had any intention of enforcing the will of the Supreme Court. No, he did not, Jackson replied. He advised Ridge to return home and tell his people to move west.

As much as he despised Jackson and loved his homeland, John Ridge left the White House convinced that removal was indeed the only hope left for his people. Moving west, he reasoned, might at least give the beleaguered Cherokees a chance to keep their nation intact. When he returned home that spring, he discovered that a number of his friends and kin, including Major Ridge and Elias Boudinot, were

majority of Cherokees, who were profoundly attached to ancestral traditions and far less inclined than the Ridges to accept change—most especially removal. Some of those traditionalists would sooner die in their cherished homeland than live elsewhere.

Both Ross and the Ridges had the interests of Cherokees at heart, but once the differences between them surfaced, the debate grew bitter. The controversy broke out into the open in July 1832 at a meeting of the national council. To avoid provoking the Georgians, Ross moved the meeting from New Echota to a place across the border in Tennessee called Red Clay. There the council delegates gathered in a rough shed shaded by oak trees. The delegates passed a resolution that called for the forthcoming Cherokee elections to be postponed and for Ross and other elected officers to remain in their present positions. Supporters defended the resolution on the grounds that holding elections would bring on a dangerous confrontation with Georgia. But the council's decision angered more than a few Cherokees, including John Ridge, who hoped to replace Ross as principal chief.

When the question of removal arose in council, the Ridges were in no mood to hide their differences with Ross. For the first time they spoke out in favor of emigrating and were met with caustic opposition from Ross and his backers. Feelings ran so high during and after the debate that Ross imposed an unprecedented restriction on Elias Boudinot, who was planning to address the controversy in his newspaper. In the interest of Cherokee unity and morale, Ross told Boudinot, the *Phoenix* must not reveal the dissension within the ranks. Within days, Boudinot resigned in protest. "I love my country and I love my people as my own heart bears me witness," he wrote to Ross. "I could not consent to be the conductor of the paper without having the right and privilege of discussing those important matters." Ross then appointed his brother-in-law, Elijah Hicks, as editor of the *Phoenix*.

This dispute between men who had long been united in defense of the Cherokees could not have come at a worse time, for the state of Georgia was making good on its threat to survey Cherokee land for distribution to white settlers. Nearly 350 surveyors were roaming 6,000 square miles of the Cherokee Nation, marking off lots of 40 acres in gold territory and 160 acres elsewhere. At first many Cherokees found the surveyors' attempts to divvy up the earth ludicrous. The Cherokee approach to land use was simple. A family could cultivate as much land as it liked, as long as its farm did not come closer than a quarter-mile to a neighboring homestead. Between the farms were woodlands where farmers could let their livestock graze freely. For prosperous families like the Ridges or Rosses, property lines were a little more formal, but for most Cherokees the idea of marking off portions of ground—and parceling them out to strangers who had never set foot there—seemed incredible.

Yet the surveyors and their supervisors meant business. To ensure that land stolen from Cherokees was distributed to whites in a fair and aboveboard manner, state officials organized a lottery. The winners were

supposed to be selected at random, but when the first drawings were made from the lottery wheel that fall, hopeful settlers noticed that choice lots were being doled out to relatives and cronies of the lottery's commissioner, Shadrach Bogan. Outraged at this assault on the integrity of the process, state officials tossed out Bogan and set the wheel spinning again.

It was up to the winners to take possession of their holdings. Some held off rather than reckon with angry Cherokees; others bluffed or bullied their way into Cherokee homes and evicted the rightful inhabitants, who sought refuge elsewhere. More than a year after the first lots were drawn, John Ross came home from yet another frustrating trip to Washington to find settlers in possession of his house. His ailing wife, Quatie, and their children had been relegated by the whites to two rooms to await his return. Ross packed them up and took them over the state line to a log cabin at Red Clay.

Major Ridge's handsome house was allotted to a Revolutionary War widow, and his son's plantation was assigned to one Griffith Mathis. But Georgia authorities knew that the Ridges were in favor of emigration and allowed them to remain in their homes until they chose to move. The special treatment the Ridges received did not endear them to Ross, or to other dispossessed Cherokees who traveled past the Ridge estates, their belongings on their backs.

Even before he lost his plantation, John Ross felt the chilling effects of the removal struggle close to home. By the spring of 1834 his own brother, Andrew Ross, had openly defied him and was engaged in unauthorized treaty talks with American officials. Andrew Ross went to Washington as part of a pro-removal Cherokee delegation that included Major Ridge and Elias Boudinot. Like Boudinot, Major Ridge withdrew from the negotiations when he learned that Andrew Ross was prepared to endorse a removal treaty that offered the Cherokees little in the way of compensation—a deal signed by few Cherokees of any consequence and later rejected by Congress. Nonetheless, Major Ridge had lent his

SPARKING SEMINOLE RESISTANCE

None of the tribes caught up in Andrew Jackson's sweeping campaign for Indian removal offered stronger opposition than the Seminoles of Florida, led by a remarkable war chief named Osceola *(right)*. The son of a Creek woman who fled to Florida with other surviving Red Sticks after their devastating defeat in 1814 at Horseshoe Bend, Osceola found a home among the Seminoles, who freely embraced fugitives, including runaway slaves. In 1834 he denounced a removal treaty some Seminole chiefs were bullied and bribed into signing that offered them a paltry two cents an acre for their land and consigned them to the Indian Territory. Indian agent Wiley Thompson tried to talk Osceola into backing the deal, but he reportedly showed his contempt for American treaty makers by driving his dagger through the documents placed before him *(below)*. "The agent has had his day," Osceola later declared after Thompson jailed him for a week to teach him a lesson. "I will have mine."

He soon made good on that vow. Commanding an elusive force of warriors that included men of Creek and African ancestry, he bedeviled one general after another sent to enforce the removal treaty. He was finally snared in the fall of 1837 and died in captivity. But thousands of Seminoles kept up the fight until 1842, when all but a small number of holdouts surrendered and headed west.

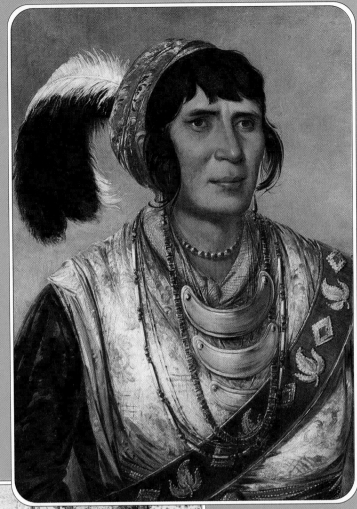

The portrait of Osceola above was painted by the artist George Catlin shortly before the chief died of a throat infection at Fort Moultrie, South Carolina, in January 1838. Osceola was confined at the fort as a prisoner of war.

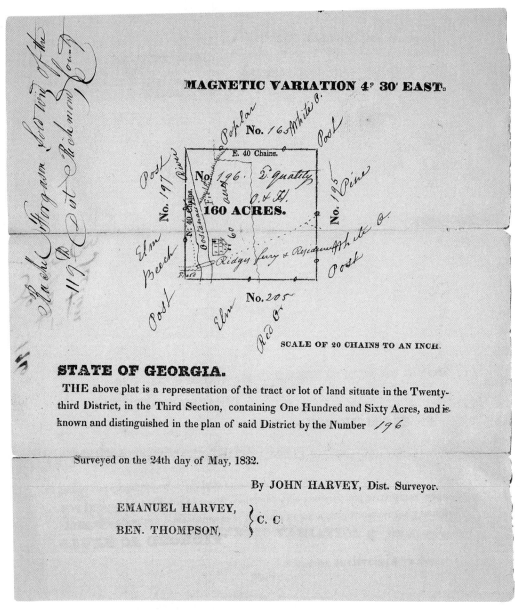

MAGNETIC VARIATION 4° 30' EAST.

No. 165

E. 40 Chains.

No. 196. 2. quality

160 ACRES.

O. & H.

No. 197

No. 195

Ridge ferry & Residence

No. 205

SCALE OF 20 CHAINS TO AN INCH.

STATE OF GEORGIA.

THE above plat is a representation of the tract or lot of land situate in the Twenty-third District, in the Third Section, containing One Hundred and Sixty Acres, and is known and distinguished in the plan of said District by the Number *196*

Surveyed on the 24th day of May, 1832.

By JOHN HARVEY, Dist. Surveyor.

EMANUEL HARVEY, } C. C.
BEN. THOMPSON,

prestige to the delegation, and he received much of the blame back home for the abortive treaty. At a meeting of the Cherokee Council in August, he was denounced as a traitor, prompting his son to rise to his defense. Was this man who had served his country faithfully, John Ridge asked, to be cast out simply for warning Cherokees of the coming storm and urging them to flee before it was too late?

As if in answer, Elijah Hicks, the new editor of the *Phoenix,* brought forth a petition calling for the

This plat of a 160-acre parcel of land owned by Major Ridge was drawn up in 1832 by a surveyor for the state of Georgia in preparation for the distribution of Cherokee land to white citizens by lottery. The surveyor noted the locations of Major Ridge's plantation house, surrounding groves of trees, and the profitable ferry he operated across the Oostanaula River.

impeachment of Major Ridge and John Ridge as representatives of the Cherokee Nation. The document bore 144 signatures, an imposing majority of the council. A court of impeachment was set for the council's October meeting. John Walker Jr., a proponent of emigration who had been in Washington when the controversial treaty was negotiated but had not signed it, left the August council early, alarmed by the hostile tone of the proceedings. Riding home in the night, he was ambushed and mortally wounded. His father blamed his death on supporters of John Ross and swore vengeance on the chief, who abhorred violence and had urged his followers to keep the peace. Now Ross felt compelled to surround himself with bodyguards. Meanwhile, menacing figures appeared in the woods around the homes of John Ridge and Major Ridge. Beset by enemies, Cherokees were beginning to war among themselves.

At the October council John Ross set aside the motion for impeachment, and when the accused asked to stand trial to clear their names, he turned down their request. At that the Ridge faction walked out and convened a council of their own at John Ridge's home. They constituted themselves as the Treaty Party, dedicated to negotiating a fair removal to western lands. In a nation of nearly 20,000 Cherokees, they could claim only 83 members. But the Treaty Party immediately attracted the interest of U.S. officials, who knew that a treaty supported by the Ridges would carry more weight in Congress than the spurious deal that Andrew Ross had endorsed.

Indeed, no less a figure than Edward Everett, the outspoken critic of Jackson's removal policy, professed sympathy for the Treaty Party. In a speech to Congress he paraphrased a statement he received from John Ridge: "They express the sorrowful conviction that it is impossible for them, in the present state of things, to retain their national existence, and to live in peace and comfort in their native region. They therefore have turned their eyes to the country west of the Mississippi." They did so reluctantly, Everett added, with a bitterness that "might naturally be expected from men placed in their situation."

Andrew Jackson sensed a breakthrough and appointed a new Indian agent to negotiate with the Treaty Party—the Reverend John F. Schermerhorn, a tall, rangy man whom the Ross party soon came to detest. The Ridges did not pretend to represent the majority of Cherokees, but they were eager to conclude a deal that could then be put before the nation as a whole. In March 1835 Schermerhorn offered them terms they considered acceptable: 4.5 million dollars for Cherokee lands in the East in exchange for 13 million acres of land in the West, plus an additional 800,000 acres valued at $500,000, bringing the total offer to five million dollars, a figure the U.S. Senate had determined to be a fair offer. John Ridge was pleased with the terms, and he was anxious to present the terms to a combined council of the Treaty Party and Ross's National Party as soon as possible.

country in hopes of catching Cherokees off guard and seizing their property. As the delegates approached the council grounds at Red Clay, Chief Ross was there to greet them. "The woods echoed with the trampling of many feet," reported John Howard Payne, an actor, writer, and composer who was visiting Ross at the time. "A long and orderly procession emerged from the trees, the gorgeous autumnal tints of whose departing foliage seemed in sad harmony with the noble spirit now beaming in this departing race." Their dress was "neat and picturesque," he noted, consisting of turbans, tunics with sashes, and long robes that evoked "old scripture pictures of patriarchal processions." A long line of delegates filed past Ross, each man pausing to take the chief's hand without speaking. The older men remained at Ross's side, while the others "withdrew to

"From the uncertainties of bettering our condition by a removal, we have determined to cling to our original rights in the country where we first drew the breath of life."

John Ross, Washington, April 14, 1834

Ross was hesitant. He had tried unsuccessfully to persuade Andrew Jackson to allow Cherokees to remain where they were as American citizens under state authority. When that proposal was turned down, he had tried to negotiate more money for the uncertain years ahead in the West but was again unsuccessful. The sum Schermerhorn offered seemed impressive, but Ross questioned whether it would be enough to keep the Cherokees afloat until they could establish themselves in a strange new country and become self-supporting. He hoped to delay action on the proposed treaty until after the presidential election of 1836, which might bring to power a man sympathetic to Cherokee interests. Nonetheless, he agreed to submit the terms Schermerhorn had offered to a combined council at Red Clay in October, trusting that most of those in attendance would follow his lead.

Delegates flocked to the council by the hundreds, some traveling on horseback and others on foot, braving the hostility of whites who prowled the

various parts of the enclosure; some sitting Turk fashion against the trees, and others upon the fences, but with the eyes of all fixed upon their chief."

John Ross remained the man most Cherokees looked to for guidance in this time of peril, and the Ridges were painfully aware of his continuing popularity. Although they believed that he was deluding his followers by holding out hopes of a better deal from the United States, they nonetheless met in civil fashion with Ross and his party in the leafy forest clearing to draw up resolutions for consideration by the council. The two sides agreed to form a joint Cherokee delegation of 20 members, which the council then empowered to conclude a treaty with the United States. But at Ross's urging the council also rejected Schermerhorn's terms, by an overwhelming margin. Members of the Treaty Party were bitter, but John Ridge and his cousin, Stand Watie, reluctantly agreed to accompany Ross and others as delegates to Washington, hoping that Ross would be content with a few minor adjustments to the proposed treaty, which was all they expected from the Americans at this point.

Before the Cherokees could leave for Washington, the Georgia militia crossed into Tennessee and arrested John Ross at his home. Taken into custody along with him was John Howard Payne. Renowned as the author of the sentimental ballad "Home Sweet Home," Payne admired Ross and drew attention to his cause by writing articles from prison describing the wretched conditions they endured there. Although the Ridges were suspicious of Payne and his dealings with Ross, they regarded the arrest of the chief as an affront to their nation and intervened on his behalf. John Ridge visited Ross in prison and helped obtain the release of the two men.

Schermerhorn, meanwhile, was fiercely intent on concluding the deal that the council had recently turned down. Shortly before the Cherokee delegation departed for Washington in early December, he called on Cherokees to meet with him later that month at New Echota to finalize a treaty. Anyone who failed to attend, he added, would be regarded as giving consent to the agreement. Ross spurned the invitation and sent runners throughout Cherokee country to tell his supporters to stay away. In the end, fewer than 400 Cherokees appeared at New Echota. Among them, however, was the one man Schermerhorn hoped for above all others—Major Ridge.

It was a summons he might easily have avoided. He could have stayed away like so many other Cherokees and waited for the delegation to complete its mission to Washington, a journey that he felt certain would end in disappointment for Ross. Yet Major Ridge had never been one to defer to others when he felt action was called for.

On the surface the gathering at New Echota resembled other recent councils that had ended inconclusively. Groups of men gathered here and there on the grounds, smoking and talking slowly, with long contemplative pauses. But Major Ridge sensed that this meeting would be decisive. The time had come, he proclaimed to the full assembly, for Cherokees to accept Schermerhorn's terms and emigrate.

"There is but one path of safety," he said, "one road to future existence as a nation." Elias Boudinot, who had resigned from Ross's delegation and come to New Echota instead, also spoke in favor of the treaty. His words were more bitter, especially when he alluded to the death threats that he and others in his family had received for advocating removal. He insisted that he was ready to die for an action he considered in the best interests of his people.

The assembled Cherokees conformed to the procedures followed earlier at Red Clay by appointing 20 of their members—including Major Ridge, Boudinot, and Andrew Ross—to act as delegates and finalize the treaty. When all was said and done, however, there was no disguising the fact that the final document drawn up at New Echota was essentially the same agreement rejected by the national council in October. By Cherokee law, anyone who signed it would be committing a capital offense.

On the evening of December 29, 1835, the 20 delegates gathered with Schermerhorn and his deputies in the dim, smoky parlor of Elias Boudinot's house near the council grounds. There, by the flickering firelight, the Cherokees listened as the familiar terms of the treaty were recited. Then it was time to sign.

Now that the moment had arrived, the delegates sat transfixed, staring at the paper and the waiting pen next to its pot of ink. Finally a Cherokee named John Gunter came forward and took up the pen. "I am not afraid," he said. "I will sell the whole country." After he signed, Andrew Ross added his name, and the others followed suit. None knew better what was at stake than Major Ridge, who had once executed a Cherokee chief for dealing away land. Ridge affixed his mark, a firm black X. Then he turned aside and remarked to his companions evenly, "I have signed my death warrant."

A short time later Schermerhorn left for Washington with Major Ridge and Boudinot to deliver the signed treaty to the Senate for ratification. When they reached the capital, John Ridge and Stand Watie promptly left the boardinghouse they had been sharing with Ross—who had made no

A GUARDIAN OF CHEROKEE RIGHTS

Adopted by Cherokees, William Holland Thomas helped his people retain a foothold in the Great Smoky Mountains that sheltered their ancestors.

Thanks in part to a white trader named William Holland Thomas *(left)*, one band of Cherokees living in the mountains of western North Carolina resisted removal from their homeland while thousands in Georgia were exiled. Under the Treaty of 1819, which placed Cherokee land in North Carolina under state authority, each family that chose to remain there was granted 640 acres and became eligible for American citizenship. In practice, however, they were denied their treaty rights. By the mid-1830s, whites were pressing them to leave home and move west along with other Cherokees. It was then that William Thomas intervened to protect a band that regarded him as one of their own.

Thomas's bond with the Cherokees went back to 1818 when he was 13 years old and working as a clerk at a trading post in Quallatown, North Carolina. His uncommon kindness toward Indian customers attracted the attention of the Cherokee chief, Yonaguska, who adopted the boy when he learned that his father had died.

Thomas grew up with one foot in the Cherokee world and the other in white society. When he was 31 years old and a lawyer and businessman, Yonaguska asked him to help the local Cherokees avoid removal. Thomas defended their rights before the state legislature and the U.S. Congress. His lobbying efforts required, in his words, "constant perseverance and the patience of Job," but they bore fruit. Yonaguska's people were officially exempted from removal, and they welcomed a number of Cherokees from Georgia who refused to move west. Known collectively as the Eastern Band of Cherokees, the group remained in North Carolina on land Thomas helped purchase for them around Quallatown, where they carried on traditions such as stickball *(below),* a version of lacrosse. Thomas could take pride in the fact that a resilient group of Cherokees persisted, as he put it, "in the land of their nativity."

headway in the latest round of negotiations—and joined Major Ridge and the others at their hotel. Like Stand Watie, John Ridge signed the treaty without hesitation, although he knew as well as his father what the risks were. Sooner or later, he predicted, he would pay with his life.

When John Ross learned of the agreement at New Echota, he was beside himself with anger. Working with his friend John Howard Payne, he quickly pulled together a massive petition against the treaty, signed by an astounding 16,000 Cherokees, and submitted it to Congress. Skeptics in Washington questioned the validity of some of the signatures, but they could not deny the fact that the treaty enjoyed the support of only a tiny minority of the Cherokee people. "The instrument in question is not the act of our nation," Ross protested in writing. "We are not parties to its covenants." In May 1836, after lengthy and heated debate, the Treaty of New Echota was ratified in the Senate by the margin of a single vote.

The Ross and Ridge parties were now divided by an unbridgeable gulf of hostility. Boudinot wrote of Ross: "He has dragged an ignorant train, wrought upon by near-sighted prejudice and stupid obstinacy, to the last brink of destruction." Many of Ross's supporters, for their part, would have been happy to see the Cherokees who signed the treaty called to account. But Ross was content to let the Ridge party slip away into exile, while he himself rode from town

The Treaty of New Echota, which led to the removal of Cherokees from their homeland, was signed and sealed by President Jackson (near left) on May 23, 1836, after the agreement was ratified by the U.S. Senate. A preceding page of the document (far left) was signed on December 29, 1835, by federal negotiator John F. Schermerhorn, Major Ridge—whose name was written out for him after he made his mark—and other Cherokees, including Andrew Ross, John Gunter, and Elias Boudinot.

to town, urging Cherokees to ignore the treaty and hold fast. That summer Andrew Jackson dispatched 7,000 federal troops to occupy their homeland, partly to protect Cherokees who were preparing to leave and partly to "overawe the Indians," as Jackson put it, "and frown down opposition to the treaty." Under its terms, Cherokees had two years in which to vacate their homeland.

Major Ridge and his son had returned home that spring to find that white settlers had already taken over parts of their estates. No matter. They were eager to move. They arranged for the sale of their disposable property and prepared for the long journey west. Major Ridge and his household, including his slaves, left in March 1837 with more than 400 other pro-treaty Cherokees, traveling mainly by boat until they reached the settlement of Fort Smith on the Arkansas River. John Ridge and Elias Boudinot left with their families later and took a different, largely overland route. Major Ridge had picked out a good spot for resettlement—Honey Creek, in the northeast corner of the Indian Territory, near the borders of Missouri and Arkansas. Although much of the Indian Territory was prairie, a kind of landscape that was alien to the eastern Indians, this corner felt a bit more like home. It was hilly and wooded, blooming in spring with the redbuds and plum trees they had known in their homeland. Creeks ran between banks of red and yellow clay, and the soil was fertile.

With the help of their slaves, Major Ridge and his son cleared land for a farm and built a store. Characteristically, one of their first acts was to open a school for the newly arrived children. In early 1838 John Ridge enrolled his 11-year-old son John Rollin as a student. Theirs was "a fine region of country abounding in springs and water and the people are thickly settled and enjoying all the comforts of life," John Ridge wrote to an acquaintance. "In a few years it will be the garden spot of the United States."

Yet even while the Ridges were settling into their new homes, they were receiving grim reports about the Cherokees they left behind. Refusing to leave voluntarily, Ross's followers were being herded by the thousands into stockades in preparation for a forced march west. The roundup of Cherokees came at the insistence of Martin Van Buren. Elected president in 1836, he continued Jackson's Indian policies, disappointing John Ross's hope that Jackson's successor would be more sympathetic to the Indians. In May 1838, when the two-year grace period expired, Van Buren appointed General Winfield Scott to supervise a forced evacuation of the Cherokee holdouts, some 17,000 people in all.

Scott was a conscientious soldier who disliked this duty, and he ordered his men to conduct the operation as humanely as possible. Nonetheless, the roundup caught most Cherokees by surprise, and they were terrified. Families were routed from their houses at bayonet point without a chance to collect their belongings. Even as they departed, whites who had long been awaiting a chance to claim their prizes in Georgia's lottery moved into their homes. Looters dug into Cherokee graves and took jewelry and other ornaments buried with the dead. One soldier from Georgia who later served with the Confederate army remarked: "I fought through the Civil War, and have seen men shot to pieces and slaughtered by thousands, but the Cherokee removal was the cruelest work I ever knew."

Soldiers marched the Cherokees into stockades on the Tennessee River. In the rising heat of summer, they awaited deportation, falling sick as they were crowded together with inadequate food and foul water. Many infants perished. By the time the first groups were herded onto boats for the trip west, more than half of the Cherokees were ill, and many were dying. John Ross appealed to Scott for a delay in the evacuation. Perhaps, he proposed, Cherokee officials could take charge of the march themselves and postpone it until cooler weather. Scott agreed, as long as every Indian was gone by October 20. As autumn closed in, group after group of Cherokees loaded their wagons and left behind the land they loved. There were not enough horses and carts to carry all the exiles, and many had to walk.

The journey proved to be even longer and harder than they had feared. Cold weather arrived early, and sickness and exposure took a fearful toll. Burial parties digging graves in the frosty ground were a frequent sight along the trail. The grieving survivors pushed ahead with grim resolve like mourners in an endless funeral procession. "Children cry and many men cry, and all look sad like when friends die," recollected one Cherokee afterward. "Looks like maybe all be dead before we get to new Indian country, but always we keep marching on." The casualties included Quatie Ross, the wife of Chief John Ross. After giving her blanket to a sick child, reported John Burnett, an interpreter for the army during the Cherokees' removal, she rode "thinly clad through a blinding sleet and snow storm, developed pneumonia, and died in the still hours of a bleak winter night."

Between January and March 1839 the depleted parties of Cherokees staggered into the Indian Territory. At least 4,000 people—and perhaps many more—died on the trek, which Cherokees called The Trail Where We Cried or The Trail of Tears. In their sorrow and bitterness, Cherokees were quick to assign blame. Some reflected angrily on the role that was played by Andrew Jackson: "If I had known that Jackson would drive us from our homes," said one old warrior who had fought with Jackson against the Creeks, "I would have killed him at Horseshoe." But most people looked for culprits closer to home. According to one missionary, "*all* the suffering and *all* the difficulties of the Cherokee people" were now charged to "the account of Messrs. Ridge and Boudinot."

The hostility increased when the newly arrived Cherokees discovered that they would have to compete with others for a foothold in the Indian Territory. Besides the Cherokees, members of four other southeastern tribes—Creeks, Seminoles, Chickasaws, and Choctaws—were also settling in the area around the same time. All of them wanted to live in the eastern part of the territory, partly because the terrain was more fertile and familiar there, but also

Joseph Vann, a wealthy planter of mixed white and Cherokee ancestry, held more slaves than any other Cherokee at the time of removal.

DEMISE OF A RECKLESS PLANTER

Although fewer than 1 in 10 Cherokees owned slaves, some of those who did lived as extravagantly as wealthy white plantation owners. Joseph Vann held 110 slaves and profited greatly by their services, but in the end he wasted his fortune, risking life and property in an act of supreme folly.

When the removal treaty became law in 1836, Vann was better equipped than most Cherokees to leave his eastern homeland and make a new start in the Indian Territory. Many of his slaves labored on the large plantation he established there, raising cotton and corn. Others manned one of the riverboats he owned that carried passengers and cargo on local waterways.

Vann might have grown old and eminent in his adopted land had it not been for his habitual drinking and gambling. In 1844 he took his paddle-wheeler, the *Lucy Walker,* on a lengthy excursion down the Arkansas River and up the Mississippi, joined by more than a dozen of his slaves and scores of gamblers and other passengers.

Reaching the Ohio River, he embarked on a race with a rival steamer for high stakes. As the two boats neared the finish line, he ordered one of his slaves to throw a side of meat into the boiler to boost the fire with fat and generate more steam. According to R. P. Vann, Joseph's grandson, the slave warned his drunken master that the engine was already carrying "every pound of steam it could stand." At that, Vann pulled his pistol and aimed it at the man, who did as his master ordered, then ran to the stern of the boat and jumped for his life, moments before the boiler exploded. Joseph Vann died in the fiery wreck, along with 12 slaves and 50 passengers.

Cherokee planters in the Indian Territory offered slaves for sale, and rewards for the return of runaways, by publishing notices like those at lower left, which appeared in 1845 in the *Cherokee Advocate*. Although many Cherokees opposed slavery and harbored runaways, slavery remained legal in the territory until the close of the Civil War, when emancipated blacks like the mother and child below, sitting in front of their cabin at Fort Gibson, became eligible for citizenship in the Cherokee Nation.

because of hostility in the west from the Osages and other tribes who had long occupied the fringes of the plains and resented the intruders. To make matters worse, Ross's followers found themselves vying for authority both with the Ridge faction and with the Old Settlers—as the Cherokees who had moved west earlier were called.

In June 1839 Ross met with John Brown, the chief of the Old Settlers, and the two tried unsuccessfully to reach an accord for a common Cherokee government. Afterward, rumors surfaced that the Ridge par-

Among the Cherokees who sided with the Confederates during the Civil War and traveled to Washington afterward to negotiate a peace treaty were several direct descendants of the Ridges and their kin, including John Rollin Ridge *(far left)*, son of John Ridge; Saladin Watie *(second from left)*, son of Stand Watie; and Elias Cornelius Boudinot *(second from right)*, son of Elias Boudinot.

ty had sabotaged the talks by persuading the Old Settlers to reject Ross's terms. For some in Ross's camp those rumors were the last straw. They set out to punish the men they blamed for signing away their country and sending Cherokees down The Trail of Tears.

The trial was held in secret, without the presence of the defendants or the knowledge of John Ross. Those in attendance listened gravely as a spokesman read aloud the law drafted by John Ridge in 1829 that made it a crime punishable by

death for anyone to cede Cherokee land without the consent of the national council. Then the fate of each defendant was decided by three jurors belonging to his clan. In the case of Major Ridge, three men of the Deer Clan found him guilty and sentenced him to die. The same punishment was decreed for John Ridge, Elias Boudinot, and Stand Watie. Then the assembled Cherokees drew lots to select those who would organize and lead the execution squads. One young man in attendance was exempted from the lottery—Allen Ross, son of the chief. He was told to go to his father's house and prevent anyone from telling the Cherokee leader about the trial and the coming executions.

On June 22 the execution squads set out before dawn. The first group of 25 men rode up to John Ridge's house at Honey Creek and surrounded it. Three men entered the house and dragged the struggling Ridge out into the yard. Sarah Ridge, who had shared in her husband's trials ever since they left the Foreign Mission School in Connecticut, ran to the door and tried to reach him, but she was forced back by Cherokees bearing rifles. Twelve-year-old John Rollin Ridge stood at her side, looking on helplessly, as several men held his father fast and another stabbed him repeatedly. The executioners then tossed him in the air and trampled him before riding off. Sarah ran to embrace him, and he died in her arms.

A short time later, in a clearing many miles away, Elias Boudinot was at work on the house that he was building for his family when four Cherokees approached him and asked for medicine for their sick relatives. Boudinot's store of medicine was at the home of Samuel Worcester, who had gone west with the Cherokees and had invited the Boudinots to live with him until their home was finished. As the group neared the missionary's house, one of the Cherokees dropped behind the others and stabbed Boudinot in the back. Another man then struck him several times with a tomahawk, splitting his skull. The executioners ran off, leaving the dying man to the attentions of his wife and Worcester, but they proved to be of no avail.

Realizing that others must also be in danger, Worcester told a Choctaw Indian at the mission to mount a fast horse called Comet and alert Stand Watie, who was at the store that he had established a mile or so away. Arriving there at a gallop, the Choctaw pulled Watie aside and, while pretending to bargain with him over a barrel of sugar, warned him in a whisper that his brother had been slain and that his own life was in peril. Watie slipped out the door, jumped on Comet, and sped off before his would-be assassins arrived.

Major Ridge was not so fortunate. After the attack on her husband, Sarah Ridge had dispatched a rider to warn her father-in-law, who was on his way to Arkansas to attend to a slave who had fallen ill there. But his executioners knew which road he was traveling on, and they got to him before the messenger. Waiting in ambush amid thick brush as Major Ridge rode by, they fired nearly a dozen rifle shots at once, and five bullets struck their target. The 68-year-old warrior fell from his rearing horse and died on the road, far from home. Some local settlers found his body and buried him in a small cemetery nearby. There he rested until 1856, when his descendants retrieved his remains and laid them beside the body of his beloved son John at Honey Creek.

By then, the fierce feuding that was spawned by the executions of June 1839 had subsided, and Cherokees were rebuilding their society under the leadership of John Ross. Tragically, their nation would again be torn apart during the Civil War, with Stand Watie and many of his kin fighting on behalf of the Confederates, while John Ross and his followers ultimately sided with the Union. After the war, as white settlers surged westward, Cherokees would once more come under relentless pressure from American authorities to relinquish their treaty rights and surrender much of the territory they had claimed at such cost. But one thing could never be taken from the Cherokee people—their devotion to the old country they left behind and to this new land they adopted in a time of grief and learned to cherish as their own. ◆

CLEARING THE CLOUDS OF IGNORANCE

"Dear Children, I often speak to you, and encourage you to continue in the pursuit of useful knowledge," a Cherokee chief told a group of young scholars at Creek Path, Alabama, in 1827. "Remember the whites are near us. . . . You must be sensible, that unless you can speak their language, read and write as they do, they will be able to cheat you and trample on your rights."

This advice represented a widespread attitude among Cherokees: Education was essential if they were to survive in a world dominated by whites. When missionaries began arriving in the Southeast to convert the Cherokees, they found many who were uninterested in Christianity but quick to place their faith in the evangelicals' schools.

One of the earliest and most successful was the Brainerd School, established in 1817 near present-day Chattanooga, Tennessee, by the American Board of Commissioners for Foreign Missions. There the missionaries instructed Cherokee boys and girls in "the rudiments of the English language, the principles of the Christian religion, and the industry and arts of civilized life."

Brainerd soon had a reputation that attracted such prominent visitors as President James Monroe, who included the school on his itinerary when he toured the western

states in 1819. The thriving establishment boasted nearly 100 pupils by 1820, and before long its alumni included *Cherokee Phoenix* editor Elias Boudinot and his brother, Stand Watie, a general in the Confederate army. Cherokee tribal leader John Ridge, whose father enrolled him at Brainerd in 1817, described how education had changed him: "The clouds of ignorance which surrounded me on all sides were dispersed. My heart received the rays of civilization and my intellect expanded and took on a wider range."

Even after being forcibly removed from their homeland, the Cherokees maintained their faith in education. By midcentury they had established an extensive network of public schools in the western territory.

A drawing of the Brainerd School shows the mission house at the center, with a fenced front yard *(below)*, the girls' dormitory next to the mission house, boys' and girls' schoolhouses, a sawmill, a gristmill, and a barn.

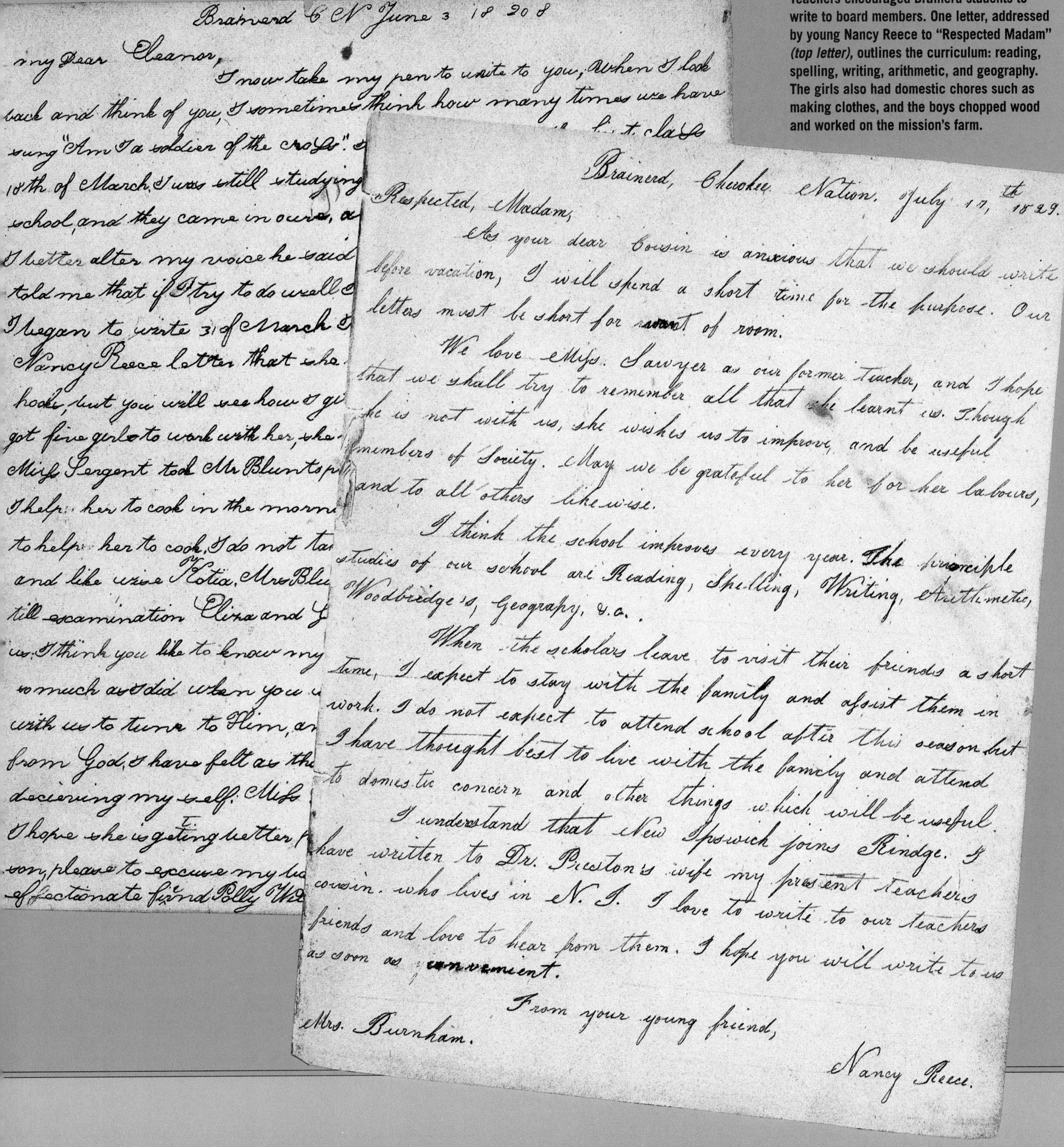

Teachers encouraged Brainerd students to write to board members. One letter, addressed by young Nancy Reece to "Respected Madam" *(top letter)*, outlines the curriculum: reading, spelling, writing, arithmetic, and geography. The girls also had domestic chores such as making clothes, and the boys chopped wood and worked on the mission's farm.

Brainerd C N June 3 18 20 8

my Dear Eleanor,

I now take my pen to write to you, when I look back and think of you, I sometimes think how many times we have sung "Am I a soldier of the cross". ... 18th of March I was still studying ... school, and they came in over, ... I better alter my voice he said ... told me that if I try to do well ... I began to write 31 of March ... Nancy Reece letter that she ... hook, but you will see how I ... got five girls to work with her, she ... Miss Sergent told Mr Blunt to p... I help her to cook in the morn... to help her to cook. I do not ta... and likewise Kotia. Mrs Blu... till examination Eliza and ... us. I think you like to know my... so much as I did when you ... with us to turn to Him, an... from God, I have felt as the... deceiving my self. Miss ... I hope she is getting better ... son, please to excuse my ... affectionate friend Polly W...

Brainerd, Cherokee Nation. July 17, th 1829.

Respected, Madam;

As your dear cousin is anxious that we should write before vacation, I will spend a short time for the purpose. Our letters must be short for want of room.

We love Miss Sawyer as our former teacher, and I hope that we shall try to remember all that she learnt us. Though she is not with us, she wishes us to improve, and be useful members of Society. May we be grateful to her for her labours, and to all others likewise.

I think the school improves every year. The principle studies of our school are Reading, Spelling, Writing, Arithmetic, Woodbridge's, Geography, &c..

When the scholars leave to visit their friends a short time, I expect to stay with the family and assist them in work. I do not expect to attend school after this season but I have thought best to live with the family and attend to domestic concern and other things which will be useful.

I understand that New Ipswich joins Rindge. I have written to Dr. Preston's wife my present teachers cousin. who lives in N. I. I love to write to our teachers friends and love to hear from them. I hope you will write to us as soon as convenient.

From your young friend,

Mrs. Burnham.

Nancy Reece.

Students gather in front of the first public school to open in Tahlequah, the Cherokee capital, which was located in what is now Oklahoma. By 1874, the year in which this photograph was

FIRST IN GENERAL KNOWLEDGE

The expulsion of the Cherokees from their homeland, although devastating, had the unforeseen benefit of placing control of education in the hands of the tribe. In 1841, after they settled in northeastern Indian Territory, the Cherokee Council provided for 11 public schools, using funds granted under the New Echota treaty governing their removal.

In just 10 years the number of schools doubled and enrollment reached 1,100. The council hired both whites and Cherokees to teach English, arithmetic, history, and geography. To one young girl her teacher seemed "a nice young man" because "he doesn't lay up in the corner and sleep, [and] tends to business all the day long." Despite such faint praise, the tribe at the time could boast of a system that had more schools, more teachers, and more students enrolled than the neighboring states of Arkansas and Missouri.

Lessons were at first taught exclusively in English because, as a member of the board of directors for Cherokee high schools explained, "a sprightly lad can learn to read his tongue in a day or even less" in the phonetic Cherokee alphabet devised by Sequoya. In later years tribal reformers introduced Cherokee language and texts to schools in communities where English was seldom spoken.

So successful were the public schools that an 1872 federal government study reported that "of all the Indian tribes, great and small, the Cherokee are first in general knowledge, in the acquisition of wealth, in the knowledge of the useful arts, and in social and moral progress."

A teacher watches over her smiling charges outside a Cherokee school *(left)*. One-room schools held children of all ages, so older students like the girls below often helped to instruct the younger ones.

ken, there were nearly 75 Cherokee schools in operation.

LIFEBLOOD OF A NATION

On the hot morning of May 6, 1851, 25 men ranging in age from 16 to 21 moved into the first nonsectarian school of higher learning west of the Mississippi, the Cherokee Male Seminary near Tahlequah. Just one day later the Cherokee Female Seminary opened its doors to 25 students in nearby Park Hill.

Pleased with the growth of their primary system, the Cherokee Council had voted to fund two high schools that were to be modeled on northeastern institutions.

Council members looked to Yale University and Mount Holyoke Seminary for instructors and a curriculum and hired a Boston firm to oversee the construction of both Cherokee seminaries.

Although many students welcomed the chance for further education, a few were more interested in mischief than mathemat-

ics. For the young men this often meant risking black marks by drinking, smoking, or slipping out after hours.

Despite such lapses in conduct, male seminarians went on to distinguish themselves as principal chiefs, educators, lawyers, physicians, and bankers. Such alumni fulfilled the promise of an 1856 student newspaper editorial describing the seminaries as "the arteries through which the life blood of our Nation's prosperity circulates."

A diploma certifies that in 1888 Phillips Rofe met the graduation requirements for the Cherokee Male Seminary, meant to prepare its students for a university education.

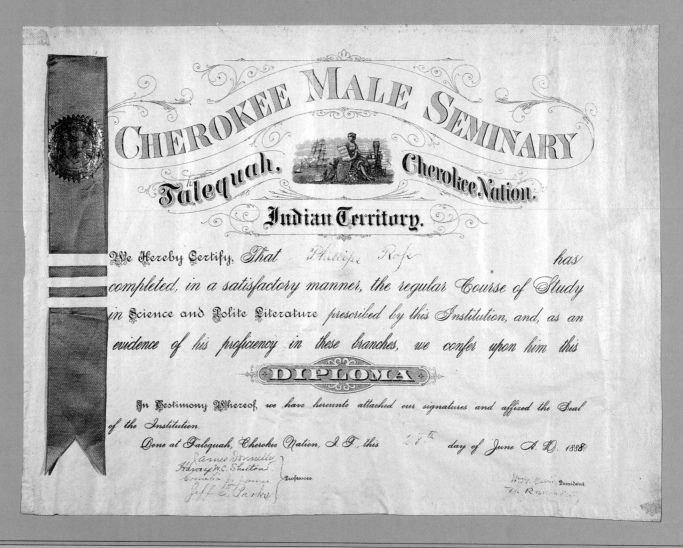

Members of the class of 1885 pose with a faculty member seated at far right in the photograph above, on the steps of the Male Seminary. The school attracted a prestigious faculty, including a graduate of Oxford University. A program *(inset)* commemorates the year's male and female joint commencement ceremony, which included a week-long festival of plays, recitals, and social events.

1850.   1885.

Annual Commencement

—OF THE—

Cherokee National Male and Female

* Seminaries, *

Thursday, June 25th, 1885.

Tahlequah, I. T.

A WREATH OF CHEROKEE ROSEBUDS

Equality reigned in the academic programs offered at the Cherokee Female Seminary in Park Hill and the male institution in Tahlequah. However, the female seminary had an additional mission: to school its students in the social graces and in what the curriculum described as the "meticulous refinements of good breeding." The young women referred to themselves as rosebuds, and an essay in the student newspaper, appropriately named *A Wreath of Cherokee Rose Buds*, declared that educated women were like flowers: "The more they are cultivated the more beautiful they become."

Although the female graduates were as proficient in academic subjects as the men, they were not expected to go on to college. It was assumed that after graduation they would teach in Cherokee schools or become the wives of the Cherokee community's leaders.

In its 40 years of operation, some 3,000 young women attended the seminary. Many did become teachers, and a smaller number took up careers in medicine, social work, and business. These women achieved the aspirations of a student who wrote, "If we would have the name of a Cherokee an honor, let us strive earnestly to value education aright."

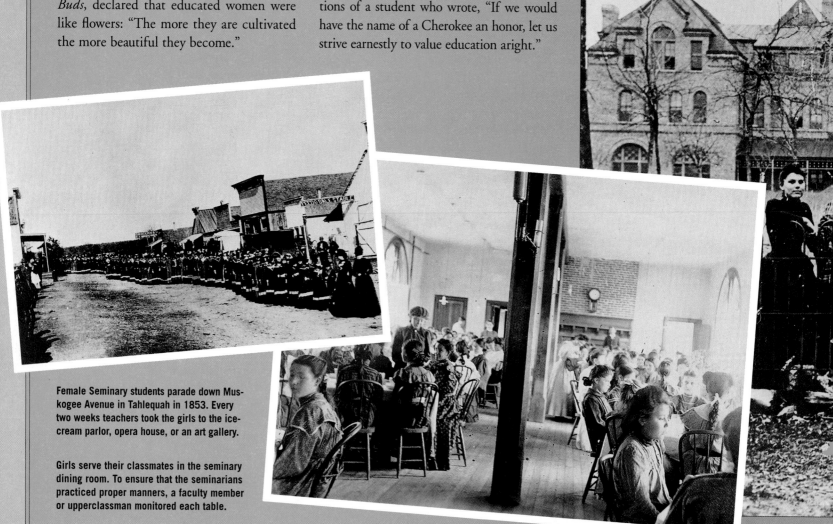

Female Seminary students parade down Muskogee Avenue in Tahlequah in 1853. Every two weeks teachers took the girls to the ice-cream parlor, opera house, or an art gallery.

Girls serve their classmates in the seminary dining room. To ensure that the seminarians practiced proper manners, a faculty member or upperclassman monitored each table.

Juniors and seniors assemble outside the gates of the second home of the seminary; the original building had burned to the ground in 1887. A program *(below)* lists the events that took place when the new building was dedicated. Now known as Seminary Hall, it is part of Northeastern Oklahoma State University.

National Female Seminary.

May 5 – 1889

Dedication Program.

1st.   Music—song of welcome.
2nd.   Prayer, by Assistant Chief gmith.
3rd.   Music Chorus.
4th.   Address by Hon. J. B. Mayes.
5th.   Music by the Band.
6th.   Address by Harvey W. C. Shelton.
7th.   Music Chorus.
8th.   Delivery of key of building from Building Committee to Board of Ed-

   cation by J. S. Stapler.
9th.   Delivery of key from Board of Education to Superintendent by Hon. W. H. Davis.
10th. Reception of key by S. S. Stephens.
11th. Dedicatory Prayer by Rev. W. L. Miller.
12th. Music Chorus.
13th. Gall speeches—meeting in hands of the public.
14th. Music by the Band.
15th. Dinner.

CHAPTER 2

THE ODYSSEY OF A COMANCHE CHIEFTAIN

"A leader's road is a hard road. Some men are good leaders of war parties. Everybody knows who they are."

QUANAH PARKER

Quanah Parker, shown here around 1880 in his early thirties, fought tirelessly for his fellow Comanches, first as a war chief defying the U.S. Army and later as a reservation leader grappling with bureaucracy and federal authorities.

Approaching quietly in the night, the Comanche raiders could see the telltale campfires of the bluecoats dwindling to embers in the distance. The cavalrymen had spent the last few hours there huddled around the low flames, whiling away another uneventful evening on the stark Texas plains. Now all but a few of them had fallen asleep, and the Comanches were ready to strike. Armed with rifles, they could have picked off a few soldiers in a rush and hurried away. But there was little glory or profit in that. The raiders were less interested in the bluecoats themselves than in their horses, tethered at the edge of the camp. More than any other prize of battle, horses brought power and prestige to the far-ranging Comanches, and cavalry horses were especially coveted because they were a larger breed than Indian ponies.

One man stood out among the raiders as they prepared to attack on the night of October 9, 1871. In his early twenties and already a prominent war leader, he was taller and leaner than most of his companions and somewhat lighter in complexion. His eyes, too, were different, startlingly gray among a brown-eyed people. His singular appearance derived from an unusual heritage. He was the son of the Comanche chief Peta Nocone and a white

woman named Cynthia Ann Parker, who was captured by Comanches as a girl. His companions knew him as Quanah, or Sweet Smell, but he would honor his mother's memory in later years by taking the name Quanah Parker.

Quanah and his fellow warriors belonged to a Comanche group known as the Quahadas, or Antelope Eaters, who subsisted in the rugged, semiarid country around the Texas Panhandle in part by hunting antelope, buffalo, and other game and in part by raiding their enemies, including white ranchers who had intruded on their territory in recent years. Their life was often harsh and uncompromising, like the land they occupied, but they had no intention of forsaking either their customs or their country.

Quanah and his band had steadfastly refused to sign a single treaty with the Americans or to accept confinement to a reservation. The cavalrymen camped in the distance had been sent to track them down and whip them into submission. But the sheer magnitude of the pursuing column—some 600 men in all, led by Colonel Ranald S. Mackenzie of the 4th U.S. Cavalry—and their carelessness in lighting fires after dark made them easy to spot. As often happened when soldiers went out after Indians, the hunters became the hunted.

In preparation for battle Quanah had daubed on his black war paint and donned the long eagle-feather bonnet that distinguished him as a war chief. Around his neck he wore the claws of a bear, a creature from which he claimed special medicine, or spirit power. Around midnight he and the others spurred their swift ponies, bred and trained especially for battle, and rode to the attack. Approaching the spot where the cavalry mounts were picketed, they did their best to set off a stampede by yelling, ringing bells, waving buffalo robes, and firing their rifles.

The commotion roused the sleeping bluecoats, who fumbled for their guns and shot wildly at the figures galloping by, adding to the frenzy of the tethered horses, which reared high and strained at their ropes, pulling the iron pickets from the ground. "Get to your horses!" officers shouted to their men, but for some of them the warning came too late. Soldiers grabbing for their mounts had to duck the sharp pickets swinging wildly in the air. A few of the men snared runaways with lariats, only to find themselves dragged along the ground until they surrendered their grip. More than 70 horses were lost to the Comanches, who were expert at roping animals on the run. Quanah singled out for his own prize a gray mount that belonged to Colonel Mackenzie. As the Comanches galloped away, recalled Captain Robert Carter of the 4th U.S. Cavalry, "the yells of the retreating Indians from the distance came back on the midnight air with a peculiar, taunting ring."

As they frequently did after a raid, the Comanches split up into smaller parties to avoid being overtaken as a group. The precaution was warranted, for Mackenzie's force still had more than enough horses to mount a strong pursuit. After daybreak, Captain Carter and a detachment of bluecoats nearly caught up with Quanah's party. Carter could see only a few Comanches in the distance, and they looked to be in no mood for a fight. They abandoned the horses they had seized and fled up a ridge, with the bluecoats in eager pursuit.

> *"The hissing and spitting of the bullets sounded viciously, and the yells of the retreating Indians from the distance came back on the midnight air with a peculiar, taunting ring, telling all too plainly that the Quahadas, Quanah's wild band of Comanches, had been among us."*
>
> CAPTAIN ROBERT G. CARTER

But Carter and his cavalrymen were being drawn into a trap. Suddenly Quanah and a small force of mounted warriors appeared atop the ridge and galloped down the slope. The troopers froze in their tracks at the sight of the oncoming spectacle. The Comanches were riding horses painted for battle and adorned with ribbons of "flannel and calico," Carter recalled, and they attacked "with jubilant, discordant yells that would have put to blush any Confederate brigade of the Civil War."

The bold charge unnerved the cavalrymen, most of whom fired a few errant shots and then turned tail. Carter and five of his men tried to make a stand, but they were pressed back by the Comanches and soon joined in the headlong retreat. One trooper named Gregg was riding a worn-out horse and fell behind the others. Quanah, pursuing on a speedy coal black horse with pistol in hand and his long war bonnet nearly sweeping the ground, closed in on Gregg like an accomplished buffalo hunter singling out the straggler in the herd. Several of Gregg's fellow troopers wheeled and fired on the chief, but he remained on the far side of Gregg, skillfully using his prey as a shield. Before Gregg could turn his pistol on his pursuer, Quanah shot him dead and galloped away.

Gregg was one of the few bluecoat casualties in the encounter, but Mackenzie was incensed by the raid on his camp and by the failure of his forces to catch the Comanches. A battle-scarred Civil War veteran who had graduated first in his class at West Point, the 31-year-old colonel had lost two fingers on his right hand and was known to his own troops as Three-Finger Jack and to Indians as Bad Hand. General Ulysses S. Grant had pronounced him "the most promising young officer in the army." But he was new to Indian fighting, and he had much to learn from his tribal opponents.

Among the first lessons he had to absorb was that despite American claims to the contrary, this was still Comanche country; he and his men were rank strangers. In the weeks to come they would follow the trail of the Quahadas across the desolate

Staked Plain—an expanse so featureless that the early Spanish explorers who crossed it purportedly marked it with stakes so they could find their way back. Extending south from the Panhandle, it was a region unmapped and hitherto untouched by the U.S. Army. But the Quahadas were thoroughly at home. They knew every slight rise and depression in the landscape and used that knowledge to frustrate their pursuers.

Another truth Mackenzie would have to reckon with was that Indian warriors were not skittish and easily intimidated, contrary to claims by some officers in the army. To be sure, chiefs like Quanah chose their battles carefully and tried to minimize casualties, for their bands were small and could ill afford to lose the services of young men who were both avid fighters and expert hunters. Most warriors, however, were fully prepared to die in defense of their homeland and kin. Quanah and his men traveled across the Staked Plain that autumn with their women and children and took great pains to protect them. Whenever the pursuing cavalry came within range of their families, Captain Carter related, warriors "began to swarm on the right and left of the trail, like angry bees, circling here and there in an effort to divert us."

Before long, Mackenzie found himself forced to do battle with the elements as well. In early November the first snow fell, and the north wind cut through the soldiers' light summer uniforms. By midmonth, the column was enveloped in a full-scale blizzard and lost contact with the Comanches. With both morale and supplies running low, Mackenzie reluctantly abandoned the chase. "We didn't look worth a damn," he said afterward of his bedraggled troopers.

Mackenzie had lost his favorite horse to Quanah, receiving in return some painful lessons in warfare on the open plains. The two were destined to meet again, however, and the next time he came up against Comanches, Mackenzie would prove to be a much more formidable opponent. In the end, relentless pressure from the bluecoats would impel Quanah to lay down his weapons and devote his prodigious energies to a far different campaign—a struggle for dignity and respect within the confines of the reservation.

That Quanah and Colonel Mackenzie first clashed over horses was fitting, for those animals, which had been brought to the New World by Europeans, transformed the lives of the Comanches and other Plains Indians and enhanced their ability to compete with whites for control of the grasslands. Spanish conquistadors introduced horses to Mexico in the 16th century, and by the mid-17th century, Pueblo Indians in the Southwest were tending large

In the early 1800s Comanches controlled a vast area called the Comanchería, outlined by the dotted line in the map below. Only after decades of fiercely resisting white intruders did the Comanches and their Kiowa allies accept confinement to the Fort Sill Reservation in the Indian Territory.

herds for their Spanish masters. During the Pueblo revolt that erupted in 1680, many of those horses ran free or were swept up by Apaches, who at the time occupied the western edge of the plains. Apache traders in turn helped disperse horses to other tribes across a vast area, from Texas in the south to the Dakotas in the north.

The adoption of the horse made Indian hunting bands on the plains far more efficient. Previously they had stalked buffalo on foot, praying that their quarry would come close enough to be driven over cliffs or into ravines, where they could be trapped and slaughtered. Now the hunters could mount up and follow the immense herds over great distances, culling them time and again. The best ponies for the purpose were light and fast and were trained to chase after stampeding buffalo without swerving or flinching; other horses served the hunting bands as beasts of burden, carrying buffalo-hide tepees and other belongings from camp to camp.

Neighboring tribes vied energetically for control of the animals. Chiefs amassed large herds of horses, and warriors prided themselves on slipping undetected into enemy encampments and making off with the prize mounts, tethered outside the lodges. Horses transformed former woodland tribes such as the Lakota Sioux, who migrated onto the northern plains from present-day Minnesota, into venturesome hunter-warriors who fought hard in order to extend their range.

No tribal group profited more from its mastery of the horse than the Comanches. Related to the Shoshones of present-day Wyoming, they broke sometime before 1700 and gradually trekked down from the mountains onto the southern plains. There they acquired horses and became dedicated buffalo hunters, developing a dependency on that creature for practically their entire subsistence—meat, shelter, clothing, weapons, tools, and even fuel in the form of buffalo chips.

As Comanche bands fanned out in pursuit of the elusive herds, they clashed with other Indians, including the Tonkawas of south central Texas, who would later provide scouts for the U.S. Army in its campaigns against Comanches. In the 1700s mounted Comanche warriors, armed with guns secured from white traders, drove the Apaches off the plains into the high desert country of the Southwest and began raiding Spanish settlements in New Mexico and down along the Rio Grande. Typically the raiders were after horses, but they also claimed lives and seized captives, and soon the Comanches and Spaniards were locked in a long and bloody vendetta.

Although Comanches acquired a fearsome reputation as warriors, they were also skilled traders and negotiators who formed durable alliances with several neighboring tribes, including the Kiowas, Wichitas, and Southern Cheyennes. They welcomed with open arms the far-ranging Spanish merchants who came to be called comancheros because of the trade they carried on with the tribe. Even some Spanish officers who dared to enter what they referred to as the Comanchería—the vast area dominated by Comanches, extending from the Arkansas River in the north to near San Antonio in the south—sometimes encountered chiefs who were willing to make peace, if the terms were right.

Spanish authorities found it difficult if not impossible to treat with Comanches as a group, however, because unlike the Cherokees, the tribe's 20,000 or so members had no central authority. Since breaking away from the Shoshones and migrating, they had lived in large, family-centered groups, or bands. Each band was in turn loosely allied with one of several branches of the tribe, such as the Kotsotekas, or Buffalo Eaters, who lived in prime bison country above the Red River, in what is now Oklahoma. The bands belonging to the same branch traveled, camped, and hunted together through the year. Periodically, they congregated for festivities and councils, and they sometimes acknowledged one man as leader of their branch. But until the reservation era, the Comanches as a whole had no principal chief.

By the time Anglo-Americans appeared on the southern plains in the early 1800s, Comanches were

"THE MOST EXTRAORDINARY HORSEMEN"

"I am ready, without hesitation, to pronounce the Comanches the most extraordinary horsemen that I have seen," wrote artist George Catlin after encountering them in 1834. "I doubt very much whether any people in the world can surpass them."

Catlin's opinion was well founded, for he visited many western tribes as part of an ambitious campaign to record the life of American Indians on canvas. He depicted the remarkable horsemanship of Comanches in the painting above, which shows warriors practicing for combat.

Catlin elaborated in his journal on the feats that he portrayed, noting that a mounted Comanche warrior would screen himself from his enemies by leaning low over the flank of his mount, "with his heel hanging over the horse's back." From that precarious position, Catlin added, the rider could right himself and dip "to the other side if necessary. In this wonderful condition, he will hang whilst at fullest speed, carrying with him his bow and his shield, and also his lance of fourteen feet in length, all or either of which he will wield upon his enemy as he passes; rising and throwing his arrows over the horse's back, or with equal ease and equal success under the horse's neck."

Such dexterity in the saddle led observers to conclude that Comanches were born horsemen, and indeed they began riding ponies at an early age. But their skills were not instinctive. It was only through rigorous training and constant conditioning that they mastered their craft and bested their rivals in mounted warfare. As Catlin observed, they were not physically superior to their opponents. Most Comanches, in fact, were rather short and stocky. "But the moment they mount their horses," the artist marveled, "they seem at once metamorphosed, and surprise the spectator with the ease and elegance of their movements."

feeling pressure from tribes that were being pushed out onto the plains by the tide of white settlement and did not have any immediate desire to add the Americans to their list of enemies. Colonel Henry Dodge of the U.S. Army discovered as much in 1834 when he led 500 cavalrymen on an expedition across the western reaches of the Indian Territory. Comanches there learned of his approach, obtained an American flag, and flew it from a pole to signal their friendly intentions. Artist George Catlin, who accompanied Colonel Dodge fully expecting a run-in with "wild and warlike Comanches," was startled not only by the sight of the Stars and Stripes but also by the willingness of the Comanches to come forward "without a weapon of any kind, to meet a war party bristling with arms and trespassing to the middle of their country."

Hopes for peace between Comanches and Americans were soon dashed, however, by the relentless westward advance of white settlers in Texas. By 1836, when the Republic of Texas won independence from Mexico, settlers were venturing from the wooded, well-watered confines of east Texas out onto the margins of the plains, where they infringed on the territory of the Comanches and allied groups such as the Wichitas, who had migrated south from Kansas. Comanches and their allies responded forcefully with raids that were aimed both at seizing horses and other prizes from the settlers and at encouraging whites to abandon the plains, if they valued their lives. Far from retreating, however, Texans fortified their outposts and launched devastating reprisals.

Neither side in this emerging conflict was inclined to show mercy to the other. In their battles with Texans, as in their raids against Spaniards and other sworn enemies, Comanche warriors often killed the men they overpowered and removed their scalps, which were preserved for display in war

Magnificently equipped with lance, bow, quiver, shield, and revolver, this proud Comanche warrior named Jesús Sánchez—a captive who was seized in Mexico as a boy and adopted by the tribe—impressed George Catlin with his "gentlemanly politeness" when the artist painted his portrait in 1834.

dances and other ceremonies. Although whites denounced scalp taking and other forms of mutilation as barbaric, they often did much the same to their Indian foes. Even more provocative to settlers than the killing and mutilating of men was the harsh treatment Comanches accorded women and children they seized. The children were often taunted and thrashed in the first days of captivity, and the women were subject to rape. Most captives survived their ordeals and were either released for ransom payments or folded into the tribe through adoption or marriage. Comanche women and children, for their part, were no less vulnerable in the struggle, often falling victim along with their men when white warriors attacked their camps.

Quanah Parker was a product of this terrible conflict, a man who carried within him the strains of two cultures that were profoundly at odds. Nevertheless, in his later years he would manage to reconcile them: He never ceased identifying himself wholeheartedly with the tribe in which he grew up, and he also came to respect the fortitude of his mother's people. Like the Comanches who first ventured down from the mountains to the plains, they too had had to fight for their place in a land of both endless promise and seemingly endless discord. While Quanah owed much to the powerful example of his Comanche father, he also derived strength from his mother and the courage that saw her through a bewildering odyssey that began in 1836 at a lonely outpost on the edge of the plains called Parker's Fort.

Some called it Indian country, but to old John Parker it was God's territory and it was intended for the strong and the righteous. Now in his late seventies, Parker was a restless farmer and itinerant Baptist preacher who had kept moving with the American frontier, like an evangelist in search of fresh prospects to redeem. Born in Virginia when it was still an English colony, he had fought in the Revolutionary War and then migrat-

Comanche shields like this one, covered with buckskin and adorned with horsehair, eagle feathers, and images of the sun and stars, were said to confer medicine, or protective spirit power, on the warriors who carried them. Comanches never willingly allowed their shields to touch the ground.

ed with his growing family, first to Georgia and then to Tennessee and Illinois. Early in 1834 he and his clan settled on the rich, rolling plains near the head of the Navasota River, some 40 miles east of present-day Waco, Texas. Their frontier community embraced four generations of the family, from the elder Parker and his wife to their great-grandchildren. Among the settlers were three of the old man's sons, including Silas Parker, who was the father of a blue-eyed nine-year-old named Cynthia Ann.

Like most of their countrymen, the Parkers and their in-laws believed that westward expansion was their right and their destiny. At the same time, they realized that Indians in the vicinity felt otherwise and took extensive precautions against attack. Profiting by the fine timber to be found along the banks of the Navasota and other rivers and streams at the edge of the plains, they built seven log cabins and then surrounded their compound of more than an acre with a stockade of split logs, placed upright and sharpened menacingly at the top. Tall blockhouses located diagonally at two of the four corners afforded good views of the surrounding terrain.

Parker's Fort, as it became known, housed 34 settlers and in an emergency offered refuge for several other families of the little colony who lived in log cabins nearby. Unfortunately, the conspicuous efforts undertaken by Americans to protect themselves only provoked neighboring Indians, who knew from experience that whites built forts not simply to fend off their enemies but also to use as bases for establishing control over the plains and the tribes living there.

On the morning of May 19, 1836, a formidable party of about 100 mounted Indians approached Parker's Fort. Most were Comanches, but the force also included some Kiowas and Wichitas. The riders were armed with bows and lances, and their horses were painted with symbols of their spirit power. To the settlers peering out through loopholes in the stockade, the Indians looked forbidding, but they were making gestures of peace. Two of the Indians rode slowly toward the front gate, one of them waving a white flag attached to his lance.

Several men of the Parker clan had left the fort early that morning to work the cornfields about a mile away near the river, but a half-dozen remained inside, along with 10 women and 15 children. All looked to Silas Parker for leadership. He was an officer of the Texas Rangers, a homegrown militia formed just the previous year to fight Indians while the regular soldiers battled for independence from Mexico. Neither Silas nor the others seemed to know quite what to do in this crisis, however. One of the settlers, E. G. Dwight, headed toward the stockade's rear door with his wife, child, and mother-in-law, whom he intended to escort to a hiding place in the woods. "Stand and fight like a man," Silas urged him. "If we have to die, we'll sell our lives as dear as we can." Dwight promised to come back when his family had reached safety.

Silas's younger brother, Benjamin, then went out the front gate to parley. Using hand signals, the Indians indicated that they were looking for a place to camp and that they were hungry and wanted some beef to eat. Benjamin returned to the fort to confer with Silas and the others. They agreed that they had no food to spare—and no intention of yielding to the demands of a large party of Indians who seemed menacing, despite their white flag. Benjamin feared the worst and warned the men to look to their arms. Then, despite Silas's pleas that he stay in the fort, Benjamin insisted on going back outside for a further parley in hopes of keeping the peace. As he walked out alone, the settlers left the gate open behind him.

The waiting warriors engulfed Benjamin and stabbed him to death with their lances, then raced into the compound. Silas Parker, who had run to his cabin to fetch ammunition for his rifle, emerged with a loud huzzah and died in a futile attempt to defend his pregnant 27-year-old niece, Rachel Plummer, and her 18-month-old son, James; both were taken captive.

Most of the settlers who had not already retreated to the woods fled out the back door, but warriors chased after them. They tracked down and killed old John Parker; assaulted his elderly wife, who barely survived; and took captive his young kinswoman, Elizabeth Kellogg. Silas's wife, Lucy, and her four children were captured as well as they tried to flee. Her two eldest, Cynthia Ann and six-year-old John, were promptly hoisted onto horses by Comanches and taken away. The rest of the family most likely would have been abducted as well had not the settlers toiling in the distant cornfield been alerted by gunfire and come running back. One of them wielded a rifle, and they looked menacing enough that the warriors remaining around the fort left Lucy and her two younger children behind and galloped off. Any relief Mrs. Parker felt at her rescue was overwhelmed by grief for John and Cynthia Ann, who were lost to the fast-retreating warriors. The Comanches split up and returned to their respective camps, and the two Parker children ended up being adopted by separate bands.

All told, seven settlers died in the attack, and five were taken captive, four of whom ultimately were ransomed. Elizabeth Kellogg was the first to be released, after six months, followed a year later by Rachel Plummer, whose published account of her ordeal, relating how she and Kellogg had been raped, further incited settlers against the Comanches. More than six years after the raid, whites learned of the whereabouts of the two boys, James Plummer and John Parker, and purchased their freedom as well. For John, however, the anguish of captivity had long since yielded to pride at being adopted by the tribe. By then in his early teens, he found white society strange and confining after his free-wheeling life as a young Comanche.

Buffalo graze placidly in the summer heat in a photograph of one of the last buffalo herds remaining on the plains in the late 1800s. Earlier in the century the hunting grounds of the Comanches and other Plains tribes so abounded with bison that Catlin reported it was not uncommon to see "several thousands in a mass, eddying and wheeling about under a cloud of dust."

For Cynthia Ann, the one unreclaimed captive, the conversion to Comanche ways was even more profound. At first, like most young captives, she was probably entrusted to the supervision of an older woman, who kept a strict watch over her and assigned her many hard tasks. Her fair skin burned and blistered in the sun, but the Comanches soothed it with buffalo grease and in time her complexion darkened, until only her pale eyes distinguished her from her companions.

As the memories of Parker's Fort faded, she grew resigned to her lot. After being watched over for a while by her guardian, she was adopted by a family and treated as one of the tribe. From her mother and other women of the band she learned how to butcher buffalo and steep her hands in the blood of that generous creature to extract tasty organs, tough sinew, and dozens of other useful parts. She also learned how to piece together buffalo skins in order to make a tepee covering and to dismantle the lodge and pack it on a travois of two poles lashed together when the band decamped to pursue bison and fresh pasture for the horses. In time she joined gladly in festivities, singing and dancing with other eligible girls when warriors returned in triumph, and anticipated the day when she too would be married to a young man rich in horses and other tokens of bravery.

The Parkers, meanwhile, were desperately trying to ransom her, offering as much as $500 in silver for her return. In 1840, when she was about 13, two whites and their Delaware Indian guide came across a girl fitting her description while trading with Comanches in the Texas Panhandle. They reportedly offered a sizable ransom in goods to her adoptive father, but he refused all offers. The girl they took to be Cynthia Ann stood by silently while they talked of her friends and kin. They thought they detected a quiver of her lips, suggesting perhaps that she understood what they said and still remembered her loved ones.

Comanche girls were considered marriageable after puberty, and Cynthia Ann evidently became a bride sometime in the early 1840s, when she was in her mid-teens. Her husband, Peta Nocone, or He Who Travels Alone and Returns, was then an avid young warrior of about 20 who was destined to become a celebrated chief. Like other prominent Comanche men, Peta Nocone acquired additional wives over time to help maintain his lodge, but that did not mean he regarded his first wife any less highly. By all evidence, she and Peta Nocone remained devoted to each other.

In 1846 two U.S. Indian commissioners, P. M. Butler and M. G. Lewis, told of encountering Cynthia Ann with her band on the Washita River in the western part of the Indian Territory. She now went by the Comanche name of Naduah, or Someone Found, and showed no interest in being reclaimed by whites. "From the influence of her alleged husband, or from her own inclination, she is unwilling to leave the people with whom she associates," the commissioners reported. "A large amount of goods and four or five hundred dollars were offered, but the offer was unavailing, as she would run off and hide herself to avoid those who went to ransom her."

Five years later, in 1851, a group of white hunters, including several friends of the Parkers, met with a group of Comanches along the upper Canadian River and recognized one of them as Cynthia Ann. They asked if she wanted to return to her kin. She shook her head and pointed to two little boys at her feet. The younger of the two was named Pecos. The other boy, a year or so older, was Quanah, the future war chief. Just how old he was then is uncertain, but he was probably born around 1848.

Quanah grew up with no knowledge of his mother's history. To be sure, he knew that she was somehow different from other women in the band, but he thought of her as a true Comanche, and she demonstrated as much through her devotion to her family. As an army officer who encountered her in 1854 put it, her husband and children were "all that she held most dear."

Although Cynthia Ann had crossed the treacherous frontier separating whites from Indians and settled into the rhythm of life on the other side, her ordeal was not over. Her husband's persistent raids made him notorious among Texans at a time when other Comanche chiefs and their followers were giving way before the white onslaught. Tens of thousands of new settlers had poured into Texas after it joined the Union as a state in 1845. White encroachment on Comanche country not only reduced the size of the buffalo range but also introduced diseases that ravaged the Comanche population—first smallpox, then cholera, spread by prospectors who were bound for California in 1849 along a trail that led from Kansas through the Texas Panhandle and connected with the Santa Fe Trail. The southernmost division of Comanches, known as the Penatekas, were so reduced in numbers and strength that they became the first members of their tribe to agree to live on a reservation, situated in central Texas. Neighboring whites refused to tolerate their presence, however, and in 1859 federal authorities removed them to the Indian Territory.

By the late 1850s some 2,500 U.S. troops were stationed at a half-dozen forts along the Texas frontier. They were augmented by a standing force of some 500 Texas Rangers and hundreds of armed settlers, loosely organized into local militias. Faced with Texans who would not rest easy until the last of the Comanches had been ousted from their state, Peta Nocone clung fiercely to his prerogatives as a hunter and warrior. He had no intention of trusting in white treaty makers and moving to a reservation, no matter how much pressure his enemies brought to bear.

In early autumn, as the full harvest moon approached, bringing with it the bright nights Comanches favored for raiding, Peta Nocone and his band prepared to resume their longstanding war on the Texans. They made their base camp for the cold months ahead along the Pease River where it approaches the Red River, west of present-day Wichita Falls. There, sand hills bordering the river afforded protection from the so-called blue northers, winter gales that swept down from Canada. Naduah and other women of the band erected the tepees and collected firewood, and the men pursued buffalo. When enough meat had been laid by to last the camp for some time, Peta Nocone and his warriors rode off to attack the burgeoning frontier settlements to the southeast.

In November 1860 he and his men made an especially deep and deadly thrust into occupied territory. They rode for hundreds of miles, passing near the decaying remains of Parker's Fort, where the

Comanche warriors traditionally wore headdresses crowned with buffalo horns like those below, wrapped in hide decorated with beadwork. Buffalo horns invested the warrior with the power of the animal that almost exclusively sustained the tribe.

In this view of a Comanche camp by Catlin, two women stretch a buffalo hide flat with stakes while another scrapes a hide clean on a frame. Once processed, hides could be fashioned into clothing or sewn together to form tepees like those in the background, painted with distinctive designs by the occupants.

chief's wife had been taken captive as a young girl, and raiding a number of ranches and homesteads in the area. In one attack—which may have been instigated by a warrior seeking to avenge the loss of a wife, mother, or child to marauding whites—Comanches descended on the log cabin of a settler named Sherman at the western edge of Parker County and singled out his pregnant wife for abuse, wounding her so severely that she died the next day after losing her child.

Amid loud cries for vengeance, authorities mounted an expedition of more than 100 men to track down and punish the notorious Peta Nocone and his band. In command was Captain Lawrence Sullivan Ross of Waco, a newly commissioned offi-

cer in the Texas Rangers. "Sul" Ross had been itching to penetrate Comanche territory and "carry the war into their own homes," as he put it, and here was his chance. In December he rode northwest with a column that included 40 Texas Rangers, a detachment of 20 troopers lent by the 2d U.S. Cavalry, and a posse of 70 volunteers. His men made slow progress through the broken landscape and a bone-chilling blue norther, but the trail was still fresh. The scouts—including a venturesome rancher named Charles Goodnight, who knew this country well and would later drive cattle through it by the thousands—found Mrs. Sherman's Bible, lost or discarded by the retreating warriors as they neared the Pease River. Following in their path, the column approached the sand hills along the river and saw signs of an Indian encampment, including flocks of screaming ravens, often attracted to buffalo carcasses. Ross and his avengers prepared to move in for the kill.

Shortly after daybreak on December 19, Sul Ross followed fresh pony tracks up a sandy knoll and found what he was looking for. Some 100 yards below him, in a little valley where the fresh waters of Mule Creek entered the cloudy current of the Pease River, lay an Indian camp. Although his view was partially obscured by wreaths of wind-whipped sand, Ross detected a burst of activity in the camp and realized with alarm that the inhabitants were packing up and preparing to move out.

Without further reconnaissance, he positioned cavalrymen to cut off the anticipated retreat of the Comanches, then led his Rangers down the hill at a

Among the fleeing warriors was the chief in the buffalo headdress. Ross felt certain that it was Peta Nocone and gave chase along with his lieutenant, Tom Kelliher. One Comanche was close behind the chief, and Ross was about to fire his pistol at that fugitive when he saw that it was a woman, holding an infant. Ross left his deputy to deal with the woman and child and continued after the chief, who also had someone riding with him, clinging to his back as he urged his horse on. Only after Ross fired and killed the chief's companion did he realize it was a girl of about 15. She fell backward, dragging the man with her.

The chief struggled to his feet and drew his bow, unleashing an arrow that struck Ross's horse and sent the animal into a frenzy. Straining to regain control of his of mount, Ross fired a blind shot that smashed into the Comanche's right arm, ren-

> *"Ross seemed to conceive the idea that the Indians were just beyond the little divide or sand dunes that came down from the hills to the creek.... When he got to the top of the sand dune, the Indians were about a hundred yards from him just mounting to break camp."*

SCOUT CHARLES GOODNIGHT

gallop. They descended with six-shooters blazing into a camp that was occupied largely by unarmed women and children, who were preparing to join their men on a hunting expedition. Most of the men had ridden off a short time before, and they raced back to the camp when they heard gunfire.

By the time they arrived, a number of their women had been gunned down by the Texans. But other women and children were fleeing for their lives, and the warriors did everything they could to protect them. Led by a chief who was wearing a buffalo headdress, they galloped in between the fugitives and the pursuing Rangers and dismounted to face the Texans from behind their horses. The warriors held out as long as they could, buying time for their kin, then retreated on the horses that had survived the Texans' gunfire, with one or two riders on each mount.

dering his bow useless. Ross then dismounted and took dead aim at his foe, shooting him twice. Gravely wounded but still upright, the chief began to sing his death song—a prayer that Indians of many tribes chanted in their final moments to the sacred powers that controlled their destiny. Ross's Mexican servant, who spoke Comanche, rode up and ordered the stricken chief to surrender. The Comanche responded by thrusting his lance menacingly in Ross's direction. Finally Ross allowed the Mexican, whose own family had been massacred by Comanches, to finish the chief off.

Sul Ross was so certain that it was Peta Nocone who lay at his feet that he took the dead chief's headdress, weapons, and shield as trophies. But Ross was wrong. The slain man was a minor chief named Nobah. Peta Nocone was miles away at the time. Never dreaming that white men would pursue his band

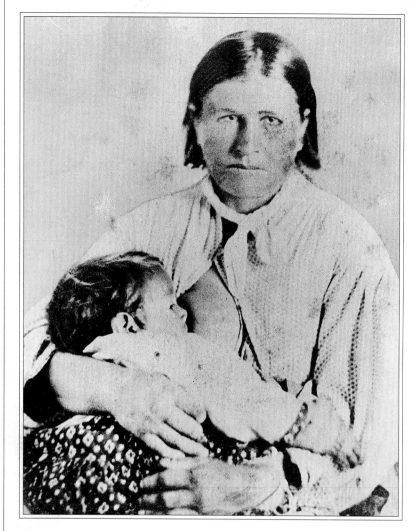

A disconsolate Cynthia Ann Parker nurses her daughter, Prairie Flower, after Texas troops recaptured the mother from the Comanches who had abducted her as a girl. According to a neighbor, she so longed to return to the tribe and her sons Quanah and Pecos that she would mingle her blood with tobacco "and burn it, and cry for her lost boys."

"was in terrible grief and distress," related Charles Goodnight. "I thought I would try to console her and make her understand she would not be hurt." Finally, the Mexican interpreter managed to learn the source of her distress. She was worried about her two sons—youngsters who had yet to reach fighting age. Through the interpreter, Goodnight reassured her that no young boys had been killed that day, and she appeared relieved.

The Texans suspected the woman might be Cynthia Ann Parker, but they could not be sure. They took her back to Camp Cooper on the Clear Fork of the Brazos River along with another captive, a nine-year-old Comanche boy whom Ross would adopt and raise. Cynthia Ann's nearest living relative, Isaac, the older brother of her slain father, was notified and hurried to the camp. At first she seemed not to recognize him or understand a word he said. But when he spoke the name Cynthia Ann, she jumped to her feet in acknowledgment.

With her infant daughter, Topsannah, or Prairie Flower, the 34-year-old Cynthia Ann went to live with Isaac near Fort Worth. The state granted her a pension of $100 a year, but she continued to work dutifully, as she had when she lived among the Comanches, chopping wood, braiding rugs, spinning cloth, and sleeping at night on the floor. After a while she began to recover some of her mother tongue and to communicate haltingly with relatives. But she remained bitterly unhappy. She grieved for her husband and two sons and her lost way of life. Indeed, she considered herself a captive of the whites and repeatedly tried to escape, forcing the Parkers to keep a very close watch on her. A former captive of the Comanches named Coho Smith visited her at one point, and she implored him in vain to help her steal some horses and return to her tribal home and the sons for whom her heart was "continually crying."

Her life came to a mournful end in 1864, shortly after her daughter succumbed to a fever. She grieved for Prairie Flower in Comanche fashion, slashing her breasts and wailing inconsolably. As her

this far into Comanche country, he had gone hunting two days previously with his sons, Quanah and Pecos, entrusting his wife and infant daughter to Nobah.

When Ross rode back to where he had left Lieutenant Kelliher and the woman, his deputy was cursing bitterly. He had run his favorite horse into the ground, and he had only a captive woman and child to show for it. Ross wrote afterward that the woman appeared "very dirty and far from attractive in her scanty garments, as well as her person." Then he took a closer look at her sun-darkened face and noticed with astonishment her blue eyes. "This is a white woman!" he exclaimed.

That night, the woman clutched her infant daughter in her arms and cried inconsolably. She despair deepened, she raised a chant that was both a lament for lost loved ones and her own death song. The Parkers buried her at a small cemetery in Henderson County, Texas, far from the Comanches she longed to rest among.

The years had not been any less trying for her husband, Peta Nocone. The loss of Naduah to Ross's men and the death at their hands of another of his wives, a Mexican woman, plunged him into despair. It was said that he never took another woman. Heartsick and weakened by an old wound that became infected, he lost his fervor for warfare. Shortly before his death, which occurred two or three years after Naduah's capture, he at last took Quanah into his confidence and told him of his mother's ancestry and how it was that she had come into Comanche hands.

At the time of his father's revelation Quanah was perhaps 15 years old and nearing the age when he would become a warrior. Since early childhood he had been trained for that role and for the related task of hunting. He had been given a small bow and taught to hit a man-sized target at a distance of up to 50 yards. As he grew stronger he learned to wield a long lance and drive it home with a vigorous underarm thrust. Raised on horseback, he practiced swooping low to retrieve objects from the ground without falling from his mount. And through it all he was steeped in stories of Comanche exploits against the Apaches, Mexicans, and Texans that infused him with brave ambitions.

Shortly after reaching puberty Quanah, like other Comanche youths, would have performed the eagle dance under the sponsorship of his father. This traditional ceremony, which portrayed young eagles leaving the nest, symbolized the young Comanche's passage from dependency to responsibility. Another mark of Quanah's coming of age was the new name that Peta Nocone gave him—Tseeta, or the Eagle. It was a fitting title for a chief and father to bestow on an aspiring warrior, but the boyish name Quanah stayed with him. No less important to him than the

"Cynthia was in terrible grief and distress... I thought I would try to console her and make her understand she would not be hurt. When I got near her I noticed she had blue eyes and light hair which had been cut off very short."

CHARLES GOODNIGHT

eagle was the protective power he acquired in a vision from the bear spirit. Those blessed with such power referred to it as medicine because they believed that it shielded them from harm and strengthened them against their enemies.

Quanah did not inherit leadership from his father, for among the Comanches, as among most other tribes, every chief had to earn his position by demonstrating courage, wisdom, and generosity, either in warfare or in peaceful pursuits. Only by living up to his father's strong example could the son of a chief attain power. For Quanah the task of following in Peta Nocone's path was complicated by the fact that some Comanches looked with suspicion on a young man with a white mother, however devoted she may have been to her band. Young Quanah was subject to taunts concerning his ancestry, but he rose to the challenge, excelling as a warrior and removing any doubt about his devotion to Comanches. In thus proving himself, he remarked later, he heeded the advice of Peta Nocone, who had told him that he must fight to become chief of his people.

Quanah rose rapidly in prestige during the mid-1860s. He traveled far with Quahada raiding parties, striking repeatedly at frontier settlements in Texas and reaching down into Mexico. Although known as a ferocious opponent in combat, this son of a captive developed a reputation for showing mercy to male prisoners and for leaving women and children alone.

As a prominent young warrior he earned a place among the Comanches who attended a big council of southern Plains tribes that was convened by the federal government on Medicine Lodge Creek in Kansas in October 1867. More than 4,000 Indians gathered there, including Comanches, Kiowas, and Southern Cheyennes and Arapahos. The government's twin objectives were to end hostilities by those tribes and confine them all to reservations, thus securing the surrounding country for the settlers and fortune hunters who were surging west after the Civil War. As yet, few whites were living on the open plains. But the wagon trails were crowded once more and railroad tracks were being laid,

threatening tribal hunting grounds and inciting raids by warriors, who exacted a steep toll from the intruders. The coming of the railroad made the grasslands especially attractive to cattlemen, who looked forward to driving their steers to rail depots and shipping them to eastern population centers. Once dismissed as a wasteland—the Great American Desert, as it was called—the plains were suddenly too rich with promise in the eyes of American authorities to be left to Indians.

At the Medicine Lodge council, Quanah and other Comanches met with stern soldier-chiefs who informed the Comanches that they "must stop going on the warpath." That in itself was no small demand, because the Comanches and the others at the council regarded warfare as an honorable pursuit that brought men lasting credit in their community. Who were these battle-proud soldier-chiefs, they wondered, to tell them to give up the glory of fighting? Still, Comanches had made peace with rival tribes in the past and might have settled their differences with the United States had not the treaty makers insisted on restricting them all to reservations. Ten Bears, chief of the Yamparikas, the northernmost division of Comanches, spoke for many of his fellow tribesmen in rejecting that idea: "I was born upon the prairie, where the wind blew free and there was nothing to break the light of the sun. I was born where there were no enclosures and where everything drew a free breath. I want to die there and not within walls."

In the end, all such eloquent protests were to no avail. American negotiators insisted that the chiefs sign the treaty or be regarded as hostile. Under the terms of the agreement, the signatories agreed to cede most of their ancestral lands to the United States and to discontinue raiding and other depre-

Shaded by an awning, army officers meet in council with Comanches, Kiowas, and members of other southern Plains tribes at Medicine Lodge Creek in Kansas in October 1867. The Americans promised to support the Indians with annuities if they adhered to reservations totaling 5,550 square miles. For people who traditionally had ranged far in pursuit of bison, Comanche chief Ten Bears told the Americans, "That which you now say we must live on is too small."

dations. In return, they were assigned reservations on land in the Indian Territory that had been confiscated from the Choctaws, Chickasaws, and other tribal groups whose members had lent some support to the Confederacy during the Civil War. Indians who reported to their assigned reservations would receive annuities of food, clothing, tools, and other forms of government aid to help them make the transition from hunting to farming—a hard task for anyone on the dry southern plains, and particularly difficult for groups like the Comanches who had never raised crops. Those who signed could at least take solace in the fact that the treaty granted them the right to hunt on land outside the reservation, "so long as the buffalo may range thereon in such numbers as to justify the chase."

Indeed, raiding only increased after the introduction of the Medicine Lodge Treaty. The Quahadas were by no means the only group involved; some of the bands that visited the reservations and collected annuities also carried out attacks on white travelers and settlers. But Quanah's Comanches came to epitomize the spirit of armed defiance, and the U.S. Army went to great lengths to track them down, assigning that responsibility to Colonel Ranald Mackenzie. The colonel's unsuccessful expedition in 1871, when he lost his horse to Quanah, was just the beginning of his campaign. That encounter taught him to "think Indian," as his troopers put it, and to train his forces in the tactics of surprise and evasion. He soon turned the 4th U.S. Cavalry into a highly effective fighting force.

"You said you wanted to put us upon a reservation, to build us houses.... I do not want them. I was born upon the prairie, where the wind blew free and there was nothing to break the light of the sun. I was born where there were no enclosures and where everything drew a free breath. I want to die there and not within walls."

COMANCHE CHIEF TEN BEARS

Many chiefs put their marks on the Medicine Lodge Treaty to avoid provoking the Americans at the council, then proceeded to ignore its terms, or to observe them selectively. In the years to come, thousands of Indians appeared occasionally at their assigned reservations—Cheyennes and Arapahos in the northwest corner of the Indian Territory, Comanches and Kiowas in the southwest part. Some stayed long enough to receive their annuities, but few settled down permanently.

Quanah and more than one-third of his fellow Comanches at the council, on the other hand, refused to sign the treaty. The Quahadas, in particular, were in no mood to play along with the proposals of the Americans. They scorned the idea of living in one place and scraping at the soil. And annuities did not hold any attraction for them so long as they could meet their needs through hunting, trading, and raiding.

During the summer of 1872 Mackenzie returned to the vicinity of his first encounter with Quanah near the Texas Panhandle. From there, with the help of 20 Tonkawa scouts and a captured comanchero—one of many Spanish traders who still trafficked with the Quahadas—the colonel and his troopers rode clear across the Staked Plain into New Mexico and back. They caught only a few glimpses of Comanches, but they learned their way around the trackless country that had confounded them the year before. Henceforth they would conduct regular patrols across the Staked Plain to break up the comanchero trade that helped the Quahadas survive outside the reservation.

In September Mackenzie stepped up his war on the elusive Comanches, setting out to find and destroy their encampments at a time when most of the men were likely to be away on their autumn buffalo hunt. Mackenzie was hardly the first American in the region to target Indians where they lived. Sul Ross had done so with a vengeance in 1860, and Christopher "Kit" Carson and other western Indian fighters had since employed the same tactic. In recent years such irregular warfare had been sanctioned by the army's top general, William Tecumseh Sherman, who bore the name of the great Shawnee leader but did all he could to crush the spirit of resistance Tecumseh exemplified. Sherman urged officers to attack the camps of chiefs who refused to report to reservations. This was total war, not unlike the campaign Sherman had waged during the Civil War, a campaign that left thousands of Southerners hungry and homeless and that crushed the Confederacy. In some ways, the attacks Sherman endorsed against Indians were even harsher, for women and children as well as warriors were often killed, and those targeted were sometimes trying to avoid hostilities.

Such was the case with Mackenzie's first attempt at total war against the Comanches. Prowling the upper forks of the Red River in the Texas Panhandle in late September, his scouts located a large encampment on McClellan Creek, near the mouth of Blanco Canyon. As it turned out, the occupants were a mixed group of Comanches, including some Quahadas and a number of Kotsotekas, led by a chief named Mow-way, who had spent time on the reservation and wanted peace with the Americans. Indeed, he was off conferring with white officials when the cavalrymen descended on his camp. Mackenzie was not required to determine who the Comanches were or what their intentions might be, since any band living off the reservation was defined as hostile.

Free to attack without further investigation, Mackenzie sent his troopers storming into the camp. They killed a reported 23 Comanches, although the actual toll was probably twice as high. A number of those killed were men who had remained behind in the village in order to protect the women and children and died fighting. Once resistance was overcome, the troopers took 124 prisoners,

mostly women and children, burned 262 lodges, and seized a sprawling herd of as many as 3,000 horses and mules.

It was no easy task to control so many animals. That night Mackenzie entrusted the herd to his exhausted Tonkawa scouts, who nodded off to sleep, allowing a party of Comanche warriors who had escaped the attack to creep near. The warriors stampeded the herd, regaining all but 50 of their animals and some of the cavalry mounts to boot. But they could not rescue their families, whom the bluecoats escorted south to captivity at Fort Concho. Quahadas found themselves in the unfamiliar position of negotiating for the release of their own people, taken captive by whites. To get them back, various Comanche bands in the region reluctantly agreed to surrender all their white captives.

Although Mackenzie could take credit for the exchange, he had yet to subdue Quanah and the main force of Quahadas. While continuing to search for the holdouts, Mackenzie and his superiors saw another way to force them onto reservations—destruction of the buffalo herds they depended on. The hunting of bison by whites had increased in recent years. In the late 1860s a young marksman named William F. Cody, hired to supply fresh meat for railroad crews working on the plains, had earned the nickname Buffalo Bill by killing a phenomenal 4,280 bison during a period of only seven months. Once the trains started running, some whites even shot the beasts for sport from their rail coaches. But the real threat to the Quahadas and other tribal groups who subsisted on buffalo was the wholesale slaughter of bison for their hides that began in 1871.

Previously regarded as an inferior source of fur, buffalo pelts increased sharply in value as a result of

Quanah Parker's splendid war bonnet—containing 60 eagle feathers, each adorned with beadwork and tipped with a plume of hair from a white horse—resembled those worn by other Comanche chiefs, who adopted this form of headdress from the Cheyennes. The feathers had special significance for Quanah, who had received the name Tseeta, or the Eagle, from his father as a token of manhood.

new processing techniques that inexpensively converted the hides into leather for apparel and for conveyor belts, widely used in eastern factories. Lured by prices that approached four dollars a pelt, hundreds of white hunters known as hide men descended on the plains. Armed with powerful new Sharps .50-caliber rifles and telescopic sights, skilled hunters could kill buffalo at a range of more than 1,000 yards. Even a hide man of only modest skill could pick off at least 40 creatures in a day, enough to provide work for three or four skinners, who claimed the pelts and left the carcasses to rot. In 1873 alone, the three railroads serving Dodge City in southwest Kansas—the shipping center for the trade—carried east more than 750,000 hides.

By that time the herds in Kansas had been decimated and large numbers of hide men had moved south into the Indian Territory. Far from discouraging the hunters from violating the spirit if not the letter of the Medicine Lodge Treaty, the generals charged with enforcing the treaty welcomed them. Wiping out the buffalo everywhere, both on and off the reservations, would, they reasoned, not only starve holdouts like the Quahadas into submission but also nullify the treaty provision that allowed Indians to leave their reservations for hunting expeditions so long as there were enough animals left "to justify the chase." Major General Philip Sheridan, the top commander in the region and a trusted subordinate of Sherman's since the Civil War, declared that the hide men were doing more "to settle the vexed Indian question than the entire regular army has done in the past 30 years. They are destroying the Indians' commissary." He was more than willing to let them "kill, skin and sell until the buffaloes are exterminated."

By the summer of 1873 the hunters were ravaging the herds around the Kiowa-Comanche Reservation and probing west toward the Texas Panhandle. Among those eager to hunt in Texas was Josiah Wright Mooar, who three years earlier as a 19-year-old fresh from Vermont had helped inaugurate the buffalo slaughter in Kansas. Now he was looking for new herds to conquer. After scouting the Panhandle

White hunters slaughter buffalo from a train in the early 1870s using the high-powered Sharps rifle. A traveler who crossed Kansas by rail in late 1868 recalled that his train often had to stop "to allow large herds to pass." Several years later on the same route, he glimpsed only a few scattered bands "of from ten to twenty buffalo."

with a fellow hunter that summer, he came back with enthusiastic reports of passing through herds that extended "as far as we could see—all day they opened up before us and came together again behind us."

Mooar and his fellow hunters were prepared to vie with Comanches and Kiowas for the right to hunt in the Panhandle. But they worried that the army might try to keep them from passing into Texas and stirring up trouble with Indians there. To feel out officials, Mooar and another hunter went to see the commander of Fort Dodge, Major Richard Dodge, whose cavalry patrolled the borders of the Indian Territory. Determined to make a good impression, the roughhewn hide men bought new suits of clothing and even went to the extreme of taking baths. They need not have fretted. Dodge, who himself liked to hunt buffalo in his spare time, received them cordially. "Major," Mooar asked at

length, "if we cross into Texas, what will be the government's attitude toward us?" "Boys," replied Dodge, "if I were a buffalo hunter, I would hunt where the buffaloes are."

Reassured, so many hide men invaded the Texas Panhandle in early 1874 that they had need of a trading post. Constructed that spring along the Canadian River near the ruins called Adobe Walls— where the frontier entrepreneur Charles Bent once traded with Comanches and Kiowas and Kit Carson later fought with them—the new post at Adobe Walls had everything that the hunters needed to destroy one of the last great Indian hunting grounds on the southern plains quickly, profitably, and securely. There were two stores where they could sell their hides to middlemen without having to journey the 150 miles up to Dodge City. A blacksmith shop kept their wagons in repair,

A mound of 40,000 buffalo hides awaits transport to factories in the East at a rail yard in Dodge City, Kansas, in 1873. Between 1872 and 1874, the so-called hide men who prowled the plains with Sharps rifles to secure such pelts killed more than four million buffalo.

a mess hall provided them with hot meals, and a saloon tended to their leisure.

By late spring, marksmen and skinners were fanning out across the Panhandle and making periodic runs back to the post with a load of hides. Out on the plains at least four hunters were killed by Indians who were incensed at their intrusions. But Adobe Walls was considered to be safe. It was situated in a broad meadow with open fields of fire for the hunters' long-range rifles, and everyone assumed that there would be security in numbers.

The hide men failed to gauge the frustration of groups like the Quahadas, who relied mightily on the buffalo in all its bounty. These Indians were prepared to take great risks in order to keep the creature from being wiped out by strangers who were so heedless and wasteful that they left the bulk of their prey to rot. Buffalo remained vital even to those bands who had reported to the reservation, where they discovered that the government could not meet its promises to feed them adequately. During the previous winter, blizzards had disrupted a system of beef rations already rendered inadequate by corruption and inefficiency. Many Indians had been forced to slaughter their precious horses to keep from starving.

Yet it was not just hunger that filled Indians with contempt for the hide men. The wasteful slaughter of buffalo was a sacrilege to tribespeople who believed that the animal was a blessing from on high, to be honored ceremonially and harvested respectfully. It was this deeper challenge to their traditions, as much as the threat to their livelihood, that impelled Quanah and other warriors to heed the words of a militant holy man named Ishatai and brave the fire of their enemies at Adobe Walls.

Quahadas gathered in May 1874 on the north bank of the Red River with Comanches from the nearby reservation for a solemn ritual of renewal. Women constructed a large circular lodge of brush and timber, and there for the first time Comanches joined in the sun dance, a ceremony that had long been observed by their Kiowa allies and other Plains Indians. Warriors began by sacrificing a buffalo to the Great Spirit above, stuffing the hide with willow twigs, and hoisting it reverently to the top of the lodge. Then the participants gave of themselves by dancing for three days and nights without any food or water. Nearing the limits of their endurance, they experienced visions and communed with the generous powers that replenished the earth.

This stirring ceremony was performed at the urging of Ishatai, who belonged to Quanah's band. Although not a warrior himself, the holy man claimed to possess medicine that would strengthen Comanches against hostile whites. Reservation authorities who learned of his promises considered them to be preposterous. "He claims that he has raised the dead to life," wrote Thomas Battey, a missionary and teacher who asked Indians to believe in a savior who could do the same. "He can make medicine which will render it impossible for a Comanche to be killed, even though he stands just before the muzzle of the white man's guns. He ascends above the clouds far beyond the sun—the home of the Great Spirit, with whom he has often conversed."

Some of what Ishatai said may have aroused skepticism among Indians as well as whites. Seasoned warriors like Quanah, for example, had reason to wonder if there was any medicine strong enough to stop the white man's bullets. Yet all Comanches knew of cases when protective spirit powers had helped people through terrible ordeals, and many had themselves experienced visions like the one Ishatai spoke of, dream journeys that carried them up into the sky and brought them in touch with the Great Spirit. Ishatai's dreams and prophecies were all the more persuasive because they spoke to the deep grievances of his people. Like many of them, he had a score to settle with whites: His uncle had been killed by cavalrymen, and he saw the sun dance gathering as a way to embolden Comanches in their struggle with intruders.

After the ceremony the assembled chiefs met in council to decide how best to repulse their enemies and salvage their homeland. Ishatai encouraged them

The Comanche holy man Ishatai, second from the right in the family photograph shown here, inspired the attack on the hide men at Adobe Walls by prophesying victory and offering warriors medicine to deflect enemy fire. In the bitter aftermath, Ishatai conceded that the hide men too had "very strong medicine" in the form of long-range rifles that allowed them to shoot today and "kill you tomorrow."

to take bold action by relating his vision. "My spirit left my body and went far away, up the path of the stars," he declared. "I came to the place of the Great Spirit; the Great Father of the Indians, who is greater and higher than the white man's God." Ishatai assured the assembled chiefs that the Great Father had promised to grant them power and success in their struggle: They would drive out the white men and the Great Father would bring the buffalo back.

There was some debate as to how this prophecy could be fulfilled. Quanah was eager to attack Mackenzie's Tonkawa scouts, who had recently killed a close friend of his. But Quanah was not in any position to tell the others what to do. In his own words, he was still a "little big man," one whose accomplishments were greater than his years. The council reached a consensus that the best way to "bring the buffalo back again" was to assault the hide men. With the help of some of their Kiowa and Cheyenne allies, Comanche warriors would launch an attack during the next full moon against the "white men's houses," as they called the new trading post in the Panhandle.

Toward dawn on June 27, 1874, a war party of perhaps 250 Comanches, Cheyennes, and Kiowas armed with lances and carbine rifles approached the compound at Adobe Walls. The younger, less experienced men were eager to attack, and it was all Quanah and the other chiefs could do to keep them in line. Then, as light streaked the eastern sky, the warriors mounted a concerted charge, raising a huge dust cloud in their wake. They wore yellow war paint that Ishatai had promised would protect them against enemy bullets. If the attack went as planned, the medicine might never be tested, for Ishatai had

Quanah Parker, pictured around 1890 holding an eagle-feather fan, appears in traditional chiefly regalia of the sort he wore before he surrendered and moved onto the reservation. Breastplates like the one covering his chest were time-honored Comanche emblems of bravery.

prophesied that the warriors would slaughter the hide men in their sleep.

As it turned out, several of the hunters were wide awake and tending their weapons when the attack began. During the night men bunked in the saloon had been roused by a loud crack like the sound of a rifle. The heavy earthen roof had put too much strain on the cottonwood ridgepole that ran the length of the building. After supervising repairs the saloon keeper, Jim Hanrahan, had rewarded his helpers with free drinks, and several then began to prepare for the day's hunt before daybreak.

One of the hunters, Billy Dixon, was loading his wagon when something caught his eye. "Just beyond the horses, at the edge of some timber," he recollected afterward, "was a large body of objects advancing vaguely in the dusky dawn toward our stock." Although he was known for his sharpshooter's vision, Dixon could not at first make out what it was. "Then I was thunderstruck. The black body of moving objects suddenly spread out like a fan, and from it went up one single, solid yell— a warwhoop that seemed to shake the very air of the early morning," the hunter recalled. "They came rushing up with our horses in front of them." Dixon fired a single shot and retreated into the saloon. Men who were sleeping on the ground outside leaped from their bedrolls, struggled into their breeches, and ran for the safety of the nearest building.

The brunt of the attack was directed at the saloon, which stood in the center of the trading post. Swarming around the saloon and the two stores at either end, the warriors tried to smash their way in. Quanah urged his mount toward a barricaded door and then whirled around and tried to back his way in. When that failed, he dismounted and pounded at the door with his rifle butt. At length he and others climbed onto the roof and poked holes in the sod to shoot down at the defenders.

The hide men in the saloon and the other buildings fired back with their pistols through the widening gaps and chinks in the log walls. The Indians were so near, recalled one of the hunters, that "we planted our guns in their faces and against their bodies through the portholes." It was a mark of the warriors' determination that they continued to fight at close quarters even when the enemy bullets defied Ishatai's medicine and began to take their toll. A splendidly attired warrior, who was the son of the Cheyenne chief Stone Calf, jumped from his horse, pressed against the wall of one of the stores, and fired his revolver through a loophole. Six men were firing back inside, along with one woman, Hannah Olds. The wife of a man who worked at the post, she was loading and shooting as steadfastly as the men. One shot from inside the store smashed into the warrior's back, and he collapsed against the wall, his legs evidently paralyzed. When a hunter went to the window to finish off the wounded Cheyenne, he shot himself to death rather than be slain by his enemies.

The only hide men stranded outside the buildings that morning were Jacob and Isaac Scheidler. When the attack began the German-born brothers were sleeping in their wagon, which was filled with hides bound for Dodge City. They pulled the wagon cover over them to elude detection, and the warriors at first swirled by them unaware. But then a curious Comanche lifted the cover with the end of his bow and was felled by a shot from one of the brothers, drawing the fury of other Comanches down on the exposed hide men. Warriors killed and scalped both brothers. Their dog, a large black Newfoundland, was killed as it tried in vain to protect its masters; the animal lost a strip of its own hide to the attackers.

All morning, as the defenders fought off charge after charge, they were mystified by the sound of bugle calls that were emanating from the ranks of the Indians. At first some hoped it heralded a troop of U.S. Cavalry coming to their rescue. When no troopers materialized, however, some who knew

> *"Just beyond the horses, at the edge of some timber, was a large body of objects advancing vaguely in the dusky dawn toward our stock and in the direction of Adobe Walls....I was thunderstruck. The black body of moving objects suddenly spread out like a fan, and from it went up one single, solid yell—a warwhoop that seemed to shake the very air of the early morning."*
>
> SHARPSHOOTER BILLY DIXON

army bugle calls suggested that the trumpeter was actually directing the movements of the Indians. Shortly before noon the bugle calls ceased and tomahawks could be heard chopping at the Scheidler brothers' wagon in search of plunder. One of the plunderers was shot dead as he ran away—a dark-skinned man who had a trumpet slung across his back. The fallen bugler, it turned out, was not an Indian at all but a black recruit who had deserted from the 10th U.S. Cavalry—one of the all-black regiments on the plains whose members were known as buffalo soldiers—and cast his lot with the Comanches.

Unable to penetrate the buildings, the warriors fell back around midday and attempted to regroup, but the defenders switched to their long-range rifles and continued to take a toll. From the stores and saloon, hide men watched in wonderment as warriors repeatedly braved fire in order to retrieve their dead and wounded. When Quanah saw a companion fall, he galloped in and, in a display of extraordinary strength, hoisted the man's lifeless body up and bore him away to make sure that his remains would not be mutilated and his spirit left to wander in agony.

At length Quanah himself went down. A few hundred yards from one of the white men's houses his horse was shot out from under him and he had to seek shelter behind a buffalo carcass. A bullet then struck the powder horn he wore around his neck and entered near his shoulder blade, leaving his right arm paralyzed for a short time. He finally managed to crawl to cover in a plum thicket, where another warrior rescued him.

The temporary loss of the fiery young war chief took much of the fight out of his comrades. At least a dozen warriors already lay dead or dying, and many more had been wounded. After repeated thrusts into the teeth of the defenses, it was clear to the attackers that their lances and carbines were not any match for long-range guns with telescopic sights.

Any lingering faith in Ishatai's prophecy was dispelled that afternoon as the holy man watched the last of the fighting on horseback with some of the elder chiefs from a knoll nearly three-quarters of a mile from Adobe Walls. Although both Ishatai and his mount were painted with yellow medicine, a stray .50-caliber bullet fired from the distant outpost struck his horse in the forehead, and he was thrown to the ground. He later blamed the devastating setback at Adobe Walls on a Cheyenne warrior who had killed and eaten a skunk en route to the battle, thus breaking a taboo and ruining Ishatai's medicine. Many Quahadas retained confidence in him, but not Quanah. In the difficult

Hide man Billy Dixon, pictured in 1876, two years after the attack at Adobe Walls, was one of the first there to see the warriors coming on the morning of June 27. Dixon, who once shot 120 bison from a fixed position, regarded the annihilation of the animal Plains Indians cherished and depended on as a simple matter of expediency: "We had to make hay while the sun shone."

years to come, he would continue to draw strength and solace from Comanche spiritual traditions. But he would never again let his actions be guided by the words of a medicine man.

The Battle of Adobe Walls sparked a larger conflict known as the Red River War that brought the Comanches and their allies up against overwhelming opposition. That summer the warriors who stormed Adobe Walls, and hundreds of others inspired by their attack, fanned out to assail white hunters, travelers, and settlers across a wide area, wreaking havoc in Texas as well as surrounding parts of New Mexico, Colorado, and Kansas. The army reacted in late summer with the most comprehensive campaign that was ever mounted on the southern plains. Five different columns, containing some 3,000 troops in total, converged on the Panhandle, where many fugitives from the reservations, fearing reprisals, had taken refuge with warriors amid the cliffs and canyons along the upper Red River and its tributaries. The pursuing cavalrymen had orders from General Sheridan to corner the Indians and force them all onto the reservations under threat of annihilation.

Quanah and his Quahadas managed to elude the army's closing pincers, but many of the other holdouts were trapped. By late September Comanche, Kiowa, and Cheyenne fugitives numbering as many as 1,000 or more had secreted themselves in Palo Duro Canyon. With steep red walls rising 800 feet or more from the valley floor, the canyon was studded with clumps of cottonwood and cedar and blessed with ample pasture for buffalo and horses. Nestled there were a string of small encampments containing a total of 200 tepees, whose occupants were sheltered from blue northers by the canyon's walls.

They thought they were safe from the cavalry as well, but at least one of the pursuing officers, Ranald Mackenzie, knew the terrain and the tactics of the warriors who inhabited it. Marching north into the Panhandle with 450 men of the 4th U.S.

Cavalry, he camped at Tule Canyon, some 20 miles from Palo Duro. Remembering previous embarrassments, he took no chances with his horses. When about 250 warriors from the Palo Duro sanctuary attacked that night, they found the cavalry mounts securely staked and hobbled and ringed with sentries who drove the raiders away.

Two days later, at dawn on September 28, 1874, Mackenzie's bluecoats reached the rim of Palo Duro and peered down on the encampments. How they located that sanctuary so readily was the subject of differing accounts. Some said they were guided there by Tonkawa scouts; others credited information obtained from José Piedad Tafoya, a comanchero whom Mackenzie had captured and ordered strapped to an upright wagon tongue until he agreed to talk.

The troopers descended into the canyon on a trail that was so steep and narrow they had to dismount from their horses and lead the animals down single file, stumbling and sliding on the rocky slope. When the lead soldiers were about halfway down, a Kiowa sentry named Red Warbonnet saw them and fired two shots as an alarm, but they went unheeded by the villagers, most of whom were still asleep.

Mackenzie's bluecoats had reached the valley floor and were galloping toward the camps before the fugitives fully realized what was happening. Warriors grabbed their guns and bought time for their families to escape by scrambling up the canyon slope on either side of the advancing cavalry and firing down at the bluecoats from behind boulders. Their quick response surprised the troopers and pinned them down for a while. "How will we ever get out of here?" cried one nervous cavalryman. "I brought you in," Mackenzie snapped back. "I will take you out!"

He made good on that promise by driving the snipers away, but he could not stop the opposing warriors from conducting their own people

A Picture in Courage

A painting of Adobe Walls done on buckskin by a Comanche named Yoke-Suite a few years after the battle pays tribute to the courage the Indian attackers displayed under punishing fire from the hide men. Warriors and chiefs, wearing long war bonnets, swarm around the stockade (center), from which bullets pour in a blue stream. At lower right Quanah Parker, having dismounted from his horse, wields his lance against a hunter firing back from a wagon. Above him a wounded comrade lies on the ground, bleeding to death.

safely out of the canyon. The fugitives left behind only four dead, but they did not have any cause to celebrate. All the belongings that they needed to get through the winter—their food, ammunition, blankets, robes, and shelters—remained on the canyon floor. Mackenzie allowed the Tonkawas to loot the lodges, then had the shelters set on fire. That left the horses, a herd of nearly 1,500. Mackenzie made sure that the Indians would not get them back this time. He deployed his troopers in a hollow square with the horses in the middle and marched the herd back to camp at Tule Canyon. The next morning, his men cut out the best 350 or so from the herd, then led the remainder to the rim of the canyon and gunned them down.

The slaughter of the horses that they cherished and depended on spelled disaster for the holdouts. In the months to come further attacks like the one in Palo Duro Canyon left the fugitives weak and demoralized, and the cruelties of winter completed what the army had begun. One by one, weary bands of Indians—hungry, horseless, and hounded relentlessly by the bluecoat columns—gave up their struggle and returned to the reservation. In February 1875 Chief Lone Wolf, the leader of Kiowa resistance, surrendered with nearly 500 of his followers. In March more than 800 Cheyennes, including Chief Stone Calf, called it quits as well. In April Chief Mow-way and nearly 200 of his Kotsoteka Comanches reported to the reservation along with a handful of Quahadas.

Colonel Mackenzie oversaw these capitulations at Fort Sill on the Kiowa-Comanche Reservation in his new capacity as commander of all troops in the Indian Territory. He waited in vain for his stubborn adversary Quanah to come in with the main force of Quahadas, who remained somewhere out on the vastness of the Staked Plain. The colonel harbored a grudging admiration for those die-hards, who could never be said to have broken a treaty because they had never signed one. Hoping to negotiate their surrender and avoid further bloodshed, he dispatched a delegation under Dr. Jacob J. Sturm, a physician and post interpreter who was married to an Indian. The delegation was guided by a newly surrendered Quahada war chief named White Horse. They rode far to the southwest, finally catching up with the main body of Quahadas on May 1 at a camp some 100 miles south of present-day Lubbock in far western Texas.

Much to the astonishment of Sturm, the Quahadas greeted him amicably, showing none of the hostility that might have been expected. Sturm watched while they met in council to consider the terms of unconditional surrender that he brought from Colonel Mackenzie. Both Ishatai, the still influential medicine man, and Quanah—whom

Colonel Ranald S. Mackenzie dealt harshly with Comanches in battle but dealt honorably with them after they surrendered, working hard to procure better rations from the government for the reservation dwellers. "I think better of this band than of any other on the reserve," he wrote of Quanah's long-defiant Quahadas. "I shall let them down as easily as I can."

Sturm characterized as "a young man of much influence with his people"—spoke in favor of giving up and accompanying the white emissary back to the reservation. Quanah knew how tired his people were of running, and he also recognized that it was only a matter of time before Bad Hand Mackenzie's relentless columns hunted them down. But before speaking in council, it was said, Quanah had sought guidance from the spirits. As he stood atop a high mesa overlooking his beloved plains with a buffalo robe drawn over his head, he had received a sign—a bird that flew northeast toward Fort Sill.

A month later, on June 2, 1875, some 400 Quahadas, the last of the Comanche holdouts, filed into Fort Sill. They threw down their arms, gave up 1,500 horses, and abandoned forever their free-roaming ways. The toll of the long struggle on the once mighty Comanches could be measured in one sad statistic—only about 2,000 of them had survived the encounter with the white man's guns and diseases, barely 10 percent of the population a century earlier. And soon the buffalo that had sustained Comanches in prosperity and adversity would be erased from the southern plains.

Quanah was already at Fort Sill when his Quahadas came in there. He had ridden ahead to carry the news of surrender to Colonel Mackenzie. Unlike some other defiant chiefs, who were separated from their bands and imprisoned, Quanah was allowed to remain with his people and treated as a worthy adversary by Mackenzie. When Quanah asked the colonel about the fate of his mother and little sister, Mackenzie could not at first enlighten him, but the colonel soon learned that Cynthia Ann Parker and her daughter had been dead for more than a decade and passed along that sad news. Quanah, grateful for the consideration shown him by his former enemy, offered to give back the prize

Comanches on the reservation sit by their tepee near Fort Sill around 1870. Although the government provided houses, many Comanches chose to live in their traditional lodges, using government-supplied canvas when buffalo hides grew scarce.

TRAVELING THE PEYOTE ROAD

To Comanches whose lives were shattered by confinement to the reservation, the peyote cult offered solace and spiritual renewal. Peyote had long been used medicinally by tribal healers in the region, but it was largely through the efforts of Quanah Parker that the cactus plant, with its mild hallucinogenic effect, emerged as the focal point of a ritual that brought reservation dwellers together in faith and harmony.

Worshipers living under galling restraints conceived of this ritual as a liberating journey down the Peyote Road. As depicted at right on a hide painting of reservation life by the Kiowa artist Silverhorn, a guide, or "roadman," equipped with a long staff and a gourd rattle, would lead the ceremonial journey, with men and women seated on either side of him around an earthen altar, raised up before the fireplace. Quanah himself served as a roadman and composed sacred songs for the ritual. When the worshipers ingested peyote to induce visions, they did so reverently and sought blessings not just for themselves but for others, praying for the sick and the needy.

Federal authorities opposed the peyote cult, but Quanah exerted his considerable influence with reservation officials to keep it from being suppressed. Seven years after his death in 1911, the peyote faith was formally chartered as the Native American Church, and its practices were protected by law.

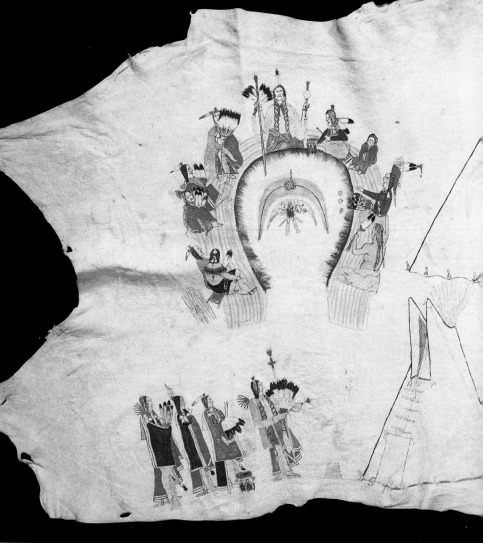

Among the Comanche worshipers assembled here in 1893 after an all-night peyote ceremony are Quanah Parker *(seated, second from left)* and two of his wives *(standing, far left and second from left)*.

gray mount he had stolen from the colonel four years before. Mackenzie, for whom the loss had been a useful lesson, paid the young chief his due by allowing him to keep the horse.

Early in 1878, nearly three years after Quanah reported to Fort Sill, he set off on horseback from the reservation with a group of Comanches and Kiowas for one last buffalo hunt. Reservation authorities had long resisted letting the occupants chase after the increasingly scarce bison, fearing that it would only bring them into conflict with whites. But Quanah and other chiefs had demonstrated that they had no intention of resuming hostilities. And the Comanches and Kiowas were finding it hard to get by on what little the reservation offered. Farming had never been a serious option for them in a country prone to drought and erosion. The land was better suited for grazing, and Colonel Mackenzie had used funds set aside for the Indians to purchase a herd of 3,500 sheep for them to tend. But they had no taste for mutton, and the sheep were easy prey for coyotes and wild dogs. Cattle raising seemed preferable, but when rations ran short, as they often did, the steers were slaughtered to feed the hungry, and the herd dwindled. People longed for the days when the buffalo brought them all they needed.

Quanah and his fellow hunters set out in late winter, a time of hunger and despondency on the reservation, with its uncertain supply system. They headed west, across the border into Texas, where many of them had hunted and hidden out before the bluecoats cornered them. Not long ago vast herds of bison had darkened the horizon, but now the riders glimpsed only bleached bones amid the snow. Around March 1 they entered Palo Duro Canyon, hoping to find some buffalo sheltered below its walls. But cattle grazed there now—part of the sprawling herd owned by rancher Charles Goodnight, who had participated in the attack 18 years earlier that separated Quanah's mother from her adoptive people.

Quanah and Goodnight were strangers to each other, and when the rancher approached the Comanche leader at his camp in the canyon, he asked him what his name was. Responding to the question in English, which he had picked up in recent years, the chief remarked tersely that he went by two names: "Mr. Parker or Quanah." He in turn was curious to know where this insistent white stranger came from. "Are you a Tejano?" he asked sharply, using the Spanish term for Texan. Goodnight knew how deeply Comanches resented Texans, and he managed to disguise his long residence in the state by swearing with some truth that he came from Colorado and supporting that claim with a detailed description of the Rocky Mountain region, which had once been home to Comanches as well. Goodnight further endeared himself to Quanah by admitting

At left Quanah Parker sits for a portrait around 1895 between a painting of his late mother and infant sister and an image of Christ, displayed in tribute to his mother's ancestral faith. The photograph was taken in the living room of his 12-room house *(above)*, with stars on the roof inspired by the emblems of the U.S. Army that Quanah came to terms with.

that the Comanches perhaps had as much right to this canyon as the Texans and offering to come to terms with the chief. After haggling a bit, they worked out a deal: Goodnight would provision Quanah's band with two cattle every other day so long as they kept the peace and respected his property.

Quanah and his companions returned to the reservation a few weeks later, having learned to their dismay that the bison had been all but extinguished. But Quanah's fruitful encounter with Goodnight demonstrated the chief's growing skill at negotiating with whites and winning concessions from them without resorting to violence. In the years ahead he would prevail on white ranchers whose cattle were straying onto the reservation to pay for grazing rights there. The arrangement benefited the reservation dwellers in general and Quanah in particular, who claimed a fee from the ranchers for administering the leases and emerged as one of the wealthiest Indians in America, with a 12-room house that rivaled the residences of white cattle barons.

Although some Comanches grew resentful of Quanah, most did not begrudge him his success. Their chiefs had long been men of property, with large herds of horses and other bounty, which they shared with their followers in times of need, just as Quanah did. And nothing he gained materially lessened his moral commitment to his people and their traditions. Time and again he made it clear that he had no intention of letting white authorities dictate every aspect of life on the reservation. Many officials denounced traditional Indian religious practices and tried to prohibit them, but Quanah promoted and protected the Comanche peyote cult, which brought worshipers visions of spirit power much like those experienced by their tribal ancestors. Some whites criticized Quanah for having several wives, after the manner of his father and other prominent Comanches in the past, but he refused to part with any of them, a gesture that the women and their kin would have regarded as meanspirited. "You come to my house," he replied pointedly to an official who urged him to choose one wife and tell the others to go. "You pick out a wife for me to keep. Then you tell 'em."

Authorities who dealt extensively with Quanah understood that he negotiated with them not as a defeated warrior but as one who believed that Comanches still had to defend their ground, albeit peacefully. If he found it easier than some former war leaders to reckon with whites, it was not out of deference to them but out of respect for his mother and her heritage—a feeling that deepened in him over the years. Not long after he came in to the reservation, Colonel Mackenzie wrote a letter on his behalf to his mother's uncle, Isaac Parker, noting that Quanah was interested in visiting his white relatives and adding that he would welcome an invitation from them in the form of a small gift, according to "Indian custom." Hostility toward Comanches in Texas prevented him from traveling to white settlements there for some time, but Quanah remained devoted to his mother's memory and set aside a corner in his house for objects associated with his mother, including a portrait based on a photograph of his mother and baby sister that was taken while they were living with their Parker relatives after being captured in the Pease River raid in 1860.

In the last years of Quanah's life, after the turn of the century, the old animosities between Texans and Comanches receded, and he went to visit his relatives in Texas and retrieve his mother's remains, which he reinterred on Comanche ground in December 1910. A few months later he was buried there beside her. Among those who honored his memory was Knox Beal, a young Texan related to the Parkers who had run away from home after the death of his mother and been taken in by Quanah as his adopted son. Beal understood that the concern Quanah had shown for him as a needy relative was simply an extension of what he had done over the years for the Comanche people who depended on him as chief. As Beal put it simply: "Quanah Parker, my father, fed a great many Comanche Indians. He had a great herd of cattle and horses in 1890, and when he died in 1911, he did not have many left because he was so generous." ◆

LEADERS IN A TURBULENT ERA

*M*ore and more white settlers and fortune seekers arrived on the western plains as the 19th century wore on to lay down rail lines, throw up fences, and stake claim to lands long held sacred by the region's tribes. Beleaguered Indian leaders trying to protect their people's interests reacted to this growing threat in a variety of ways. Some refused to accept the white incursion and fought it to the bitter end. Others chose the path of accommodation in hopes of preserving at least some of their territory and traditions. Circumstances sometimes dictated a shifting policy, with peacemakers often forced to take up arms and warriors opting for peace.

In the end none of them succeeded in turning back a conquering culture intent on dominating the continent and subduing its native peoples. The tribes were, as artist George Catlin put it, "fast traveling . . . towards the setting sun."

Among the leaders favoring passive resistance over armed conflict was Chief Joseph, whose band of Nez Perce had long lived in Oregon's fertile Wallowa Valley. With the discovery of gold there in 1860, whites began pressuring the Indians to move to a reservation in Idaho. Joseph, an imposing, eloquent man, quietly refused. "I see the whites all over the country gaining wealth," he said, adding pointedly that they wanted "to give us lands which are worthless."

Frustrated by Joseph's intransigence, officials called in the army to force the Nez Perce off their lands. At this point the chief backed down and agreed to take his people peacefully to the reservation. However, a few drunken Nez Perce warriors went on a rampage and killed several whites. Fearing retaliation, the entire band fled, and as the band's leader, Joseph felt obligated to join them. After trekking for 1,700 miles across the Bitterroot Mountains toward Canada, engaging in repeated skirmishes with the pursuing troops, and losing more than half his braves, Joseph finally surrendered in 1877. Exiled to a reservation in Washington State far from his beloved Wallowa Valley, the great chief died in 1904, reportedly of a broken heart.

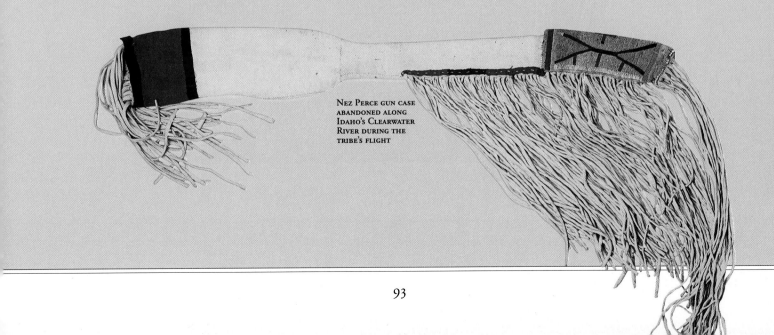

NEZ PERCE GUN CASE
ABANDONED ALONG
IDAHO'S CLEARWATER
RIVER DURING THE
TRIBE'S FLIGHT

A government doctor traveling the southern plains to inoculate Indians against smallpox in 1864 spent four days at the village of Kiowa chief Satanta on the Arkansas River. Satanta, who impressed the doctor as "a fine-looking Indian, very energetic and sharp as a briar," offered the visitor three meals a day in his lodge: "He puts on a great deal of style, spreads a carpet for his guests to sit on. . . . He has a brass horn which he blew vigorously when the meals were ready."

But within months of the physician's visit, the once genial host had changed his cordial stance toward whites as thousands of emigrants, headed for California by way of the Santa Fe Trail, began crossing Kiowa territory and killing buffalo by the score. Some even staked out homesteads on the Kiowas' hunting ground. Fiercely attached to his land and his heritage, Satanta vowed to stop them. He became the Kiowas' principal war chief and one of the government's staunchest foes. "We have to protect ourselves," he said. "We have to fight for what is ours. We have to kill those men who drive away our buffalo." True to his word he launched repeated attacks against whites even though many Kiowas felt that victory was unattainable.

Cutting a striking figure at council meetings with his tall, broad-chested body painted a bright red, Satanta was an eloquent orator who spoke four Indian languages, as well as Spanish and English. He explained why he kept fighting: "I love the land and the buffalo and will not part with it." But the depletion of game, timber, and prairie grasses quickened with the burgeoning of white settlements. Witnessing the changes, Satanta once confessed, "I feel as though my heart will burst with sorrow."

Still, the implacable warrior refused to lay down his arms. Imprisoned in 1871 for the murder of seven wagon train drivers, Satanta was freed after two years. In 1874 he violated his parole and was sent back to prison. Apparently unable to endure confinement, in 1878 he leaped to his death from a prison window. Satanta had once said of his people, "When we settle down, we grow pale and die."

1870 KIOWA BONNET
OF EAGLE FEATHERS

When Washakie was still a boy, he spent a season herding ponies for a group of white fur trappers near his home in southwestern Wyoming. At the end of the season, the trappers presented an old musket to the youth. He later recalled his friends' reaction to the gift: "After that, all the young men of my tribe followed me, because I could shoot farther than they."

Marked for leadership from that time on, Washakie became the principal chief of the eastern Shoshones sometime in the 1840s. He continued his tribe's longtime policy of befriending whites, helping to rescue their livestock, and assisting them in fording rivers as they passed through the tribe's territory on the way to California and Oregon.

Washakie's stance toward whites was a thoroughly pragmatic one. Recognizing that the Shoshones could never defeat them, he instead sought their friendship in order to provide protection against his people's enemies. He could pursue a peaceful course with the whites without fear of criticism because he was a relentless warrior, and no one doubted his personal courage. On one occasion, for example, he tracked a Blackfeet war party for 600 miles, returning with many of their scalps along with the horses they had stolen from his people.

Washakie won from the government nearly three million acres in Wyoming's Wind River Valley as a reservation for his people. In addition he was given assurances that the U.S. Army would protect them against their enemies. But in spite of these concessions he chafed at the inequity that had been forced on the eastern Shoshones: "The white man, who possesses this whole vast country from sea to sea, who roams over it at pleasure and lives where he likes, cannot know the cramp we feel in this little spot."

Nonetheless, Washakie sent his warriors to fight alongside the army against the Sioux in the 1870s. To reward Washakie for his loyalty, the government changed the name of the Wind River's military post from Fort Brown to Fort Washakie and granted him a lifelong pension. In addition, President Ulysses S. Grant presented him with a saddle.

In February 1900, as he lay dying, the chief sent a message to an old friend: "Washakie has found the right trail."

MEDAL AWARDED TO CHIEF
WASHAKIE BY PRESIDENT
ANDREW JOHNSON

Captain Jack, known as Keintpoos to his fellow Indians, lived quietly with a band of some 50 Modocs near the Lost River on California's northeastern plateau. Jack, seen at right in the photograph on the opposite page, dressed like the white settlers and was contentedly assimilated into their culture. "I have always lived like a white man, and wanted to live so," he said. But the Modocs' land was coveted by whites who forced Jack and his band to abandon their farms for the Klamath Reservation in southern Oregon in 1865. "See the good land . . . that is taken away from me and my people," he lamented.

In 1870, fed up with the bullying of the Klamaths, who were longstanding enemies of the Modocs, Jack and some of his followers left the reservation and returned to their old land. When army troops arrived and surrounded the Modocs to return them to the reservation, Jack offered to go peaceably. But firing broke out between the fidgety soldiers and Indians, and the band fled in panic to a barren expanse of lava beds riddled with caves and fissures on the southern edge of Tule Lake. A few months later an army unit tracked them down, but Captain Jack and his men successfully repulsed their pursuers. However, the Modocs had no hope of prevailing for long against the army. Desperate for a peaceful solution, Jack agreed to parley with a team of white negotiators. Begging for a separate reservation for his people, he said that even the barren lava beds were an acceptable site, but his pleas were rejected. "You white people have driven me from mountain to mountain, from valley to valley, like we do the wounded deer," Jack said.

With the peace talks at an impasse, Jack was goaded by a militant faction of his band to take decisive action. During a meeting on April 11, 1873, with chief negotiator General Edward Canby, Jack and five other warriors, including John Schonchin *(far left on the opposite page)*, whipped out their pistols and killed him.

Canby's death prompted a manhunt for Jack, who was captured after three months by turncoat militants. At his trial he said, "You white people conquered me not: My own men did." Along with Schonchin and two other Modocs, Captain Jack was hanged in October 1873.

CAPTAIN JACK'S FRINGED
BUCKSKIN SHIRT

PLENTY COUPS AT AGE 60

A nine-year-old Crow boy had a dream in the late 1850s while attending a tribal gathering in what is now Montana: A huge herd of buffalo suddenly disappeared, and a terrific storm swept across the land, uprooting all the trees in its path but one, in which a chickadee perched. The boy related his dream to the tribe's spiritual leader, Yellow Bear, who explained it: The buffalo stood for the Indian way of life, which was to vanish before the storm of the white man's might. The overturned trees represented the Plains tribes who resisted the storm. The one left standing was the Crow people, who, if they paid heed like the chickadee, could "escape this and keep our lands."

The boy whose dream helped solidify tribal policy toward whites grew up to become a highly honored warrior named Plenty Coups. Repeatedly demonstrating bravery in battle, he earned the rank of chief while in his thirties. Eager to cement an alliance against the Crows' enemies, such as the Sioux and the Cheyennes, his tribe had long befriended fur traders and aided travelers on the Bozeman Trail. Plenty Coups strengthened this alliance by sending warriors and scouts to assist the army in fighting the Sioux.

As his boyhood dream had foretold, Plenty Coups's people did obtain a reservation on their own ancestral lands; they were one of few tribes to do so. He later proclaimed, "When I think back, my heart sings because we acted as we did. It was the only way open to us."

CHIEF PLENTY COUPS'S EAGLE-FEATHERED WAR BONNET REFLECTS HIS WEALTH AND STATUS.

CHAPTER 3

THE SPIRIT OF SITTING BULL

*"These soldiers have come shooting. They want war.
We must stand together or they will kill us separately."*

SITTING BULL, 1876

Chief Sitting Bull posed for this portrait in 1883, two years after he surrendered to U.S. authorities and went to live on the Great Sioux Reservation. He and his Lakota followers put up some of the stiffest resistance the army encountered on the western plains.

A few Lakota Sioux scouts urged their ponies across the parched Montana plains on an August day in 1872. Sent to look for enemies, they were hurrying back to their encampment near the Bighorn River, one of several streams that fed snowmelt from the slopes of the Bighorn Mountains northward to the Yellowstone River and on to the broad Missouri. Amid the sere yellow of the surrounding plains, the green banks of the Yellowstone and its tributaries, rimmed with cottonwoods and willows, offered inviting campsites for the Lakotas and fine browsing for their horses and for the herds of bison that the tribe depended on. But other groups prized this country as well, and the scouts had just encountered a rival force of alarming strength.

These hard-riding wolves, as the scouts were known to their people, had been out prowling for Crow warriors, tribal foes whom the Lakotas had clashed with repeatedly in recent times and driven west of the Bighorn River. Instead, they had spotted a more threatening presence: bluecoats of the U.S. Army, stationed by the hundreds on the north bank of the Yellowstone to protect a party of surveyors dispatched by the Northern Pacific Railroad. The scouts knew what had happened elsewhere on the plains when railroad tracks were laid: Whites appeared in droves, and the buffalo vanished. Having battled rival warriors for this fine hunting ground, Lakotas were not about to let white men drive a wedge through it without a fight.

Reaching their encampment, the scouts dismounted from their horses and hurried to the lodge of a chief named Sitting Bull. A man of great resolve, he exercised a degree of influence that was unprecedented among his people. Like the Comanches of the southern plains, the Lakotas were a loose alliance of seven self-sufficient divisions, or branches, including Sitting Bull's Hunkpapas. Each branch had its own council and leaders, but Lakotas as a whole had never seen fit to elevate one chief above the rest.

In 1869, however, after the federal government negotiated a treaty with some Lakota leaders and assigned the entire tribe to a reservation in the Dakota Territory, Hunkpapas met with members of other branches opposed to that pact. During their deliberations they looked to Sitting Bull for guidance and leadership. Although he wielded no more power than other chiefs, his moral authority was deeply respected among the Hunkpapas and the other branches of the Lakotas as well.

The Lakota Sioux once dominated the northern plains from the Missouri River west to the Rocky Mountains *(right)*. Within that territory, the stronghold of Sitting Bull's branch of the Lakotas, the Hunkpapas, lay south of the mouth of the Yellowstone River, where the U.S. Army established one of its forts. The red stars mark clashes between the Lakotas and U.S. troops.

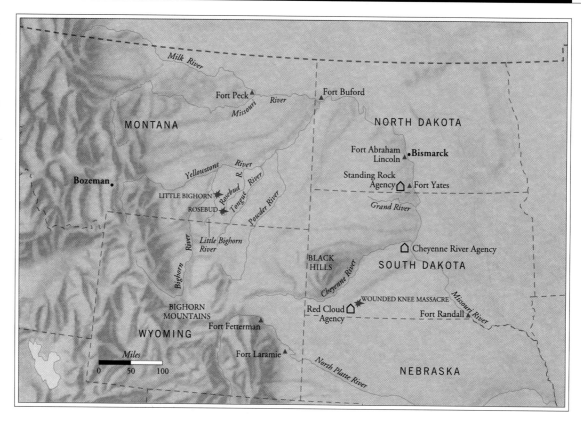

Sitting Bull was well equipped to assume such a prominent role and to deal with challenges like the armed intrusion his scouts informed him of. Short in stature and solid in build, he had expressive features that could pass in an instant from glowering intensity to the warmest of smiles. Now about 40 years old, he owed much to the example of his father, a prominent war chief whose raids on rival tribes had made him a wealthy man with "a great many ponies," as Sitting Bull recalled proudly in later years. Uncles were as important as fathers in the upbringing of Lakota boys, and one of Sitting Bull's uncles, Four Horns, was a trusted officer who helped to enforce the decisions that were made by the Hunkpapa council.

Aside from the lessons in leadership that he absorbed from his male elders, Sitting Bull derived authority from visions he began experiencing at an early age that put him in touch with a supreme spirit Lakotas called Wakan Tanka, or the Great Mystery, a power that pervaded the universe and in-

spired all living things. By one account he was only six years old when he experienced a revelation of the sort most boys did not achieve until the age of puberty, when they embarked on a grueling vision quest by fasting and praying under the stars. While tending his family's horses one day, Slow (as Sitting Bull was known in childhood) walked to the top of a ridge and saw a great buffalo bull seated on its haunches, staring at him. After they had gazed at each other for a while, the bull heaved itself to its feet. Before departing, the animal spoke, blessing the boy for taking pity on him. "Thank you," the buffalo said. "I respect you."

Slow's father was greatly impressed with this vision, which he believed conferred on his son the buffalo's power to endure hardship and sustain the tribe and also foretold his success as a hunter and warrior. The boy went on to prove that power in battle by counting coup for the first time at the age of 14, galloping after a Crow warrior and knocking the man from his horse with a tomahawk. Whether the enemy was struck with a weapon, a bare hand, or a coup stick, the gesture was a daring way to mortify an opponent, and Slow's father marked his precocious achievement by giving him a new name—Sitting Bull. Sitting Bull also earned the right to wear an eagle feather for his first coup and for every one that he counted thereafter. Eventually, his ceremonial war bonnet grew to contain 63 eagle feathers, along with several red feathers signifying wounds received in battle.

For all his accomplishments and prestige, Sitting Bull could not issue commands to his people, even in times of crisis. When he learned of the soldier force that was camped north of the Yellowstone, he met with other chiefs in council on August 14 to consider a response. Because he was leader of the Lakotas off the reservation, his words carried extra weight in the council. But every opinion voiced there had to be pondered carefully, and no action could be taken until the chiefs reached a consensus. Among those present at the conclave was Crazy Horse, a brilliant war leader of the Oglala branch who deferred to Sitting Bull in matters of policy but yielded to no one when it came to planning attacks.

The meticulous deliberations of the council strained the patience of younger warriors in camp who were eager to take action. Before dawn on the following day, while the chiefs were still engaged in discussion, a group of young men slipped away undetected by the warriors who policed their camp, splashed across the Yellowstone River on horseback, and launched a series of uncoordinated attacks on the soldier force.

Their impromptu action left the chiefs little choice but to commit the rest of the warriors to battle. By early morning the entire force had crossed the Yellowstone. Many of the Lakotas ascended the bluffs north of the river and aimed their rifles at the white men in the valley below. Outnumbered nearly 2 to 1, the

A SINGER OF SONGS

Sitting Bull often sang at tribal gatherings, accompanying himself on this box drum, which he painted with the likeness of the buffalo. He was a versatile composer, creating songs for sacred ceremonies, to honor a friend or relative, or to voice his love of nature. "He would imitate the songs of birds," a friend recalled. "He was said to understand what the meadowlarks say."

troops and surveyors abandoned their exposed camp and fell back to the edge of the river, where they were screened from the attackers by trees and brush and shielded by an embankment carved by high water. Time and again small groups of warriors dashed at them on horseback, yelling and firing. But their fitful daring failed to dislodge the bluecoats.

Looking on with Crazy Horse from high ground, Sitting Bull considered what he should do. If he mounted a concerted attack against the soldiers, he risked heavy casualties—something no chief took lightly. But if he failed to challenge the enemy, he might well lose the confidence of the young men and dampen their fighting spirit.

Sitting Bull came to a decision. Taking his pipe and tobacco, he walked down alone from the bluffs into the valley, seated himself calmly on the ground amid the puffs of dust raised by enemy bullets, and began to smoke. He shouted an invitation to other warriors to come down and join him, and four men answered his call, including his sister's son, White Bull, whom Sitting Bull had helped rear.

As they passed the pipe from hand to hand under fire, White Bull could feel his heart pounding in his chest like a drum. But he drew strength from his uncle, who sat there like the splendid creature he was named for, resolute and immovable. After smoking the last of the tobacco, Sitting Bull carefully cleaned his pipe, returned it to its pouch, and walked at a deliberate pace back to safety while his companions scurried ahead. All five came through unscathed. In organizing this "smoking party," White Bull remarked afterward, Sitting Bull had performed "the bravest deed possible."

His heroics heartened the warriors and allowed them to withdraw with pride after Crazy Horse mounted one last charge against the soldiers. Although the surveyors and their military escorts had suffered only two dead and two wounded, they were much shaken by the attack and retreated to the safety of a distant fort. The Lakotas were left to relish their victory and extol Sitting Bull for the eloquent gesture that had inspired his followers, shamed their opponents, and added luster to his reputation.

Sitting Bull's people, the Lakotas, were the westernmost tribe of the Sioux, whose ancestral homeland was around the headwaters of the Mississippi River. By the early 19th century the Lakotas had split off from their eastern cousins, the Dakota Sioux, and migrated out onto the northern plains. There they acquired large numbers of horses and flourished. Superb riders and hunters, they could bring down a stampeding buffalo with a bow and arrow while riding bareback at full speed. The great herds they pursued through the year kept them well supplied with food, shelter, tools, and clothing.

Like the Comanches, Lakotas ranged far in pursuit of their prey and clashed frequently with other tribes. Crossing the Missouri River and coursing over the rolling plains extending from what are now the western Dakotas into eastern Wyoming and Montana, they collided with the Crows and the Assiniboins and ousted them from some of their finest hunting grounds. Those tribes remained mortal enemies of the Lakotas and ultimately furnished the U.S. Army with scouts to help track them down. Yet the Lakotas were not indiscriminately warlike. Over the years they formed durable alliances with other tribal groups, notably the Northern Cheyennes, who later joined them in battles with the bluecoats.

At first Lakotas had little trouble with the white men who ventured across the northern plains in small numbers in the early 1800s to trade or trap beaver. But the *wasichus,* as Lakotas called whites, became a problem in the late 1840s when they began crossing Wyoming by the thousands on the Oregon Trail, spreading disease and disrupting the hunting grounds of Lakotas and their allies. U.S. Cavalry units who were dispatched to protect the

General William Tecumseh Sherman, leaning forward third from left, was among the government officials who met with Indian chiefs at Fort Laramie in 1868 to negotiate a treaty. He took a hard line against traditionalists and declared, "All who cling to their old hunting grounds are hostile and will remain so till killed off."

travelers from Indian raids clashed sharply with Lakota and Cheyenne war parties during the 1850s.

Then, in 1862, a new and different fuse was lighted when the Dakotas back in Minnesota found that conditions on reservations there were intolerable and lashed out at surrounding whites. When state and federal troops struck back, many Dakotas fled west onto the plains and sought refuge with Lakotas, embroiling Sitting Bull and other chiefs in conflict with pursuing soldiers. Sitting Bull emerged from those punishing battles keenly aware of the army's firepower and determined to pick his fights with the bluecoats carefully.

Another cause of conflict on the northern plains in the 1860s was the discovery of gold in the southwestern part of the Montana Territory. To reach the gold fields located there, prospectors left the Oregon Trail at Fort Laramie in southeastern Wyoming Territory and followed the Bozeman Trail, which cut through fine hunting grounds watered by the Yellowstone River and its tributaries, including the Powder, the Tongue, the Rosebud, the Bighorn, and the subsidiary Little Bighorn. The Lakota branch that was most directly affected by the surge in traffic on the Bozeman Trail was the Oglalas. Led by their chief, Red Cloud, with a mighty assist from Crazy Horse, the Oglalas raided the trail so persistently that an exasperated federal government decided to negotiate with the defiant Lakotas. It made a concession without precedent, declaring that it would abandon the army posts on the trail.

Federal commissioners sat down with Lakota chiefs at Fort Laramie in 1868 to hammer out a treaty. However, a number of prominent figures were

RED CLOUD'S WAR

When gold was discovered in Montana's Bitterroot Mountains in the early 1860s, miners and profiteers began pouring up a trail blazed by a scout named Bozeman through the Powder River country of Wyoming and Montana. This was the heart of Oglala territory, and Chief Red Cloud feared the heavy traffic would destroy the game his people depended on. Determined to stop the influx, he proclaimed, "The Great Spirit . . . raised me in this land, and it belongs to me."

Red Cloud and his Oglala warriors launched a war of harassment against travelers. In the face of the attacks, in 1866 the army built several forts to protect the "bloody Bozeman." But the military presence did not stop Red Cloud. He cut off the mail routes, destroyed wagon trains or forced them to turn back, and boldly raided the posts.

In 1868 the government yielded to Red Cloud's demand to abandon the Bozeman Trail forts. That summer, after the signing of the Fort Laramie Treaty, the soldiers marched out of the forts, and the triumphant Oglalas moved in to burn them down.

not in attendance. Distrustful of American authorities, Sitting Bull, Red Cloud, Northern Cheyenne chief Two Moons, and other like-minded leaders had refused to appear, and their absence signaled problems ahead for the government.

Its objectives at Fort Laramie were much the same as at Medicine Lodge Creek in Kansas, where treaty makers had tried with limited success in 1867 to compel tribes of the southern plains to cease hostilities and accept confinement to the reservation. Under the terms of the Fort Laramie Treaty, federal authorities set aside the western half of present-day South Dakota as the Great Sioux Reservation, where the inhabitants would receive regular disbursements of food and other necessities at one of several agencies, or administrative centers. All the Lakotas were expected to settle down there eventually, learn to farm, and live by the white man's laws and customs. The treaty conceded the right of the Lakotas to hunt in the Yellowstone country, outside the reservation, "for as long as the buffalo range thereon in such numbers as to justify the chase," the same clause that appeared in the Medicine Lodge Treaty and encouraged the wholesale slaughter of bison by whites.

Although Red Cloud had not attended the parley, late in 1868 he led his people onto the reservation after the government fulfilled its promise to abandon the Bozeman Trail posts. But any hopes the Americans harbored that his compliance would leave the Lakotas without a commanding resistance leader were dashed when Sitting Bull emerged as the chief of those opposed to the treaty and attracted the support of Crazy Horse and other defiant warriors. Roughly a third of the

Lakota people followed Sitting Bull's lead and refused to live on the reservation. During the summers their ranks were swelled by others who left the agencies for the season to hunt where they pleased, as the treaty allowed.

Sitting Bull did all he could to ensure that there would always be ample herds of buffalo and other game off the reservation to sustain his people and "justify the chase," as the treaty makers put it. As the surveyors for the Northern Pacific discovered in August 1872, not even a sizable escort of troops could shield them from attack if they trespassed on the tribe's favorite hunting grounds.

The war that Sitting Bull and his allies waged to preserve their homeland and their way of life was defensive. They did not make it a practice to venture outside their territory to raid Americans, and they much preferred to count coup on their tribal foes. Nevertheless, by attacking intruders like the railroad surveyors and their military protectors, Sitting Bull and his people incurred the hostility of the army's toughest soldier-chiefs. General William Tecumseh Sherman declared in Washington in March 1873 that building a railroad across the northern plains was a vital national enterprise, and he pledged to protect employees of the Northern Pacific from the Sioux. They were, he warned, perhaps "the most warlike nation of Indians on this continent, who will fight for every foot of the line."

By this time, the Northern Pacific line had reached the Missouri River in present-day North Dakota, fostering a boom town called Bismarck and a military post nearby, Fort Abraham Lincoln, which served as headquarters for a newly arrived regiment, the 7th U.S. Cavalry. In command of the 7th was a lieutenant colonel named George Armstrong Custer, a 33-year-old former Civil War hero who was known to Lakotas as Long Hair for his shoulder-length, blond tresses. In late June 1873 Custer and his cavalrymen headed west as part of a larger force to guard the railroad surveyors as they resumed the task interrupted by Sitting Bull and Crazy Horse the year before.

As always, the Lakota wolves were keeping a keen lookout. Sitting Bull's people were camped along the Yellowstone when the wolves brought word that the bluecoats were back and heading in their direction. While the women and children packed up the lodges and prepared to flee, the warriors made ready to attack. Unlike the haphazard assault that had driven the surveyors and soldiers away the year before, this one was well coordinated. A portion of the warriors would show themselves to Custer's men, then retreat in the hope of drawing the bluecoats into an ambush.

A bold and impetuous commander who underestimated the capacity of Indians to stand and fight, Custer took the bait. At first sight of the Lakota decoys on August 4, he galloped after them with his troopers, leaving behind the main force of infantry under Colonel David Stanley. Before the warriors could close the trap, however, Custer sensed danger and sought shelter with his troopers in a grove of trees. As they waited there for the infantry to come up, Custer had the regimental band strike up his favorite battle song, an old Irish drinking tune called "Garry Owen."

Once Stanley's foot soldiers reached the grove in force, the warriors no longer held the advantage and fled westward along the Yellowstone. For 36 strenuous hours they kept just ahead of Custer's pursuing cavalry. Then, when the Lakotas were nearing the mouth of the Bighorn River, they swam their horses across a deep and swift section of the Yellowstone. It was a feat the white troopers, less agile and more heavily laden, could not duplicate. The two sides shot at each other across the river for another day before the Lakotas slipped away.

For Custer the encounter had been a close call, but he saw no reason to alter his tactics. Unlike Colonel Ranald Mackenzie and other adaptable officers who respected the fighting abilities of Plains Indians and learned from them, Custer remained convinced that tribal war parties would crumble under pressure. The key to defeating them, he believed, was bold and relentless pursuit.

It would be some time before Custer came up against another large force of Lakota warriors. The financial panic of 1873 brought work on the Northern Pacific to a halt for several years, temporarily removing that project as a source of conflict. In the meantime, however, the colonel was in the vanguard of a new invasion that inflamed Lakotas on and off the reservation.

There was not any part of the Great Sioux Reservation that meant more to Lakotas than the Black Hills—a treasure, Sitting Bull called them. Rising from the surrounding prairie like islands in a sea of grass, their pine-forested slopes drew plentiful moisture from the passing storm clouds. Clear streams tumbled down from the heights through lush valleys where bison, deer, and elk grazed in an abundance rivaled only by the Yellowstone country. The craggy peaks, haunted by eagles and mountain goats and often wreathed in mist, became places of pilgrimage for young Lakotas, who sought power in visions from the spirits. To invade these hills was to strike at the tribe's very heart.

In July 1874 Custer led an expedition of more than 1,000 men and 100 supply wagons into the Black Hills. Officially his objective was to locate a site for a fort that the army could use to patrol the reservation. But Custer also brought along geologists and mining men, who confirmed rumors from earlier white travelers of sizable deposits of gold in

A reconnaissance mission led by Lieutenant Colonel George Custer snakes its way through the Black Hills in 1874. An especially rich hunting ground, the area had been set aside as part of the Great Sioux Reservation only six years earlier, and the massive intrusion alarmed and angered Indians.

the hills. Newspaper reporters accompanying the expedition at Custer's invitation promptly publicized the find, and white prospectors began invading the Black Hills by the thousands, in blatant violation of the Fort Laramie Treaty.

As the gold fever intensified, American authorities launched an effort to purchase the Black Hills from the Lakotas. In September 1875 they convened a council at the Red Cloud Agency on the Great Sioux Reservation, where the Oglala chief and his followers were living. The Americans sent a delegation to Sitting Bull at his camp by the Tongue River to invite him to the council. But he declined, informing the interpreter that he was no "agency Indian" and would never consider selling the land of his people. He asked the interpreter to tell the white men at the council that Sitting Bull "declared open war and would fight them wherever he met them from that time on."

He made sure that the agency Indians, largely dependent on the Americans for food and supplies and thus more willing to deal with them, knew of his bitter opposition to ceding the Black Hills. A few hundred Lakotas who felt as Sitting Bull did joined the 10,000 or so agency Indians at the council and agitated against any deal, making the American commissioners and their small military escort extremely nervous. At one point, when they thought they were close to an agreement, an Oglala warrior with close ties to Crazy Horse and Sitting Bull rode between the commissioners and the assembled Indians and vowed to "kill the first chief who speaks for selling the Black Hills." In the tense moments that followed, armed Lakotas opposed to the deal faced down the cavalrymen, and the commissioners retreated to safety. No shots were fired, but the opponents prevailed. The assembled Lakotas refused to sell their heritage.

By now, 15,000 miners were openly flouting U.S. law by digging and panning for gold in the Black Hills. After the Lakotas refused to sell, President Ulysses S. Grant and his advisers decided that they would simply let the prospectors have the hills and

instructed the army to abandon the few feeble efforts it had been making to keep white intruders from entering. All military resources in the region would henceforth be devoted to forcing Sitting Bull's Hunkpapas and their fellow holdouts onto the reservation. This offensive defined all bands living off the reservation as hostile and made their encampments subject to attack. Sitting Bull and his allies—including Northern Cheyennes who refused to report to the reservation they were assigned to—would have to submit to the government's will or face annihilation.

Before commencing hostilities, the army dispatched messengers carrying an ultimatum in the dead of winter to the defiant hunting bands camped below the Yellowstone. They were to report to one of the agencies by January 31, 1876, and if they failed to comply, soldiers would come after them. The order made little sense to the Indians, who could not imagine packing up their lodges at the coldest time of the year and trekking to the inhospitable agencies. One messenger told of being welcomed amicably by holdouts who promised to come in to the agency in the spring and talk over their differences with the government then. Few who received the ultimatum thought that the bluecoats would pursue them any time soon. What kind of chief would drive his men to war through blizzard winds?

On February 1, the day after the deadline passed, General Philip Sheridan, commander of the army's Division of the Missouri, ordered his subordinates in the field to march against the holdouts from various forts around the region—a directive that ignored the snowdrifts and frozen rivers that made travel across the northern plains perilous, if not impossible. Only one commander managed to get going before the winter was out: Brigadier General George Crook, who rode north on March 1 with more than 700 men from Fort Fetterman in eastern Wyoming. Now 48 years old, the six-foot-tall West Point graduate had served with distinction in the Civil War and won renown as an Indian fighter in the Northwest and Arizona. An eccentric who disdained uniforms and

The tepees of a Lakota village pitched on the rolling prairie along White Clay Creek in South Dakota in 1891 evoke the era when the Indians of the northern plains were still nomads following the buffalo herds.

wore moccasins and shabby clothing in the field, he had acquired a healthy regard for the fighting skills of his tribal opponents and pursued them deliberately and with due caution.

At dawn on March 17 a detachment of Crook's cavalry charged with rifles blazing into a winter camp on the Powder River occupied by several hundred men, women, and children—mostly Cheyennes, with some allied Lakotas. Although forced nearly unclad out into sub-zero cold, the warriors fought back fiercely, killing four soldiers and wounding six while suffering only a few casualties of their own. The cavalrymen ravaged the encampment, however, setting the lodges on fire and making off with the horses.

The army's offensive was predicated on the assumption that holdouts who survived such blows would be forced to give up and submit to life on the reservation. Instead of being cowed by the destruction of their village, however, the warriors tracked the cavalrymen back to their camp and recaptured many of the band's horses. Then the Indians rode off to seek refuge with Crazy Horse and Sitting Bull, who could barely restrain their angry followers from seeking immediate revenge for the attack. Sitting Bull and the other chiefs understood that pitched battles favored the army: They would fight only if the women and children were threatened. It seemed clear that the bluecoats meant to force the issue, however. "These soldiers have come shooting. They want war," Sitting Bull concluded. "We must stand together or they will kill us separately."

In the weeks ahead the scattered hunting bands did just that, converging on Sitting Bull's village near the Powder River to form one vast encampment. "We supposed that the combined camps would frighten off the soldiers," the Cheyenne Wooden Leg recalled. "We hoped thus to be freed from their annoyance. Then we could separate again into the tribal bands and resume our quiet wandering and hunting." As it happened, the army knew nothing as yet of Sitting Bull's growing encampment. Crook was resting and reinforcing his weary,

frostbitten troops, and General Sheridan had conceded to the elements for the time being and would not resume his combined offensive until late spring.

By early May nearly all the Indians off the reservation were camped with Sitting Bull. The lodges spread as far as a mounted man could see—461 of them in all, with each branch forming its own circle. There were 154 tepees in the Hunkpapa circle, and 100 in the Cheyennes'. In all, some 3,000 people, roughly 800 of them warriors, bustled about their chores, played games, and held councils in the vast village. They were so numerous that within a week or so they exhausted the grass and game in the area, and they struck camp and moved to a new location.

By late May they were camped along the Rosebud River not far from its confluence with the Yellowstone. Sitting Bull's responsibilities had never been greater. Looking to him for support were his Hunkpapas and the allied circles as well as the extended family of 13 people who shared his lodge: his mother, sister, two wives, two adolescent daughters, three sons (including infant twins), two stepsons, a brother-in-law, and a nephew, One Bull. His other nephew, White Bull, lived nearby.

As a holy man, Sitting Bull prayed and sought visions that would help him bear the burden of leadership and shield his people from misfortune and calamities. One day in May, Sitting Bull fell asleep while meditating and saw in a dream a great dust storm swirling out of the east, followed by ranks of mounted soldiers. The storm spent its fury without doing harm, and Sitting Bull took the dream to mean that soldiers would launch a futile attack on the village from the east. He prayed to the Great Spirit that his people would be spared and would find plenty of game through the coming year. In supplication he promised to sacrifice a buffalo to Wakan Tanka and give of his own flesh and blood in the forthcoming sun dance.

Although Lakotas performed the sun dance every June to give thanks for the blessings that sustained the tribe and to ensure future bounty, this year's ceremony had special meaning. Others would partic-

"If you do this for me, I will sun dance two days and two nights and will give you a whole buffalo."

SITTING BULL PRAYING TO WAKAN TANKA

ipate as well, but Sitting Bull would make a conspicuous sacrifice by offering up what the Lakotas called a scarlet blanket to inspire divine pity and protect the encampment from misfortune. Before dancing he sat against the sacred pole in the center of the dance circle while an assistant used an awl and knife to gouge bits of flesh from his arm. The operation was repeated until blood welled from 100 small wounds, 50 on each of his arms.

Then, extending his bleeding arms—his scarlet blanket—to heaven, Sitting Bull danced, hour after hour, circling the sacred pole while staring at the sun. The sun went down, and he danced on through the night and into the following day. Around noon Sitting Bull suddenly went rigid, as if transfixed. Other dancers laid him gently on the ground and sprinkled him with water. When he regained consciousness, he told of the vision that had come to him.

Obeying a voice that instructed him to fix his gaze just under the sun, he had seen in the distance a plague of white soldiers on horseback charging an Indian village. But the mounted figures were upside down, their heads toward the earth, their hats falling off. "They are to die," the voice explained. Sitting Bull could see that a few Indians in the village were also inverted, but every one of the whites had his feet toward the sky. As instructed by the voice, Sitting Bull told his people not to claim any of

A SACRED SKULL

To invoke the animal's protective spirit, Sitting Bull kept this sacred buffalo skull near him during the sun dance and other important tribal ceremonies. As was the custom, when the skull was still intact he would fill its eye and nose cavities with grass as a symbolic offering to the animal so essential physically and spiritually to the Lakotas' way of life. Useful though every part of the buffalo was, from fur to bone, Sitting Bull occasionally would shoot one and leave the animal where it fell, as an offering to the Great Spirit, Wakan Tanka.

the dead soldiers' belongings in the coming battle, or they would be cursed.

The triumphant vision of Sitting Bull's swelled the feeling of confidence among his people, who were inspired to draw images in the dirt of the dead soldiers he had seen falling into the village. On June 8, a few days after the ceremony, they left their camp near the mouth of the Rosebud and moved southward up the river valley. A week or so later, in pursuit of buffalo, they turned west through a pass in the Wolf Mountains toward the Little Bighorn River. Before they reached the Little Bighorn, however, some Cheyenne wolves trailing behind spotted a big column of soldiers marching north along the Rosebud from the direction of Wyoming.

It was George Crook, back for another shot at the holdouts who had eluded his grasp in March. Now consisting of more than 1,000 blue-coated cavalry and infantry and a few hundred Crow and Shoshone auxiliaries who had enlisted to fight against their Lakota foes, Crook's force was just one of three columns moving against Sitting Bull's encampment. Colonel John Gibbon was heading east from Fort Ellis at Bozeman, Montana, and General Alfred Terry was marching west from Fort Abraham Lincoln near Bismarck with a force spearheaded by Custer's 7th U.S. Cavalry.

Crook was "bristling for a fight," in the words of a newspaper correspondent who talked with him before he renewed his pursuit in late May. And the warriors in Sitting Bull's camp were inclined to oblige the general. Although Sitting Bull and the other chiefs once again sought to avoid a confrontation by counseling their followers to leave the soldiers alone unless they attacked, hundreds of young men slipped away on the night of June 16, heading back toward the Rosebud to challenge the bluecoats. Seeing that their advice had been rejected, Sitting Bull and Crazy Horse hastened to support their warriors.

Shortly after sunup, while Crook's bluecoats were lounging about and sipping coffee at their camp beside the Rosebud, they came under concerted attack. The warriors advanced "in flocks or herds like the buffalo," observed Captain Anson Mills of Crook's cavalry, "and they piled in upon us."

steep toll for a small population—but they were prepared to take the same risk again if the soldiers persisted in coming after them.

Technically, Crook could claim victory in the Battle of the Rosebud, because his men had repulsed the attack, at a cost of some 30 casualties. But he knew that his opponents were far from defeated, and his men lacked ammunition and provisions to pursue the holdouts. Crook retired south to his base camp near the Wyoming border the next day and would not advance again until he was resupplied and reinforced.

The spirits of Sitting Bull's people had never been higher, and as Crook's force retreated they made their way through the pass in the mountains to the banks of the Little Bighorn. There they were joined by bands that had recently left the reservation

"The Indians came not in a line but in flocks or herds like the buffalo, and they piled in upon us until I think there must have been one thousand or fifteen hundred in our immediate front...."

CAPTAIN ANSON MILLS DESCRIBING THE BATTLE OF THE ROSEBUD

Nearly overrun, the bluecoats were bolstered by their Crow and Shoshone allies. When the attack began, they were out front probing for opposition and helped stem the tide, enabling the rest of Crook's force to form a strong defensive line. Even after the Lakotas and Cheyennes lost the advantage of surprise, however, they fought with extraordinary fervor and persistence, mounting charge after charge. Captain Mills concluded that he was up against "the best cavalry in the world."

Sitting Bull, his arms still painfully swollen from the 100 cuts of the scarlet blanket, did not take part in the fight. But Crazy Horse played a commanding role, rallying warriors when they grew discouraged and leading daring counterattacks. The battle raged for six hours. "It was a hard fight," White Bull remembered, "a really big battle." In the end, the exhausted warriors withdrew, having demonstrated to Crook that they were in deadly earnest. They had lost more than 30 men killed and 60 wounded—a

for the summer in a defiant mood, having suffered from short rations through the winter and learned of the army's punitive campaign against the holdouts. Without the Black Hills to fall back on, they needed this hunting ground all the more, and they were prepared to fight for it if necessary. As they poured in, Sitting Bull's encampment swelled to more than 1,000 lodges housing 7,000 people, including 1,800 warriors. In search of game and fresh pasture, they soon moved to a new site along the Little Bighorn, several miles north of the pass.

The pursuing commanders, meanwhile, had only a vague idea of the encampment's location and size. With Crook out of the picture, the campaign was left to Colonel Gibbon and General Terry, advancing along the Yellowstone from the west and the east, respectively. On June 21 the two officers met where the Rosebud enters the Yellowstone to plan an attack. From the reports of their Indian scouts the officers knew that the holdouts had recently moved west from the Rosebud to the Little Bighorn, but they were unaware that reinforcements from the reservation were flocking to join them. Terry assigned Custer and his 600 or so cavalrymen to follow Sitting Bull's trail southward along the Rosebud and over to the Little Bighorn. Gibbon, meanwhile, progressing at a slower pace with infantry, would move south up the Bighorn to the mouth of the Little Bighorn and position his troops to block the anticipated retreat of the fugitives when Custer swung north and attacked them. The plan called for Gibbon to be in place by June 26.

Custer and his cavalrymen headed up the Rosebud on June 22, encountering abundant evidence of Sitting Bull's progress. Reaching the site where the chief had performed his sun dance earlier that month, Custer's Indian scouts found ominous signs, including the dead soldiers Sitting Bull's people had drawn in the dirt after he related his vision. The scouts also spotted fresh horse droppings and lodgepole tracks, indicating that bands of Indians had headed west through the pass in the mountains over the past few days to swell Sitting Bull's camp on the Little Bighorn. One scout warned Custer that he faced a "damn big fight," but the colonel forged ahead, hurrying his men up the east side of the pass on the night of June 24.

Early the following morning, from a peak overlooking the Little Bighorn Valley, Custer and his scouts saw smoke rising in the distance from the Indian camp. The intervening trees and hills prevented them from observing the camp itself or gauging its extent, but they did see a party of Indians on horseback riding toward the rising smoke—bearing word, Custer assumed, that his soldiers were moving in this direction. Thinking that the Indians would promptly pack up and leave when they learned of his presence, Custer spurred his regiment into action without scouting the village or waiting a day for Colonel Gibbon to reach his blocking position at the mouth of the Little Bighorn. So eager was Custer to attack that he and his troopers galloped ahead of the packtrain with

the reserve ammunition, which would make its way down from the hills at a slower pace.

Custer and his troopers reached the eastern edge of the valley around midday. Although the encampment was still out of view to the northwest, across the tree-shaded Little Bighorn, Custer deployed his forces for battle. Concerned that there might be more Indians off to the southwest, he dispatched three companies under Captain Frederick Benteen to reconnoiter in that direction. He then further divided his command by ordering Major Marcus Reno to take three of the remaining eight companies across the river and attack the village from the south.

Custer never had the chance to explain his battle plan, but he evidently thought that Reno's small force would be enough to overcome initial resistance and panic the villagers. While Reno's attack was unfolding, the colonel himself would lead the other five companies north along the crest of the ridge overlooking the river's east bank and sweep down around the far end of the encampment to crush any lingering opposition and trap the villagers. Without Colonel Gibbon nearby to block their expected retreat, Custer had to deal with that contingency himself. Far from anticipating a big fight from the Indians, he seemed largely concerned with stemming their flight.

The Indian encampment was quiet. For the past week, the nights had been filled with dancing, feasting, and celebration, and many of the revelers were slow to awaken. A few early risers were smoking their pipes contentedly when a visiting party of Lakotas who had left camp around dawn returned hurriedly and told of seeing bluecoats off in the distance. Those who offered the warnings were not trusted scouts, however, and no one they talked to could believe that the bluecoats would dare attack such a formidable force of warriors in broad daylight.

As the sun rose high in the sky, many in the village continued to doze, including Sitting Bull. Sometime after noon, he recalled years later, he was lying in his

lodge when he heard men shouting, "Get up. They are firing into the camp." Elsewhere in the camp some sleepers were rudely awakened by the gunfire itself. One woman was startled by "a terrific volley of carbines. The bullets shattered the tepee poles."

The attack was coming from the south, along the streambed of the Little Bighorn, straight at the camp circle of Sitting Bull's Hunkpapas. While warriors hurried to meet the challenge, the chief and his nephew One Bull mounted their horses and conducted women of their family to safety in the low hills west of the village. Returning to the tepee, Sitting Bull retrieved his most precious articles of war—the shield his father had designed for him, his bow and arrows, and his war club—and presented them to his nephew. "Go right ahead," he said, urging the younger man into battle. "Don't be afraid, go right on." One Bull in turn gave his pistol and rifle to his uncle. As befitted an elder chief responsible for the encampment, Sitting Bull would remain in the village throughout the battle, helping to defend the women and children still in the camp and bracing the warriors with strong words. "Brave up, boys," he shouted to the men as they gathered for battle, "it will be a hard time. Brave up."

Major Reno and his men, meanwhile, were facing a severe test of their own courage. Not until he forded the Little Bighorn did Reno get a clear look at the Indian camp. To his great shock, he saw hundreds of tepees stretching off into the hazy distance. Any thoughts of rushing headlong into the village were abandoned. Reno ordered his men to dismount and form a skirmish line. They advanced boldly toward the tepees, firing their carbines, but the gathering warriors soon overwhelmed them. Angry Hunkpapas from Sitting Bull's circle swept around Reno's flanks and pressed his men back.

Brash, impulsive, and hellbent for glory, George Armstrong Custer once boasted, "I could whip all the Indians on the continent." In the photograph at left he wears the uniform of a major general, the brevet rank he achieved during the Civil War. After the war, when he went west to fight Indians on the plains, he reverted to his regular army rank of lieutenant colonel.

Just before the battle at the Little Bighorn Custer dictated a message to his adjutant, W. W. Cooke, whose hurried scrawl appears below at right. Addressed to Captain Frederick Benteen, the message directed him to bring reserve ammunition supplies, or packs, for Custer's men. Benteen later transcribed the message—Custer's last—in the neater hand seen above Cooke's.

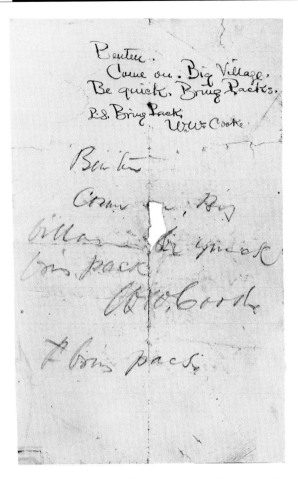

a very large force of warriors who showed no signs of retreating. From his high vantage point, Custer dispatched an urgent note to Captain Benteen, who was still off reconnoitering to the south, ordering him to speed to the scene and bring along the ammunition train. Sometime later, Benteen succeeded in linking up with Reno, but after venturing tentatively from the bluff with their men and encountering large numbers of Indians, they returned under fire to their defensive position.

When the warriors who had routed Reno learned that more bluecoats had been spotted east of the camp, they rode back to the village to meet this new threat. There they saw troopers moving down a ravine across the river, and others higher up on the slope. Custer's men, still hoping to hold the Indians at bay and envelop the huge encampment, were firing into the lodges, and many in the village feared that hordes of bluecoats were about to descend on them. Sitting Bull, seated on his horse at the northern edge of the village, where women and children had flocked during Reno's attack, heard the bullets droning "like humming bees." Once again he urged the gathering warriors to take heart and rise to the defense of their families.

Led by Crazy Horse and other war chiefs, more than 1,000 warriors forded the river with shrill battle cries, drove the cavalrymen back up the ravine, and engaged Custer's greatly outnumbered troopers from all sides. The fighting atop the ridge was furious, raising clouds of dust and gun smoke that shrouded the battleground and left Sitting Bull and others down below unsure as to the outcome. The chief briefly considered telling the women to strike the lodges in case the warriors were repulsed. But then a young man returned from the battleground to inform Sitting Bull that his vision had been fulfilled: "Every white man is killed."

Indeed, not one of the 210 soldiers Custer had led north along the ridge remained alive. Toward the end some of the men had thrown down their guns and begged for mercy, warriors related. But as one woman in the village explained later, the Lakotas

Then scores of Oglalas with Crazy Horse in the lead galloped into the fray and forced the soldiers to retreat with their horses deep into the woods along the riverbank.

As warriors pressed in on them through the trees and brush, the desperate soldiers mounted up and bolted, heading for the ford they had crossed earlier, south of the camp. Lakotas chased after them exuberantly, shooting down bluecoats and clubbing them from the saddle. Those troopers who escaped back across the river took refuge on a bluff above the east bank.

Of the 175 men who had followed Reno into battle, more than a third were dead, wounded, or missing. The major himself survived, but his battered force would be of no help to Custer, who had hurried his companies north along the ridge and now confronted the startling truth in the valley below—

SCOUTING FOR CUSTER

When George Armstrong Custer began his pursuit of renegade Sioux and their Cheyenne allies in May 1876, he needed experts familiar with the land to lead the way. So just as he had done in previous campaigns, he first enlisted some Indian scouts. There was no shortage of recruits; many Indians considered their tribal rivals to be greater enemies than the white man. In addition, by scouting for the bluecoats, warriors could prove their courage in battle and sometimes obtain a more favorable deal from the U.S. government for their tribe.

Custer enlisted 45 Indian scouts, mostly Arikara and Crow—both fierce enemies of the Sioux and the Cheyennes. One of the Crows, named White Man Runs Him, explained, "We loved our land so we consented to go in with the soldiers and put these other tribes off the land. The soldiers and I were fighting in friendship, what they said, I did and what I said, they did. So I helped my tribe. Land is a very valuable thing and especially our land. I knew the Cheyennes and Sioux wanted to take it by conquest, so I stayed with the soldiers to help hold it."

Custer generally paid close heed to his scouts' advice. But when he came upon the Sioux and Cheyennes at the Little Bighorn, his egotism got the better of him, and he ignored the scouts' warning that a major fight was looming. For his reckless charge in the face of overwhelming odds, he and the 7th Cavalry—along with some of his scouts—paid with their lives.

Arikara scout Bloody Knife points to the map on George Armstrong Custer's lap during a railroad survey expedition in 1873. Three years later Bloody Knife was shot in the head and killed at the Little Bighorn while fighting under the 7th Cavalry guidon shown at right.

Before mounting his attack on Sitting Bull's village, Custer released his Crow scouts. Years later White Man Runs Him (right) observed, "Had Custer not ordered me to go, the people who visit Custer Field today would see my name on the monument."

Curly, a Crow scout, survived the slaughter at the Little Bighorn. According to one account, he hid inside the carcass of a horse until the battle was over.

and their allies had a score to settle with the attacking bluecoats: "The blood of the people was hot and their hearts bad, and they took no prisoners that day." Not until after the hectic battle did the victors discover that the force they had annihilated was commanded by Long Hair, who now lay dead. He was stripped of his clothing and mutilated, as were many of his men. "He thought he was the greatest man in the world," a Hunkpapa warrior named Bad Soup said to his companions as they viewed what remained of Long Hair, "and there he is."

Once Custer's companies had been wiped out, warriors renewed their assault on the bluecoats who had taken shelter on the bluff to the south. There the soldiers led by Reno and Benteen had dug deep trenches, burrowing into the ground "like prairie dogs," in the words of one Lakota, and offering the warriors little to shoot at. The soldiers remained under siege until noon the next day, June 26, when Sitting Bull informed the warriors that it was time for the entire encampment to move on. "Let them go now," he said of the besieged bluecoats, "so some can go home and spread the news." The decision to move was prompted by reports from scouts that more troops were on their way from the north—the forces of Colonel Gibbon, who had expected to corral the fugitives after Custer destroyed their camp but instead ended up collecting the shattered remnants of the 7th U.S. Cavalry.

That afternoon the Lakotas and Cheyennes hastily packed up and left, heading southwest. On the fourth night after the battle, when they knew they were safe from pursuit for the time being, they staged a dance to celebrate the greatest victory they had ever won over the bluecoats—a spectacular coup that would be recounted by the participants time and again, in words and pictures (pages 133-143). The triumph had been costly, however. At least 30 warriors had been killed, and dozens wounded. Sitting Bull lamented their loss, as well as the steep enemy toll, which was bound to bring retribution. "I feel sorry that too many were killed on each side," he said. "But when Indians must fight, they must." The outcome had confirmed the power of his vision. But he regretted that his people had ignored his stern warning not to claim the clothing and keepsakes of the dead soldiers and feared that it meant they would "always covet white people's belongings."

Word of Custer's stunning defeat reached the East Coast in the midst of celebrations commemorating America's 100th birthday. While the Centennial Exhibition in Philadelphia extolled the nation's inexorable progress, out west a cavalry corps led by one of America's most promising young officers had been crushed by a band of so-called savages, a term that persisted in the press despite the evident skill and dedication of Custer's opponents. Newspaper accounts branded his defeat a massacre, fostering the misconception that Custer and his men were the hapless victims of Indian treachery.

Amid public outrage, President Grant and his military commanders stepped up their campaign against the Lakotas, targeting not only the bands involved in the fighting but those who had remained behind on the reservation. In July the agencies there were placed under strict military control; officers were empowered to imprison men they regarded as hostile and to confiscate horses, weapons, and ammunition. In August Grant signed a measure that withheld food and other forms of government aid from any Lakota branch engaged in hostilities, including people who had remained near the agencies. Soon all the reservation dwellers would lose their allocations, the government warned, unless their chiefs agreed to cede the Black Hills and other territory that had been granted to them in perpetuity just eight years earlier.

Sitting Bull and his allies knew little of these disturbing developments at the time. They remained on the open plains, having divided into smaller hunting groups a month or so after the battle to better sustain themselves and avoid pursuit. In late summer some of the bands decided to return to the agencies, but Sitting Bull and Crazy Horse held out with their respective followers, hunting in the country north of the reservation.

By mid-August Generals Crook and Terry had been reinforced and were pursuing the holdouts with a combined force of 4,000 soldiers. The two generals soon quarreled, however, and went separate ways. As fall approached their men grew increasingly hungry, weary, and wary. Terry gave up the chase in early September with nothing to show for his efforts. Crook fared little better. On September 9 a detachment of his men stumbled across a small encampment of Lakotas at Slim Buttes in present-day North Dakota and launched an attack that cost the lives of women and children as well as those of a few warriors and only stiffened the resolve of the survivors. Instead of returning to the reservation, as they had planned, many remained at large with Sitting Bull, who had rushed to the scene from his nearby camp with several hundred men to defend those under attack. "What have we done that the white people want us to stop?" he asked after Crook's troops withdrew.

During the prime hunting days of September and early October, Sitting Bull and his people moved back toward the Yellowstone country in pursuit of buffalo. On October 10 his scouts spotted a train of 86 wagons heading west along the Yellowstone River to the mouth of the Tongue River, where Colonel Nelson A. Miles and his men were building their winter quarters. The next morning Sitting Bull's warriors attacked the wagon train, killing or running off so many mules that the drivers were forced to turn back. Four days later, however, the wagons reappeared, this time with an escort of 200 soldiers. Although Sitting Bull's warriors sniped constantly at them and set a grass fire in their way, the drivers pressed forward.

Sitting Bull had with him an interpreter who could write English, and together they composed a note to the intruders and impaled it on a stick in the path of the wagon train. "I want to know what you are doing traveling on this road," the note read. "You scare all the buffalo away. I want to hunt on the place. I want you to turn back from here. If you don't, I will fight you again." But Sitting Bull made it clear that he wanted to avoid fighting. "I am your friend," he assured the whites.

The note set the stage for talks. In the days to come, Sitting Bull twice met in parleys with the bluecoats—first with the commander of the wagon guard, Lieutenant Colonel Elwell S. Otis, and later with Colonel Miles, who hurried to the scene with the entire 5th Infantry Regiment. Finding the wagon train safe, he marched to Sitting Bull's encampment up a tributary of the Yellowstone called Cedar Creek and deployed his men in a line of battle outside the chief's village of some 400 tepees on October 20. Then the colonel rode forward with his staff to talk with Sitting Bull and other chiefs. It was a clear, cold day, with a touch of winter in the air. A cannon brooded over the camp from a nearby hill, and a line of mounted warriors waited not far behind Sitting Bull. The tension was thick, and there were many on both sides who itched for battle. Miles dismounted to extend his hand, and Sitting Bull met the man he would have to contend with for some time to come.

Born just four months before Custer, Miles had much in common with the late colonel. Both had won distinction in the Civil War, rising to the exalted rank of major general while still in their twenties before reverting to colonel in the smaller postwar army. Both were energetic and intensely ambitious. But Miles was a more disciplined and diplomatic officer than Custer—qualities that would help him become commander in chief of the army in later years. He was not one to spoil his hopes by taking his Indian opponents lightly.

He certainly did not underestimate Sitting Bull, whom he described in a letter to his wife as a

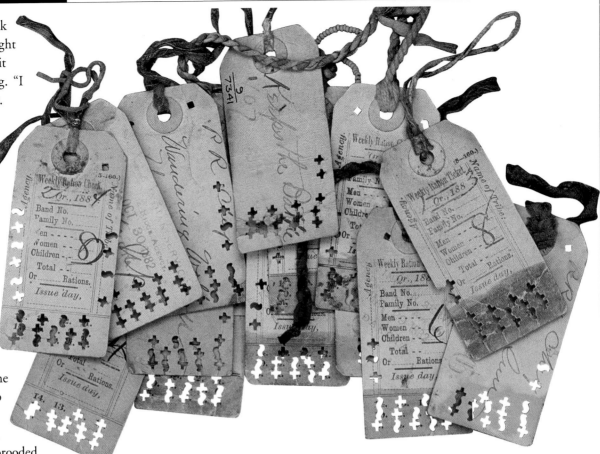

A MEAGER DIET

Government agents punched ration cards, like those shown above from the Pine Ridge Reservation, each time they handed out supplies of beef, sugar, or flour. Hunger was a chronic problem because rations were always scanty and stealing and corruption were widespread among agents and contractors.

man of great influence and intelligence. But he also sensed that the chief was deeply troubled and unsure of what path to follow: "I should judge his great strength is as a warrior. I think he feels that his strength is somewhat exhausted and he appeared much depressed, suffering from nervous excitement and loss of power." It remained to be seen whether Sitting Bull would try to reassert that power through warfare or whether he would affirm his strength as a leader in other ways.

The two men sparred verbally all afternoon. Miles demanded the return of the mules driven off from the wagon train, to which Sitting Bull responded by demanding the return of the buffalo that the wagon train had scared off. Sitting Bull told Miles to dismantle his forts, abandon the Yellowstone country, and leave his people alone. Miles told Sitting Bull he must surrender unconditionally and bring his people in to settle on an agency.

Although he exuded defiance, Sitting Bull was facing strong opposition from Miles, and his people were no longer of one purpose. In addition to his Hunkpapas, there were other Lakotas in his camp, and they urged him to be conciliatory—some even talked about surrendering. "At times," Colonel Miles wrote, "he was almost inclined to accept the situation, but I think partly from fear and partly through the belief that he might do better, he did not accept." They broke off the talks overnight, during which time each side considered attacking the other but thought better of it.

They made no progress the next day, either, as Sitting Bull sat in silence, torn by conflicting emotions. Finally, Miles delivered an ultimatum: If the Lakotas did not surrender without any delay, he would order his men to attack. Sitting Bull angrily broke off the meeting and left with the chiefs who had accompanied him.

As the bluecoats now advanced, they were peppered with fire from warriors who had stolen up into the surrounding hills overnight. The women in the camp had already packed up the tents and prepared for flight, and after a brief firefight the Lakotas slipped away, with Miles in hot pursuit. Within a few days, however, a large contingent decided to surrender to Miles and return to the reservation rather than face the hardships of a fugitive existence over the coming winter. With 30 steadfast Hunkpapa families, Sitting Bull traveled north.

Sitting Bull's grand alliance was shattered, his enormous gathering of warriors shrunk to a loyal few, his vast hunting territory occupied by a permanent enemy force. The people who remained with him were short of food and ammunition. Even the weather turned against them, with a series of unusually harsh blizzards and sharp cold spells. Nonetheless, Sitting Bull considered such hardship preferable to a life of confinement and dependency at the agencies. "When there are no more buffalo or other game I will send my children to hunt and live on prairie mice," he insisted, "for where an Indian is shut up in one place his body becomes weak."

Late in the winter, still harried by Miles, Sitting Bull and his people decided to seek refuge in Canada. Approaching the border in northeastern Montana, they came upon an interpreter from nearby Fort Peck. Hoping that the army had abandoned that lonely outpost, they asked if there were still soldiers there. The interpreter answered yes, prompting a response that summed up the fugitives' plight: "Damn soldiers everywhere."

Things seemed better across the border at first. Sitting Bull and his people entered Canada in May, undetected and unchallenged, and found buffalo grazing in abundance on the fresh green plains of present-day Saskatchewan. Their first contact with the representatives of Canada's Grandmother—as Sitting Bull called Queen Victoria, the ruler of this British dominion—came in astonishing form. Soon after they had established their village, a party of seven white men, five of them wearing the scarlet tunics of Canada's North West Mounted Police, rode nonchalantly to the outskirts of the camp. Ignoring the presence of scores of potentially hostile warriors, they pitched their own tent and requested a conference. Never before, one warrior told them, had white men dared to impose on Sitting Bull in such a fashion.

At the meeting, Major James M. Walsh of the mounted police, a compact, dark-haired, bearded officer who seemed not to know the meaning of the word fear, laid down the law. The White Mother would embrace and protect all people who obeyed her laws, he said. The Lakotas were welcome as long as they committed no transgressions, either in Canada or back in the United States. Walsh drove his point home by arresting a warrior in the camp in possession of some horses the major's scouts recognized as stolen. As Walsh was about to clap the culprit in leg irons, the man surrendered the horses and was set free. Sitting Bull had met the first white man, and one of the few, he ever liked and respected.

South of the border that year, the U.S. Army all but crushed Lakota resistance. Crazy Horse, after

leading his people back to the reservation in May to spare them further suffering, was bayoneted to death by a soldier when he resisted arrest. Not all Lakotas returned to the agencies or remained there, however. Some joined Sitting Bull's people in Canada, and by the summer of 1877 there were about 1,000 living there much as they had to the south before the bluecoats descended on them. The hunting was good, the traders in the area were fair, and the police dealt with them firmly but respectfully.

Despite the improvement in the fortunes of his people, Sitting Bull mourned the loss of his homeland and felt that he had failed as a leader. "I am nothing," he told the people he met, "neither a chief nor a soldier." Yet his followers relied on him more than ever. Walsh noted the "universal confidence which is given to his judgment. They listen and obey."

Sitting Bull's presence worried higher Canadian authorities, who feared that the Lakotas would clash with one of Canada's resident tribes or cross back into the United States and cause trouble there, raising diplomatic tensions. With encouragement from the Canadians, American officials sent General Terry north to try to talk Sitting Bull into returning and surrendering. The chief refused at first even to meet with the enemy commander: "We cannot talk with men who have blood on their hands," he said. At Walsh's insistence, he at last sat down with Terry, who promised that if the fugitives gave up their weapons and agreed to live on the reservation they would not be punished. "You come here to tell us lies," Sitting Bull replied dismissively. "Go back home where you came from."

By the spring of 1878 there were as many as 5,000 fugitives in Canada with Sitting Bull, including recent refugees from the strife-torn Lakota agencies and forlorn members of the Nez Perce tribe who had fled north the year before when their leader, Chief Joseph, surrendered to pursuing feder-

Sitting Bull posed with Buffalo Bill Cody for this photo taken in Montreal in 1885. For four months that year, the chief toured with Buffalo Bill's Wild West Show, visiting more than a dozen cities in the United States and Canada.

al troops *(pages 92-101)*. Buffalo became scarce around the crowded Canadian encampments, and the hunters began to stray south across the border, where they took not only bison but the occasional horse, supply wagon, and scalp, when whites or some of their old tribal foes got in their way.

During the summer of 1879 the army dispatched Miles to drive the Lakotas in northern Montana back into Canada. With 700 soldiers and 143 Indian auxiliaries, Miles came upon Sitting Bull and a large party of buffalo hunters, women, and children on the Milk River. One Crow auxiliary named Magpie rode out ahead of the rest and challenged Sitting Bull to individual combat. Sitting Bull readily accepted, and the two aging warriors galloped their ponies toward each other. Magpie tried to take the first shot, but his rifle jammed. Sitting Bull then fired one shot in return, and blew off the top of Magpie's skull. The regular soldiers soon arrived and joined the fight with cannons blazing, and the Lakotas fled back to Canada.

Sitting Bull had shown that he could still make war, but he could not save his people from the forces that now pressed in upon them. The Canadian government offered them no more help or encouragement, and in 1880 Major Walsh was reassigned on the grounds that he had become too friendly with the Lakotas. The buffalo were gone, the horses were dying of mange, and the people were afflicted with scurvy and close to starvation.

Sitting Bull's allies began to drift away, back to the reservation agencies, where they would find no dignity or freedom but would at least find something to eat. In early 1881, as the despair mounted and the camps dwindled, Sitting Bull began to think seriously, agonizingly, about surrender.

The morning of July 19, 1881, Sitting Bull rode south to submit to federal authorities at Fort Buford, just east of the border between the Montana and Dakota Territories. Of all the chiefs who had once heeded him, only his paternal uncle Four Horns and a few others remained at his side. Of the thousands of warriors who had once followed him, a mere 44 trailed behind him now, accompanied by 143 women and children. Of the sprawling herds of

Sitting Bull pleads his people's cause before a panel on tribal matters at the Standing Rock Agency in 1889. The bearded man sitting to the right behind the table is Indian agent James McLaughlin, with his wife at his side. During his seven years at Standing Rock, the chief fought efforts to reduce the size of the reservation. He was such a persuasive debater that McLaughlin and other officials often tried to prevent his speaking.

ponies that had once been the strength of his people, fewer than 100 gaunt mounts remained. Five years after achieving the pinnacle of victory at the Little Bighorn, Sitting Bull and his people filed dejectedly into the parade ground of Fort Buford at noon. "Nothing but nakedness and starvation has driven this man to submission," remarked Captain Walter Clifford, the officer in charge of prisoners at the fort, "and that not on his own account but for the sake of his children, of whom he is very fond."

Sitting Bull was suffering from an eye infection, and he peered out from under a bandanna tied around his head. He wore a soiled calico shirt and black leggings, with a tattered old blanket knotted around his waist. Some of his people were "literally naked," noted Major David Brotherton, the fort's commander, "and with most of them the clothing is falling off from pure rottenness."

Sitting Bull refused to yield his battered Winchester, hoping to postpone the dreaded moment of surrender a while longer. Major Brotherton told him to bring his warriors to his office the next morning. At the appointed time, Sitting Bull and his men entered the room and sat on the floor. With his five-year-old son Crow Foot at his side, Sitting Bull laid his Winchester down and signaled for the boy to carry it to Brotherton. "I surrender this rifle to you through my young son," said Sitting Bull. "I wish it to be remembered that I was the last man of my tribe to surrender my rifle. This boy has given it to you, and he now wants to know how he is going to make a living."

Major Brotherton and others had explained to Sitting Bull and his followers that they would be shipped down the Missouri River to the Standing Rock Agency, near Fort Yates in the eastern part of the Great Sioux Reservation, where they would join some of their friends and relatives who had already surrendered. But Sitting Bull found it hard to grasp that he was no longer free to do as he pleased. He asked for the right to visit Canada and to live with his followers on a reservation of their own. His requests were denied, and he began to reckon with the fact that others now controlled his destiny. That evening he composed a song, as he often had before at crucial moments in his life: "A

The rarely photographed ghost dance was secretly caught on film by a Chicago newspaperman who hid a camera inside his coat to get this shot at Standing Rock. As the ghost dance swept the reservation, Sitting Bull set up his tepee to the right of the dance circle and refused to comply with the agency's orders to halt the practice.

warrior I have been," he chanted. "Now it is all over. A hard time I have."

On July 29 Sitting Bull and his ragged band walked up the gangplank of the steamer *General Sherman* and journeyed to a world transformed beyond their comprehension. Two days later they stopped off briefly at Bismarck, North Dakota. On a siding at the levee sat smoking and chuffing something that Sitting Bull had long hated and opposed but never seen—a locomotive, hitched to a private railroad car. The general manager of the Northern Pacific had provided the car to transport Sitting Bull into town. Dubiously he examined it, then asked to see it move. When the engineer complied, he declared that he would rather walk.

In Bismarck the city fathers had laid on a formal dinner in the ornate Merchants House. Hundreds of onlookers were surprised as Sitting Bull, along with his sister, uncle, and several chiefs, received the repast with relaxed good humor and gamely wielded knives and forks. Sitting Bull did not try to conceal his astonishment at the dish of ice cream he was served for dessert, muttering that he could

not see how such stuff "could be frozen in hot weather." During this visit Sitting Bull discovered another strange thing: Whites would gladly pay him for his signature, which he had learned to write while in Canada.

Then it was back on the steamer for the trip downriver to the Standing Rock Agency. Sitting Bull and his chiefs stood at the bow of the steamer as it approached the dock, raising a sad chant as friends and relatives gathered to greet them, held back by a line of soldiers. Although allowed to visit with loved ones around the agency, Sitting Bull and the nearly 200 new arrivals were lodged separately there while the army reconsidered their fate. After three weeks, in defiance of promises made to Sitting Bull in good faith by Major Brotherton and others, troops threw a cordon of bayonets around the little band, herded them back on the steamer, and took them farther down the Missouri to Fort Randall, where they were held under guard as prisoners of war for nearly two years.

Sitting Bull's repeated pleas to the government to honor the pledges it had made to secure his surrender were ignored until December 1882. Then an elderly Lakota chief named Strike-the-Ree wrote a letter to Robert Todd Lincoln, the son of President Abraham Lincoln, now serving as secretary of war in the administration of President Chester Arthur. "My friend," wrote the chief, "what has Sitting Bull been convicted of doing that you hold him a prisoner for so many long moons? His moaning cry comes to my ears. There is no one else to speak for him so I plead his cause."

Moved by this appeal, Lincoln intervened, and on May 10, 1883, Sitting Bull and his people returned to Standing Rock. His spirit unbroken by his long confinement, he fully expected to resume his former role as principal chief there. On meeting the agent in charge, James McLaughlin, Sitting Bull explained his intentions: He would receive and distribute all rations for his Hunkpapas; he would not plant any crops the first year, but would think about doing so the next; he wanted his former followers who were living at other agencies brought to him at Standing Rock; he had prepared a list of the subchiefs who would form his council; and he expected a house to be built for him.

McLaughlin was a veteran agent with little regard for Indian traditions. A stern authoritarian, he was bent on transforming the reservation dwellers into God-fearing farmers. He was not about to help a staunch traditionalist like Sitting Bull regain power. "I heard this inflated nonsense through to the end," McLaughlin recalled of that first meeting. Then he told Sitting Bull bluntly to draw his rations, plant his crops, and live by the rules like everyone else.

The two men were sharply at odds from that moment on. Sitting Bull went along with some of the programs McLaughlin instituted when he felt that they might be

Bedecked with eagle feathers and celestial symbols, this shirt is typical of those worn by the ghost dancers. Made of muslin and stitched with sinew, the shirts were believed to protect the wearer from all harm, including white men's bullets.

of help to his people. But he refused to bow to the agent's authority or renounce his ancestral beliefs, and McLaughlin came to regard him as a trouble-making obstructionist.

McLaughlin laid out farming districts and appointed an Indian "boss farmer" to oversee each district. Far from opposing the plan, Sitting Bull recognized that it would make reservation dwellers less dependent on government handouts, and he took up farming himself at the cabin he shared with his extended family on the Grand River, near the place of his birth. Within a few years he possessed dozens of cattle, a large flock of chickens, a well-stocked root cellar, and productive fields of oats, corn, and potatoes. Similarly, Sitting Bull saw something to be gained from the education available on the reservation. He put all the children in his family into a day school run by Protestant missionaries near his home, believing that they would be better prepared to deal with whites if they learned to read and write English.

When it came to the matter of religion, McLaughlin and Sitting Bull were worlds apart. The agent wanted all the Indians on the reservation to become practicing Christians, and Sitting Bull was just as determined to preserve the traditional beliefs of his people. "He hated Christianity," recalled a missionary who in spite of that fact became his friend, "and found great satisfaction in taking my converts back into heathendom while of course I felt equal satisfaction in converting his heathen friends."

Sitting Bull's strong faith made him contemptuous of a legal system on the reservation that outlawed sacred tribal practices. Indian police under the command of the agent could take people into custody not only for such obvious transgressions as theft and assault but also for various offenses deemed by the government to be "demoralizing and barbarous," including the sun dance and other rituals.

Many Indian police looked the other way when people in their community adhered to age-old religious customs. But the officers tried to enforce other statutes such as those governing the use of weapons. Sitting Bull ran afoul of the law one day when another chief took umbrage at his comments and attacked him with a knife. Sitting Bull drove his assailant off with a tomahawk, and both men were then hauled into court, where the knife and the tomahawk were confiscated. This was hardly Sitting Bull's idea of justice, but something happened a few days later that seemed to be a judgment from on high: His assailant was struck by lightning and killed. Lakotas saw this as further proof of Sitting Bull's remarkable medicine—a spirit power stronger than the law. Reported the exasperated McLaughlin:

"The event had a tremendous effect in restoring the waning prestige of the old medicine chief."

Hemmed in by the agent and his regulations, Sitting Bull looked with interest to the world beyond the reservation, where he was notorious as Custer's vanquisher and the implacable enemy of white settlement. Having seen the wonders of Bismarck, Sitting Bull was eager to learn what else the white man had wrought. McLaughlin allowed him to travel outside the reservation now and then, and in 1884 he accompanied the agent on a trip to St. Paul, Minnesota, where he witnessed one marvel after another, including a printing press, a telegraph office, and a fire station. Sitting Bull was no less fascinating to the citizens he met. They thronged around him, clamored for his autograph, and asked countless questions.

The spectacle inspired more than one enterprising person to think about cashing in on the chief's celebrity. When the owner of a St. Paul hotel proposed mounting an exhibition featuring

Frustrated by Sitting Bull's refusal to stop the ghost dancers, Standing Rock agent James McLaughlin sent the letter below ordering the reservation police to arrest the chief before daylight the following day. His postscript admonished: "You must not let him escape under any circumstances."

Sitting Bull in New York City and Philadelphia, McLaughlin replied that he thought he could get "the old fool" to do it, and proceeded to make the arrangements while fending off another entrepreneur, William F. Cody, better known as Buffalo Bill, who wanted Sitting Bull for his own Wild West Show.

The exhibition McLaughlin helped bring about featured a tepee onstage, with Sitting Bull and a handful of other Indians in full regalia acting out their customs and exploits while a lecturer explained it all in lurid and often misleading terms. The show drew 6,000 people on its first day in New York and played to packed houses for weeks. Despite the carnival atmosphere, Sitting Bull retained a measure of dignity during the show and made earnest speeches in his native language. On one occasion he declared that the days for fighting had come to an end and that it was necessary now for young Indians to become educated. The lecturer pretended to translate his remarks for the audience, twisting them into a spurious tale in which the chief villainously ambushed Custer.

A year later Sitting Bull embarked on another tour, this time with Cody, who respectfully refrained from including the chief in the mock battles other Indians in the troupe performed. Sitting Bull got along well with Cody and with another famous member of the company, sharpshooter Annie Oakley. He was paid $50 a week for his appearances, and earned more from the sale of pictures and autographs. But as was his lifelong custom, he gave most of his money away, often to beggars he encountered on the streets, many of whom were children. "The white man knows how to make everything," he remarked to Annie Oakley, "but he does not know how to distribute it."

When he returned to Standing Rock, Sitting Bull spent what little remained of his income hosting feasts for his friends and recounting his adventures. McLaughlin considered such generosity to be uncivilized. Like some other agents and reformers of the day, he thought that the Indians would adapt more readily to life in white America if individuals learned to keep their wealth for themselves instead of sharing it, as Sitting Bull had done. He forbade any more tours by Sitting Bull, concluding that the chief was "too vain and obstinate to be benefited by what he sees, and makes no good use of the money he thus earns."

Some authorities thought that the only way to draw the Lakotas and other Indians fully into American society was to sever the ties that bound them to their tribe and make them private landholders. In 1887 Congress passed the General Allotment Act, which called for land on reservations across the country to be removed from collective tribal ownership and parceled out to Indian families, each of which would typically receive an allotment of 160 acres. The remaining tribal land would be sold to white settlers, with the proceeds held in trust for the Indians. For the Lakotas, this meant that the Great

Crow Foot, one of a pair of twin boys born shortly before the Battle of the Little Bighorn in 1876, was Sitting Bull's favorite son. A thoughtful, sober boy, he began attending councils with his father by the time he was five years old.

Sioux Reservation would be carved up and their territory greatly diminished. Families would receive allotments on one of six small reservations located around the scattered agencies, leaving nine million acres of the tribe's land to be sold to white settlers for just 50¢ an acre.

Sitting Bull protested bitterly. Even McLaughlin thought that the proposal was unjust, but there was little that he could do to change it. After Sitting Bull and other chiefs managed to negotiate a somewhat higher price for the land sold to settlers, the government rammed the deal through in early 1890, even as Lakotas were suffering from a reduction in the food rations that were mandated by Congress. For many, it was the bleakest time since the army pursued them across the plains. They yearned for a chance at redemption and found it in the promises of a distant holy man.

A Lakota named Kicking Bear, a member of the tribe's Miniconjou branch from the nearby Cheyenne River Agency, arrived at Sitting Bull's settlement on the Grand River on October 9, 1890, with news of a momentous development in the life of the people. Hunkpapas gathered that night to hear him speak, and as they listened they felt something they had not experienced for many years—a thrill of hope.

That summer their situation had grown more desperate. Many families found that their allotments of land were woefully small for subsistence. Now Kicking Bear stood before them to say that all they had lost to whites over the years would soon be restored to them. The previous winter he had traveled to Nevada with a Lakota delegation sent to investigate reports of a prophet who offered hope for all Indians. The holy man, a Paiute named Wovoka, spoke the truth, Kicking Bear proclaimed. Wovoka had experienced a great vision at a time when "the sun died," most likely a reference to a solar eclipse that had occurred on January 1, 1889. Wovoka said that he had died with the sun and was taken up into heaven, where he was shown the way to salvation.

Then he had returned to lead other Indians to paradise, where they would be reunited with their departed ancestors and live with them in eternal harmony. There would be no white people in paradise, and no reservations. It would be like the world they once knew, boundless and filled with buffalo.

To reach that promised land, Wovoka said, Indians must never lie or steal, must live in peace with one another and the whites, and must perform regularly a sacred ghost dance that would put them in touch with their departed kin. The next spring, Wovoka promised, the Great Spirit would come. The transforming power of that spirit would sweep over the world like a flood, drowning the whites but lifting up faithful Indians.

Wovoka's vision, echoing both Christian teachings about the apocalypse and age-old Indian prophecies of paradise in the hereafter, inspired the Hunkpapas and other Lakotas. The ghost dance they began to perform bore a similarity to their old sun dance. After purifying themselves in a sweat lodge, the participants danced for hours in a circle around a central pole. Men and women joined in the ceremony, and as they sang and prayed, they felt themselves drawing close to paradise and their lost loved ones. The dancers wore so-called ghost shirts decorated with emblems of spirit power that were believed to protect the wearer from harm, including white men's bullets. Although the ghost shirts invoked the same kind of medicine that warriors had long relied on for protection, Lakotas wore them not because they planned to attack anyone but because they feared retribution for practicing their faith and prophesying doom for whites.

Tragically, those fears were borne out. Some authorities worried that this prophecy, like those of the Comanche Ishatai and other militant medicine men in the past, would lead resentful Indians to rise up in arms against their white oppressors. But agent McLaughlin was more concerned that "this absurdity," as he called the ghost dance movement, would undermine his campaign to Christianize the Lakotas and strengthen his archrival Sitting Bull.

He dispatched Indian police to eject Kicking Bear from Sitting Bull's settlement, and then recommended to superiors that Sitting Bull be dispatched to a military prison.

In fact, Sitting Bull was not the "high priest and leading apostle" of the ghost dance movement that McLaughlin took him to be. The chief was initially skeptical of Wovoka's prophecy, for he did not believe that it was possible for a dead man to return and live again. As the fervor of the ghost dancers increased, however, Sitting Bull reached out to them. He erected a tepee on the edge of the dancing ground and helped the dancers interpret the visions that came to them as they reached the point of exhaustion. Finally, in late October, Sitting Bull stepped into the circle himself and took part in the ceremony, much as he had performed the sun dance in times past.

Word of Sitting Bull's involvement strengthened the appeal of the movement to Lakotas and intensified white fears of an uprising. Other Indian agents joined McLaughlin in urging strong action against the ghost dancers and their leaders. The Interior Department, in charge of the reservations, turned the matter over to the army, which promptly occupied the Pine Ridge and Rosebud Agencies, situated near the Badlands of South Dakota. Many of the ghost dancers fled into the Badlands and continued to practice their faith.

McLaughlin hoped to avoid a similar flight from his agency by using his police force to suppress the ghost dance. He still considered Sitting Bull to be personally responsible for the spread of this "pernicious system of religion." Although any attempt to seize the chief might turn violent, McLaughlin felt that Sitting Bull had to be silenced, even at the cost of his life. On December 14 the

Sitting Bull's death was headlined across the country in approving newspaper articles like the one at right, which makes an ugly play on the saying "The only good Indian is a dead Indian." Reporters heaped praise on the Indian policemen sent to arrest Sitting Bull. Their leader, Lieutenant Henry Bull Head (top right), a Sioux whose badge is shown here, fired one of the shots that killed the chief in the ensuing scuffle.

SITTING BULL IS DEAD.

The Old Chief and Seven of His Followers Killed in an Engagement with Police.

Sitting Bull was Preparing to Start for the Bad Lands and His Arrest was Ordered.

The Indian Police Start From Yates, Followed by Two Companies—Cavalry and Infantry.

When the Arrest was Made, Sitting Bull's Followers Attempted a Recapture.

In the Fight That Ensued, Sitting Bull, His Son and Six Indians Were Killed.

On the Other Side, Four of Police were Killed and Three Wounded.

The Cavalry Then Arrived on the Scene, and the Indians Fled Up Grand River.

A Lengthy Account of Major McLaughlin's Last Trip to Sitting Bull's Camp.

He's a Good Indian Now.

CHICAGO, Dec. 15.—At 9 o'clock to-night, Assistant Adjutant General Corbin of General Miles' staff received an official dispatch from St. Paul, saying Sitting Bull, five of Sitting Bull's men and seven of the Indian police have been killed. Thirteen casualties were the result of the attempt by the Indian police to arrest Sitting Bull.

HOW IT HAPPENED.

ST. PAUL, Dec. 15.—The report was received in this city this afternoon that Sitting Bull had been killed ... Indian po-

agent dispatched orders in writing to Lieutenant Henry Bull Head, who was the chief of his police force, instructing him to arrest Sitting Bull without delay, and concluding ominously, "You must not let him escape under any circumstances."

For Bull Head, the assignment was the culmination of an improbable career. A quarter-century earlier, as a young Hunkpapa warrior, he had fought with distinction alongside Sitting Bull against the bluecoats. Later, when the struggle was over and the Americans were in command, he had enlisted with them as a reservation policeman. It was a role with honorable precedent among the Lakotas. In the old days, each camp had been governed by *akicitas,* or soldiers, who enforced discipline and kept young hunter-warriors from acting selfishly or impulsively. Reservation policemen served their communities in similar fashion by prohibiting the sale of alcohol and restraining other disruptive activities. But under agents like McLaughlin they also became embroiled in feuds with

Indians who resented white authorities and the police who worked for them. By the time Bull Head received orders to arrest Sitting Bull, he had long been at odds with the chief and needed little prompting to go after him.

Before dawn on December 15 Bull Head led 42 agency policemen on horseback to Sitting Bull's village, where they dismounted and surrounded the chief's cabin. Bull Head and several other policemen entered in the dark and laid hands on the chief. His wife screamed in alarm, but Sitting Bull put up no resistance. He simply asked for a chance to get dressed before they took him away.

In the meantime, the commotion had awakened neighbors, and an angry crowd gathered outside the cabin to confront the policemen. Several of Sitting Bull's supporters brandished guns. Nervously, Bull Head grasped Sitting Bull with one hand and a revolver with the other and led the chief out the door toward the waiting horses, followed by a police sergeant, Red Tomahawk, who held a pistol at the chief's back. "You think you are going to take him," shouted Catch the Bear, one of Sitting Bull's armed followers. "You shall not!" Among those who were looking on in dismay was Sitting Bull's son Crow Foot, who had surrendered his father's rifle to the white soldiers nine years before at Fort Buford. "You always called yourself a brave chief," the 14-year-old cried to his father. "Now you are allowing yourself to be taken."

Stung by the youngster's words, Sitting Bull pulled up. After a pause he said vehemently, "I shall not go." When the police tried to prod him forward, Catch the Bear raised his rifle and shot Bull Head in the side. Before collapsing, Bull Head shot Sitting Bull in the chest, and Red Tomahawk fired point-blank into the back of the chief's head.

In the chaotic fighting that followed, a number of Sitting Bull's supporters and several policemen perished. Some of the surviving policemen took refuge in Sitting Bull's cabin, dragging Bull Head with them. Inside, they found Crow Foot hiding under a bed and pulled him out. "My Uncles," he pleaded, using the traditional Lakota term of respect, "do not kill me." But the mortally wounded Bull Head blamed the youngster for the debacle and refused to spare him. One policeman clubbed the boy with his rifle, and others poured bullets into him. Crow Foot was one of 13 people to die in the clash along with Sitting Bull.

Far from resolving the crisis, McLaughlin's attempt to arrest Sitting Bull increased tensions and contributed to an even greater tragedy two weeks later. When ghost dancers at the Cheyenne River Agency learned of Sitting Bull's death, they feared that they would also be punished and fled to join the other believers in the Badlands. Troops of Custer's old regiment, the 7th Cavalry, went after them and surrounded their camp at Wounded Knee Creek. There, on December 29, a move to strip the Lakotas of their weapons provoked resistance. In response the bluecoats turned Gatling guns on the crowd and took the lives of more than 200 men, women, and children, many of whom died while trying to escape.

Sitting Bull's death and the ensuing carnage at Wounded Knee seemed to leave Lakotas with no hope of redemption, in this world or the next. The ghost shirts had failed to protect believers from the soldiers' bullets, and the fervor of the surviving ghost dancers soon withered.

Despite the devastation that had been inflicted on the Lakotas, future generations managed to restore their sense of nationhood. They did so in part by honoring the memory of chiefs like Sitting Bull who suffered terrible setbacks yet preserved their faith and their fighting spirit. Lakotas and other Indians would celebrate Sitting Bull not just as the visionary who inspired the triumph at the Little Bighorn but as the chief who urged his people in defeat to resist the white man's way and hold to their own true path. "The life my people want is a life of freedom," he once said. "I have seen nothing that a white man has, houses or railways or clothing or food, that is as good as the right to move in the open country, and live in our own fashion." ◆

VICTORY AT GREASY GRASS CREEK

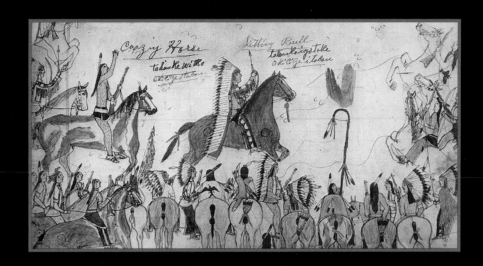

"The greatest leader of all was the chief of the Hunkpapa—Sitting Bull. As long as we were all camped together, we looked on him as head chief. We all rallied around him because he stood for our old way of life and the freedom we had always known. We were not there to make war, but, if need be, we were ready to fight for our sacred rights."

DEWEY BEARD (WASA MASA), PARTICIPANT IN THE BATTLE OF THE LITTLE BIGHORN

Seven thousand Lakota Sioux and Cheyenne Indians made camp on the banks of a Montana stream they called Greasy Grass Creek in late June 1876. Led by Sitting Bull and Crazy Horse, both pictured in the drawing above, it was the largest congregation of Plains Indians—men, women, and children—in history. Their village stretched for four miles along the Greasy Grass, called the Little Bighorn River by whites.

The two tribes had come together in order to put up a common defense against the U.S. Army troops that had been sent into southeastern Montana to round up or kill any hostiles refusing to settle on the reservations. The bluecoat strategy was to advance on the Indians in three widely separated columns that would then close in on them and attack simultaneously.

But one of the columns, the fast-moving 7th U.S. Cavalry Regiment under Lieutenant Colonel George Armstrong Custer, got ahead of the others. Early on June 25 his regiment spotted an Indian encampment in the distance. Fearing that the Indians might scatter at his approach, Custer decided to attack without determining the strength of the opposition. This rash decision set the stage for what would prove to be the greatest Indian triumph in their long struggle against whites on the western plains.

Some of the warriors present that day were interviewed by white reporters and historians in later years. Their recollections are included here and on the following pages, along with battle scenes by Indian artists. Two of the artists whose work is shown, Red Horse and Kicking Bear, took part in the battle, whereas Amos Bad Heart Buffalo was only seven years old in 1876 and based his work on stories his uncles told him. These words and images vividly portray the Indian perspective of the Battle of Greasy Grass Creek.

Kicking Bear *(far left)* and another Indian fire on the cavalrymen commanded by Major Marcus Reno as they charge toward the village. Unaware of how badly his 600-man cavalry was out-numbered, Custer had divided his force and ordered Reno to lead the first assault. The Sioux inscription on Amos Bad Heart Buffalo's drawing summarizes the battle's opening episode.

> *"Along this stream is the head of the Greasy Grass. They came in this fashion, all abreast. This is they who started shooting first and surprised the Indian tribes. All those who pretended to be men got their horses and got ready and met them with a shout and charged."*

AMOS BAD HEART BUFFALO, FROM THE INSCRIPTION ON THE MAP BELOW

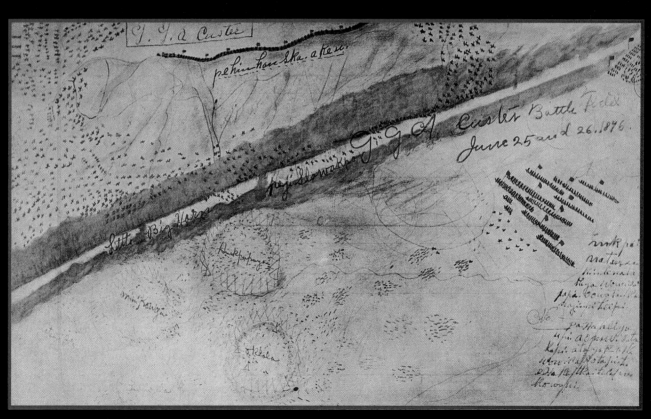

Amos Bad Heart Buffalo's map of the battlefield shows Reno's cavalrymen riding abreast of one another in orderly ranks with flags flying at right center. The Indian camp can be seen as a series of tepees arranged in circles at left center, just below the river. The battalion under Custer's personal command is ranged along the top of the ridge on the opposite side of the Greasy Grass *(top center)*

Forced back by the Indians, many of Reno's troops were unhorsed when they tried to ford the steep-banked, swiftly flowing Greasy Grass Creek. Warrior Henry Oscar One Bull described the rout of the cavalrymen: "We rode right into them, chasing them into the river. We killed many on the river bank and in the water."

Reno's retreating force rides back over its own tracks in Red Horse's pictograph. Chief Runs the Enemy admired Reno's courage and observed that he "only had a few soldiers and our camp was a great camp, and he came rushing into the camp with his few soldiers. In all the history of my great-grandfather I have never known of such an attack in daylight."

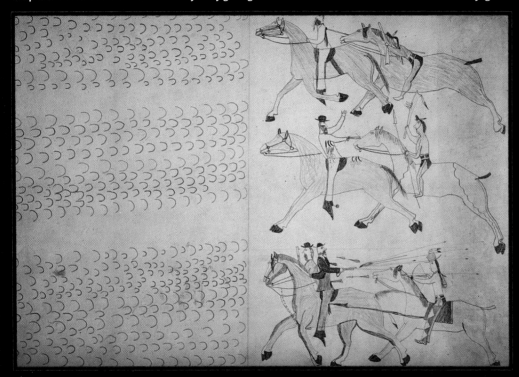

"Indians covered the flat. They began to drive the soldiers all mixed up—Sioux, then soldiers, then more Sioux, and all shooting. The air was full of smoke and dust. I saw the soldiers fall back and drop into the river-bed like buffalo fleeing." CHIEF TWO MOONS

After driving Reno back, warriors rushed to the other end of the village to meet Custer's battalion. Red Horse, who drew this pictograph of the ensuing fight, recalled that the Indians drove the cavalry "in confusion; these soldiers became foolish, many throwing away their guns and raising their hands, saying, 'Sioux, pity us; take us prisoners.'"

*"This new battle was a turmoil of dust and warriors and soldiers, with
bullets whining and arrows hissing all around. Sometimes a bugle would sound
and the shouting would get louder. Some of the soldiers were firing
pistols at close range. Our knives and war clubs flashed in the sun. I could hear
bullets whiz past my ears. But I kept going and shouting, 'It's a good
day to die!' so that everyone who heard would know I was not
afraid of being killed in battle."* DEWEY BEARD

Three Indians close in on cavalrymen moving forward to attack, as indicated by the hoofprints' direction in Red Horse's drawing. At the onset of the clash Sitting Bull stiffened the warriors' resolve by urging them to act like a bird that "spreads its wing to cover the nest and eggs and protect them. We are here to protect our wives and children, and we must not let the soldiers get them."

His body painted with marks representing hail to protect him in battle, Chief Crazy Horse leads his warriors against Custer's troops on the ridge overlooking Greasy Grass Creek in this drawing by Red Horse. Indians who participated in the action reported that Crazy Horse gave the battle cry "Ho-ka hey! It is a good day to fight! It is a good day to die! Strong hearts, brave hearts, to the front! Weak hearts and cowards to the rear!" Said White Bull, the soldiers ran "like scared rabbits."

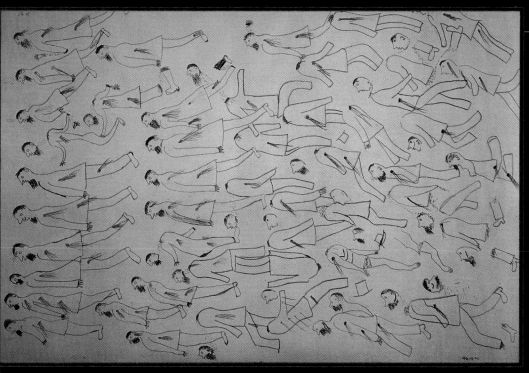

Red Horse depicted the bleeding and beheaded bodies of soldiers on the battlefield after Crazy Horse's charge.

Cavalry horses, identifiable by their free-flowing tails, surround a fallen flag. Indians tied up their mounts' tails for battle.

"Smoke rolled up like a mountain above our heads. The soldiers were piled one on top of another, dead, with here and there an Indian among the soldiers. Horses lay on top of men and men on top of horses."

CHIEF RUNS THE ENEMY

"After we had killed Custer and all his men I did not think very much about it. The soldiers fired first and we returned the fire. Sitting Bull had talked to us and all the tribes to make a brave fight and we made it. When we had killed all the soldiers we felt that we had done our duty, and felt that it was a great battle and not a massacre." **CHIEF RUNS THE ENEMY**

Although this drawing shows Custer impaled on a warrior's lance, he was actually killed by bullet wounds to the chest and head. Another inaccuracy is Custer's streaming hair, which he had cut short before the campaign began. None of the Indians recognized him in the thick of battle.

In this watercolor painted by Kicking Bear in 1898, four victorious Sioux chiefs stand amid fallen cavalrymen and warriors—Sitting Bull *(left)*, Rain in the Face, Crazy Horse, and, at right, Kicking Bear himself holding the scalp of one of Custer's Indian scouts. Custer, who is clad in a buckskin suit and has his hat sitting on the ground near his head, lies to the left of the chiefs. The uncolored figures are spirits in the process of rising from the bodies of the dead.

CHAPTER 4

GERONIMO AND THE WHITE EYES

"I never do wrong without a cause."

GERONIMO, 1886

Pen in hand, a small, dapper man by the name of S. M. Barrett waited on a bitter, blustery day in January 1906 at his home in the town of Lawton, some 10 miles from the Fort Sill Indian agency in what was soon to become the state of Oklahoma. Barrett, the superintendent of schools in Lawton, had been working on a unique project for the past three months. With the help of an Indian interpreter, he was chronicling the life of the 19th-century Apache war chief and medicine man Geronimo, as told by the old warrior himself.

Just 20 years earlier Geronimo had been locked in a brutal contest with Americans in the desert Southwest. At the head of a small band of warriors, the Apache leader had carried out deadly raids on his white enemies that earned him the epithet the Apache Terror. Now he was an old man with a creased face and white hair, tilling the soil near Fort Sill, the agency for Quanah Parker's Comanches and their Kiowa allies. Geronimo and his small band had been sent here, far from their homeland, after spending years in exile in Florida and Alabama under military guard. Technically Geronimo was still a prisoner of war. In order to interview him, in fact, Barrett had been required to obtain permission from President Theodore Roosevelt.

As the north wind howled that January day and Barrett waited, a visitor knocked at the door. It was Asa Daklugie, the Apache interpreter and a relative of Geronimo's, come to inform Barrett that the chief was suffering from a severe cold and had been urged to remain at home. Daklugie was warming himself by the fire before riding home when he glanced out the window. Motioning to Barrett he pointed to a solitary figure, approaching on horseback at a gallop. Geronimo had promised to meet with Barrett that day, and true to his Apache heritage, he was keeping his word. When the chief arrived, Barrett gently suggested to him that he should be in bed recuperating and that the story could wait. Geronimo stood there silently for some time. Then, abruptly, he turned and left, enduring another long, cold ride back home with the satisfaction of having honored his commitment.

After his cold passed, Geronimo spent another six months relating the story of his life to Barrett. He spoke in Apache; Daklugie translated his words into English. Geronimo chose each day's topic and spoke about it in a clear, brief fashion. He refused to answer questions on a subject on the day he introduced it, but agreed to review what had been written later as Daklugie conveyed it to him, amending and adding material as necessary.

Grim-faced Chiricahua Apache Geronimo posed for the camera in 1884, during his residence at San Carlos Reservation. A fellow tribesman called Geronimo, who led the last Indian war against the U.S. government, "the embodiment of the Apache spirit, of the fighting Chiricahua."

The story that unfolded was one of great devotion and determination. Geronimo reckoned that he was born in 1829, though it may actually have been several years earlier. He belonged to the Bedonkohe band of Apaches, whose rugged homeland of forested peaks and winding river valleys straddled what is now the Arizona-New Mexico border, northeast of Tucson. "The scattered valleys contained our fields," he recalled, "the boundless prairies, stretching away on every side, were our pastures; the rocky caverns were our burying places." There as an infant he rolled about freely on the dirt floor of the family's lodge or lay bound in his cradle, swinging from the bough of a tree. As befitted his placid upbringing, his childhood name was Goyahkla, or One Who Yawns. From his mother he imbibed the legends of his people and learned about the supreme spirit Usen, who watched over

Apaches and heard their prayers. From his father, an accomplished warrior and hunter, he learned of "the brave deeds of our warriors, of the pleasures of the chase, and the glories of the warpath."

Geronimo began hunting when he was around nine years old. "To me this was never work," he observed. Gadding about on their ponies, he and his companions tracked small game, including wild turkeys. After driving the clumsy birds to the point of exhaustion, the boys would dash in and snare them "by swinging from the side of our horses." The fledgling hunters also pursued the deer, antelope, and elk that roamed the region. "It required more skill to hunt the deer than any other animal," he recalled. "Frequently we would spend hours in stealing upon grazing deer. If they were in the open, we would crawl long distances on the ground, keeping a weed or brush before us, so that our approach would not be noticed."

Such stealthy pursuits during his childhood taught Geronimo skills that would later serve him well as a warrior, and he honed those reflexes by playing at war with his companions. Yet his homeland was blessedly secure from enemies. He and his kin could gather nuts and berries in the forests and plant corn, melons, and pumpkins in the fields without any fear of being attacked. The region then was claimed by Mexico, but it was unorganized territory. Mexican priests and soldiers confined themselves to scattered outposts such as Tucson, and Anglo-Americans had not yet penetrated Apache country in significant numbers. "During my minority we had never seen a missionary or a priest," Geronimo told Barrett. "We had never seen a white man. Thus quietly lived the Bedonkohe Apaches."

The first indication of the sorrows that lay in store for Geronimo came when he was still just a small boy and illness claimed the life of his father. When Geronimo recalled the solemn Apache burial ritual in later years the detail remained vivid: "Carefully the watchers closed his eyes, then they arrayed him in his best clothes, painted his face afresh, wrapped a rich blanket around him, saddled his favorite horse, bore his arms in front of him, and led his horse behind, repeating in wailing tones his deeds of valor as they carried his body to a cave in the mountains." There he was laid to rest along with his weapons. The mourners sacrificed his horse, gave away his possessions, and sealed the opening of the cave with stones.

After his father's death, Geronimo assumed the responsibility for the care and support of his mother. The two of them went to live with relatives among the Nednhi Apaches to the south, and it was there that Geronimo was admitted to the council of warriors at the age of 17 or so. "Then I was very happy," he remembered. "When opportunity offered, after this, I could go on the warpath with

Mimicked by a diminutive but powerful clown, four Apache dancers wearing masks representing mountain spirits perform the mountain dance, an appeal for success in pursuits such as warfare, hunting, and healing *(opposite)*. The cross and the dark triangles on the wood-crowned buckskin mask below probably symbolize the four cardinal directions and mountains, whereas the jagged orange band represents lightning.

my tribe. This would be glorious. I hoped soon to serve my people in battle."

Admission to the council of warriors also meant the young man could marry. Geronimo met a slender, delicate Nednhi girl named Alope and secured her from her father with a gift of ponies. The couple soon had three little children to care for in their lodge. At night, the family slept under mountain lion pelts claimed by Geronimo.

Despite the peacefulness of Geronimo's youth, Apaches had been fighting the Spanish for centuries, and the conflict had continued without abating when Mexico achieved independence from Spain in 1821. In a ruthless campaign to end Apache raids on ranches and settlements in the northern Mexican states of Sonora and Chihuahua, officials there offered a substantial reward for the scalps of Apache warriors and a smaller bounty for those of Apache women and children. The grim work of the self-appointed scalp hunters was reinforced by Mexican troops, who hunted down Apache bands and attacked their camps.

One such incident would mark Geronimo for life. Amid the hostilities, he and his people continued to trade with Mexicans periodically, as Apaches had in the past. Sometime around 1850, lured by the prospect of trade, Geronimo and his family camped with other Apaches outside of the town of Janos in Chihuahua. Each day most of the men ventured into town to barter, while the women and children stayed behind, guarded by a few warriors. Late one afternoon, as the trading party was returning home, they were met by a frantic group who had just fled the camp. Mexican troops, the fugitives related, had surprised the guards and cut them down, and destroyed the supplies. Most of the women and children were either slaughtered or captured and sold as slaves.

Fearing discovery, the men waited until nighttime to steal back into camp. There among the dead, Geronimo found his mother, wife, and three small children. "I silently turned away and stood by the river," he recalled. "How long I stood there I do not know, but when I saw the warriors arranging for a council I took my place." The chief of the Chihenne band, a leader of great strength and resolve named Mangas Coloradas, counseled patience. He knew that his Apaches were surrounded by Mexicans and were too few in number to seek immediate revenge. The troops who overran their camp, they learned, had crossed over from the neighboring state of Sonora. The Apaches would need to gather supplies and reinforcements before pursuing and punishing them. As the band started for home, Geronimo remained behind for a while, paralyzed by grief. "I did not pray, nor did I resolve to do anything in particular, for I had no purpose

left," he recalled. In the days ahead, his anguish sharpened into keen hatred for Mexicans and a driving passion for revenge.

His people spent the months after the massacre at Janos preparing to strike back at the Mexicans. Sometime during this period Geronimo had a transforming experience. He was alone, reflecting on his loss, when a voice that seemed to come from another world assured him that no gun would ever claim his life. "I will take the bullets from the guns of the Mexicans, so they will have nothing but powder," the voice said. "And I will guide your arrows." Geronimo drew spirit power from this experience, and from then on he fought with an abandon that earned him the admiration of his followers.

He played a major role in organizing the retaliatory raid against the Sonorans, traveling among various Apache bands and soliciting their aid. "We are the same men as the Mexicans are," he assured them. "We can do to them what they have done to us." About 200 warriors answered the call and assembled for the expedition, with their faces painted for battle and buckskin headbands restraining their long, unbraided locks.

They had chosen as their target the town of Arizpe, where Sonoran troops were stationed. The warriors journeyed to their destination on foot, which allowed them to traverse terrain too barren or steep for horses and helped them elude detection. Each day they walked for 14 hours, covering as many as 45 miles. They were camped near Arizpe when they confronted a party of eight Mexicans who had come out to negotiate and killed and scalped them all. This was done "to draw the troops from the city," Geronimo explained, "and the next day they came." Among the approaching soldiers, he felt sure, were the men who had killed his family, and the elder war chiefs allowed him the honor of directing the battle.

At the time, Geronimo was a muscular young man in his twenties with a broad, square-jawed face. Like the other warriors, he fought bare chested. Arrayed in a crescent, the 200 Apaches faced a

The nomadic Apaches roamed southern Arizona and New Mexico and northern Mexico until the early 1870s, when the U.S. government created reservations in Arizona and New Mexico. By the end of the decade all the Apaches west of the Rio Grande were relegated to San Carlos, and the other reservations there were shut down.

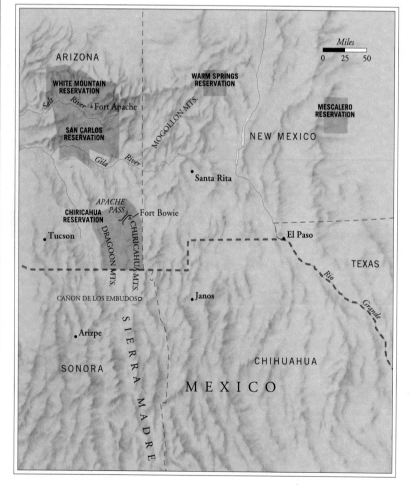

Mexican force about half that size, with the Sonoran infantry up front and the cavalry in reserve. After assigning a small group of warriors to harry the Mexican rear and divert the cavalrymen, Geronimo led a frontal assault—an unusual tactic for Apaches, who preferred to fire from behind cover and pick off a few enemies at a time. The warriors were armed mainly with bows and arrows, spears, and knives, but those weapons could still be devastatingly effective against troops wielding firearms that were often inaccurate and took time to reload.

Geronimo led repeated charges, first brandishing his spear, and after burying it in the body of a Mexican, attacking with his knife. "I fought with fury," he recalled. "In all the battle I thought of my murdered mother, wife, and babies . . . and my vow

against the tribe's enemies would expand to include the Americans who defeated Mexico in 1848 and claimed much of the Apache homeland as their own. He would strike fear into this new foe just as forcefully as with the Mexicans.

The Apaches who lived in Geronimo's day were among the most rugged and resilient of American Indians. A loosely knit group that numbered perhaps 6,000 to 8,000 at their peak, they were spread over vast portions of what is today northern Mexico and the American Southwest. Many of them had once occupied the plains but had since been driven to this mountainous terrain by the expansive Comanches. Through their ordeals, Apaches had acquired a toughness of body and

"My feelings toward the Mexicans did not change. I still hated them and longed for revenge. I never ceased to plan for their punishment."

GERONIMO, FOLLOWING THE ATTACK ON ARIZPE

of vengeance." By one account his terrified enemies cried for help to their patron saint, Jerome—or Geronimo, in Spanish—and thus endowed the young Apache war leader with his adult name.

In the end, the field was littered with dead Mexicans. Those who had not been felled had fled. At first Geronimo was overwhelmed with the "joy of battle, victory, and vengeance," as he put it. But soon his elation faded, and the longing for retribution returned. If the spirits had blessed him with special power in battle, they had also burdened him with a profound grievance that could not be soothed by a single triumph. Others in his band felt satisfied and returned to their peaceful pursuits, but Geronimo continued to seek redress in battle for an unassuageable loss. "My feelings toward the Mexicans did not change," he confided. "I still hated them and longed for revenge. I never ceased to plan for their punishment."

In years to come Apaches would have pressing need of war chiefs of great physical and spiritual fortitude like Geronimo. His relentless vendetta

mind essential to survival in an unforgiving land.

The basic unit of Apache society was a group consisting of several extended families who lived together in one encampment through the winter and ventured to various hunting and foraging spots in the warmer months. Each group was largely self-sufficient, but they sometimes joined with their neighbors in bands of 200 to 300 people to trade, hunt, or make war on common enemies. A tribe was made up of bands that regularly cooperated and intermarried with one another. The Bedonkohe and Nednhi bands, for example, were part of the Chiricahua tribe. Chiricahuas kept their distance from other Apache tribes such as the Mescaleros of southeastern New Mexico and the Western Apaches of central Arizona.

Each band had its own chief. Often, a man whose father had been a chief was selected to succeed to the chieftainship, but only after he had demonstrated his wisdom, bravery, generosity, and honesty. Apaches expected the chief—or *nantan*, meaning "he who talks or advises"—to speak frankly and forcefully at all times. Apache leaders believed in keeping their word, to each other and to outsiders who made deals with them, and few things angered them more than being lied to.

The chief's overriding responsibility was to protect his people and avenge any losses that they suffered at the hands of enemies. Calls for vengeance arose frequently among Geronimo's people because raiding and its attendant risks were part of their livelihood. To be sure, they gleaned all that they could in peaceful fashion from their rugged homeland, which was creased with steep ridges and deep canyons whose waters sometimes ran dry under the summer sun. They harvested nuts, berries, roots, and the flesh of the mescal cactus, which they could bake and dry for later consumption. In fertile spots, they cultivated small gardens, raising corn and other crops and brewing a mild corn beer known as tiswin that enlivened their rituals and festivities. And they hunted tirelessly, stalking mainly deer—their prime source of meat and hide. Tribes farther east, such as the Mescaleros, pursued buffalo, which roamed the sparse grasslands of the Southwest in small numbers.

For all their resourcefulness, Apaches inhabited a land in which bounty was limited and they were forced to endure seasons of want. Inevitably they cast hungry eyes on encroaching white settlers, with their sprawling herds of cattle and horses. Often Apache raiders contented themselves with seizing livestock; much of the catch was then slaughtered to feed the band, while the better horses were spared to serve as mounts. Other prizes coveted by raiders included weapons and European-style clothing, which many Apaches had adopted in whole or in part by the 19th century.

Not all raids were easy or bloodless. If ranchers resisted and claimed the lives of Apaches, chiefs were then morally obligated to avenge them. Until they did so, neither the spirits of the deceased nor the hearts of their grieving kin would rest easy. Apache women were as insistent on vengeance as the men. They raised their young boys to be tough

in battle by immersing them in icy streams, chided men who failed to retaliate promptly for losses to the enemy, and sometimes assuaged their grief over the death of a kinsman by joining in the execution of male captives who were brought back to the camp. In other cases they adopted youngsters seized from the enemy to replace their lost loved ones.

Raiding provided Apaches with more than subsistence or the solace of retribution. It was the established way for a man to attain honor and demonstrate his value to his people. Asa Daklugie, Geronimo's interpreter and the son of his brother-in-law Juh, a Nednhi chief, recalled one successful assault Juh carried out on a Mexican village to avenge a group of Apache women and children who had been out harvesting mescal when men from that village attacked them, killing some of the boys and enslaving the rest of the group.

Juh and his warriors slipped into the Mexican village on Sunday morning while most of the people were at worship and burned the church to the ground, with the occupants trapped inside. Then they freed the Apache captives and made off with booty, arriving home with mules laden with guns, knives, ammunition, blankets, saddles, clothing, and metal cooking utensils. Geronimo, as Juh's kinsman and ally, was present for the ceremony welcoming the warriors back to camp. He heaped praise on his brother-in-law and confederates. "They have avenged the deaths of their people," he said. "Much honor is due Juh."

No Apache tribe prosecuted its vendettas with Mexicans and Americans more vigorously than the Chiricahuas. Their mountainous homeland, extending south along the New Mexico-Arizona border into northern Chihuahua and Sonora, afforded them splendid refuge from pursuing troops. And they profited from the leadership of charismatic chiefs whose reputation and authority extended well beyond their own bands—including Mangas Coloradas of the Chihenne band, Cochise of the Chokonen band, and Geronimo himself, one of the last great Chiricahua resistance leaders.

For many years after defeating the Sonoran troops at Arizpe in the early 1850s, Geronimo remained preoccupied with the Mexicans and was little known to Americans. But through his dealings with Mangas and Cochise—older chiefs who were at the peak of their power in the early decades of American rule in the Southwest—Geronimo came to despise the White Eyes, as Apaches called the Americans. Among the lessons he learned from his elders was that the White Eyes seemed always to promise one thing and do another. Ultimately, in the early 1880s, Geronimo emerged as a merciless foe of the Americans and one of the most determined tribal opponents the U.S. Army ever faced. He took that uncompromising stance not simply because of challenges by Americans to his own authority and the welfare of his band but because of the indignities and betrayals suffered by other Chiricahua chiefs over more than a quarter of a century.

John Bartlett, one of the first American officials to enter Apache territory, received a visit from Mangas Coloradas in June 1851 at the camp Bartlett's party had set up at Santa Rita, an abandoned Mexican copper mining town in the southwestern corner of New Mexico Territory. Bartlett was there as head of a commission to chart a firm boundary between the United States and Mexico, as called for by the treaty that ended the war between the two nations and ceded this area to the Americans. Mangas was unaware of Bartlett's purpose, but as chief of the local Chihenne band, he kept a close and wary eye on intruders. His relations with the Mexicans had been poisonous, and he and his warriors had done much to reduce Santa Rita to a ghost town.

Bartlett could see at once that Mangas was a figure to be reckoned with. Now around 60 years of age, the chief stood more than six feet tall, with a full chest, broad shoulders, and thick, dark hair that reached nearly to his waist. Americans were often struck by the long, luxuriant hair that Apache men retained into old age. Apaches, for their part, were surprised by how much hair

Geronimo's headdress of buckskin, ribbons, and sacred feathers symbolized his role as a medicine man. "I don't know that [he] ever told his warriors that he had supernatural protection," said a nephew, "but they were with him in many dangerous times and saw his miraculous escapes, his cures for wounds, and the results of his medicine."

American men had on "their faces and bodies and how little of it they had on their heads," as Asa Daklugie put it. "People with all that hair where it didn't belong were repulsive to us," he added. "They looked too much like bears."

Mangas assured Bartlett through an interpreter that he was a friend of the Americans. During the recent war he had allowed American troops safe passage through his territory so that they could attack the Mexicans. But Mangas was perplexed and disappointed when Bartlett informed him that the United States was now bound by treaty to stop Apaches from crossing into Mexico for hostile purposes—and also was required to return any Mexicans whom the Apaches held captive. The chief promised to keep peace with the Americans, but he would not make any compromises when it came to his old enemies south of the border. As Bartlett noted after meeting with Mangas, "Why we should defend the Mexicans, after being at war with them, was to him incomprehensible."

The first test of the American treaty commitment came later in June when two young Mexican captives who had been adopted by the Chihennes ran away from the band and sought refuge with the Americans. Angry words were exchanged when Mangas and his followers learned that Bartlett meant to return the boys to their Mexican kin. Hoping to avert bloodshed, Bartlett offered $250 worth of goods to the warrior who had claimed the boys as his own to compensate and pacify him. Mangas endorsed the deal and preserved the peace, but he and Bartlett soon had a more serious problem to contend with. A Mexican worker employed by the Boundary Commission shot an Apache warrior, who subsequently died. Once again Bartlett defused the situation by offering compensation to the victim's kin and putting the accused in chains. But the Chihennes were losing patience. As the summer wore

Raiders drive a herd of stolen horses down a mountain trail in this painting based on an 1888 drawing by Frederic Remington. "Stealing horses was fun," one Apache recalled. "I was not quite old enough to get in on that, and how I envied those who were! It was usually the boys, too, who shot the fire-arrows to set houses ablaze."

on, some of them stole mules and horses belonging to Bartlett's party. Besieged by resentful Apaches, the commission left the area late in August.

More trouble for Mangas and his people arrived around this same time, however, in the form of American prospectors, who struck gold near Santa Rita at a place called Pinos Altos and overran the area. Some Apaches responded by attacking the miners or stealing their livestock, but Mangas still hoped to avoid an explosive feud with the oncoming Americans. In the fall of 1851 he rode into Pinos Altos with a few of his followers and offered to lead the prospectors to a richer gold field in Sonora if they would leave these moun-

tains to the Chihennes. In response the miners seized Mangas, tied him to a tree, and beat him mercilessly. Never before had anyone dared to strike the chief, observed one of his followers, and there was "no humiliation worse than that of a whip."

The results of the Americans' attempt to shame the Apache chief into submission were predictably disastrous. Once his wounds had healed, Mangas called upon Chihenne warriors and recruits from other Chiricahua bands and embarked on a rampage against the White Eyes that went on until the following summer. No mining camp or stagecoach was safe from their fury. Yet anger did not blind

Mangas to the fact that an endless war with the Americans would be calamitous for his small band. Once he had avenged the wrongs that had been done by the foolhardy prospectors to his satisfaction, he and other chiefs sat down with American officials and worked out an accord. As often happened during such negotiations, however, the chiefs either were misled about the terms of the treaty or simply misunderstood them. It was not until he put his mark on the document that Mangas was clearly told that by doing so he agreed to cease raiding into Mexico. "Are we to be victims of treachery and not be avenged?" he asked pointedly.

Aside from the thirst for vengeance, Apaches sorely needed the booty that came to them through raiding at a time when whites were infringing on their territory and reducing their hunting and foraging grounds. One American official tried to reinforce the treaty by promising Mangas and other chiefs regular supplies of food and livestock as long as they kept the peace. But Congress refused to allocate the necessary funds, and hungry Apaches were soon raiding ranches and settlements on both sides of the border. U.S. Army troops struck back at them by destroying their winter camps, exposing them to the twin privations of cold and starvation. To spare his band further hardship, Mangas agreed in 1855 to settle with them on a reservation along the Mimbres River in New Mexico in return for disbursements of food and supplies.

But the establishment of the reservation failed to bring peace. Mangas and his men continued to raid into Mexico, and American settlers and soldiers hostile to Apaches pressed in on the Chihennes. In 1862, Mangas, then about 70 years old, heeded the calls of angry young warriors and joined with the defiant Cochise in attacks on the bluecoats, whose forces were spread thin by the demands of the Civil War. Mangas fell wounded that summer dur-

Even after acquiring firearms, Apache warriors continued to carry sacred lances and rawhide shields like those shown here in the belief that the spirits would offer them physical protection. The shield displays a stylized thunderbird flying amid jagged bolts of lightning.

ing an attack on soldiers at Apache Pass, a strategic defile in the Chiricahua Mountains of southeastern Arizona that the army hoped to secure. Repulsed, Chihenne warriors retreated into Mexico with their wounded chief and forced a doctor there at gunpoint to treat Mangas.

Six months later, in 1863, Mangas was invited to peace talks with American officers and accepted, against the recommendations of many of his people. The White Eyes were not to be trusted, they warned him, but he longed for peace and thought the chance worth taking. When he arrived in Pinos Altos for the council, clad in blue overalls, a checkered shirt, and a sombrero, he was immediately seized by soldiers displaying a white flag of truce, taken to a nearby fort, and placed under guard. His jailers were told by their commander to treat Mangas as a murderer and to make sure that they kept a tight grip on him, "dead or alive." That night, they heated their bayonets and applied the blades to the chief's legs and feet. When Mangas could bear it no longer and tried to resist, the soldiers shot him point-blank, scalped him, and dumped his body into a shallow trench.

It was an act of treachery that Geronimo would never forget. He later called the murder of Mangas "perhaps the greatest wrong ever done" to his people.

In fact, the act was one in a long string of betrayals. The recent conflict between Apaches and bluecoats had been precipitated in part by the attempt of an American officer to deceive Cochise. In 1861, at the invitation of Lieutenant George Bascom, Cochise had agreed to meet for talks at Apache Pass. Seated in the lieutenant's tent for what he thought would be a friendly conversation, Cochise was sipping coffee when the lieutenant abruptly accused him of kidnapping the stepson of a white rancher. The chief denied responsibility, but Bascom ordered his soldiers to seize him with the intention of holding him as ransom for the boy. Cochise escaped, however, by slashing through the tent with a knife he had concealed in one of his moccasins and fleeing into the hills under fire in a getaway that became legendary among Apaches. Bascom's duplicity earned the Americans the enmity of another powerful Chiricahua chief and set the stage for bloody clashes with Cochise's forces.

Geronimo reportedly had joined with Cochise and Mangas in the fighting against American troops around Apache Pass in 1862, but he was still primarily concerned with his old foes in Mexico. He had taken two wives in recent years, only to lose one of them and another child to marauding Mexicans in a terrible repetition of the murder of his family at Janos. He redoubled his efforts against the people he blamed for his sorrows, using new tactics. Increasingly he and his raiders traveled on horseback, which broadened their range and made it easier for them to herd stolen cattle back to their camps. And they now fought with firearms, many of which they seized from Mexicans and then turned against them. The best guns for the purpose were those that could be wielded handily from horseback, such as the Colt .45 pistol that Geronimo carried.

Only gradually did it become clear to him that the White Eyes posed a greater threat to his people than the Mexicans. After the Civil War, American miners, settlers, and soldiers poured into the Southwest, and federal authorities stepped up their efforts to confine all the bands there to reservations. Some Apaches felt the need for a reservation as a refuge against hostile settlers, who tended to disregard what little law there was on the frontier when it came to dealing with Indians. White vigilantes out to avenge neighbors or family members killed by warriors sometimes targeted the first Indians they came upon without bothering to determine their guilt or innocence. A murderous incident of this kind occurred in 1871, with far-reaching implications for Apaches throughout the region.

A cavalry patrol departs from southeastern Arizona's Fort Bowie, which served as the army's headquarters in its campaign to defeat Indian leaders such as Cochise and Geronimo. Built in 1862, the fort was situated near the critical Apache Pass in the Chiricahua Mountains.

In March of that year a lieutenant named Royal Whitman had established an unofficial reservation near the army post of Camp Grant, about 60 miles north of Tucson. Some 500 Apaches, most of them members of the Aravaipa band led by a chief called Eskiminzin, were living peacefully at the site, where the proximity of troops presumably offered them some protection against vigilante action. But early on April 30, while many were still sleeping and a few Apaches stood guard, a mob of 150 men from Tucson attacked in retaliation against Apache raids. Many in the camp managed to escape, but more than 100 Apaches were caught in the rampage and killed. Some of the women who fell victim were first raped. Whitman was five miles away at Camp Grant, and by the time he learned of the attack, all he could do

praising the vigilantes for taking the law into their own hands. But officials in Washington feared that unchecked vigilanteism could lead to anarchy and set out to establish firm boundaries between whites and Apaches. Brigadier General Oliver Otis Howard, a devout Christian and humanitarian, was dispatched to the region to convince Apache leaders that it was in the best interests of their people to report to reservations and remain there.

Howard focused his attentions on Cochise, the most prominent Chiricahua chief and a staunch defender of the rights of his people. Now more than 60 years old and often in pain from a serious stomach ailment, he still exuded defiance. Mindful of the trick Lieutenant Bascom had played on him, he kept an armed guard around him at all times and

"I found that I should have but little use for wagon and medicine. Those who had been wounded in the first instance had their brains beaten out with stones....Nearly all of the dead were mutilated."

DR. CONANT B. BRIESLY AFTER THE CAMP GRANT MASSACRE, 1871

to help was dispatch the post surgeon. "I found that I should have but little use for wagon and medicine," the doctor reported. "Those who had been wounded in the first instance had their brains beaten out with stones. . . . Nearly all of the dead were mutilated."

Chief Eskiminzin escaped with a daughter, but his two wives and five other children were among the dead. A month later Eskiminzin visited at the home of a nearby rancher. After dining with his host—who had been his closest friend among the White Eyes—Eskiminzin picked up his gun, shot the man dead, and made his escape. The deed was uncharacteristic of Apaches, who prided themselves on loyalty to their friends. But as Eskiminzin explained, "I did it to teach my people that there must be no friendship between them and the white men."

The perpetrators of the Camp Grant massacre went unpunished. After deliberating for less than 20 minutes, the jury found them innocent. Arizona newspapers painted the incident in glowing terms,

refused to enter any building or military tent. He would meet with Americans only in the open, seated on a blanket.

For all his determination, Cochise understood that his people might not survive if he failed to reach some sort of accommodation with the populous and increasingly hostile Americans. In March 1872, before meeting with Howard, he noted sadly: "On me depends their future, whether they shall utterly vanish from the land or that a small remnant remain for a few years to see the sun rise over these mountains, their home."

General Howard was something of a curiosity to Cochise and his followers. He had lost an arm in the Civil War and was given to dropping down on one knee and praying at almost any time—a practice that caused Apaches to wonder if he was some kind of medicine man. He expected Apaches to trust him implicitly, despite all their recent troubles with the White Eyes. He asked one chief if he

THE BLUE-EYED APACHE

An army officer who accompanied General George Crook to Mexico in search of Geronimo in 1886 made an interesting discovery when he arrived at an Apache camp at Cañon de los Embudos. One of the boys at play caught Captain John Bourke's eye: "He was about ten years old, slim, straight, and sinewy, blue-gray eyes, badly freckled, light eyebrows and lashes, much tanned and blistered by the sun, and wore an old and once-white handkerchief on his head which covered it so tightly that the hair could not be seen."

Under Bourke's persistent questioning, the boy *(below, foreground)* reluctantly told his story. He was Santiago McKinn, the child of an Irish father and a Mexican mother. The previous September he and his brother had been herding cattle near their home in New Mexico when Geronimo's warriors had swooped down upon

them. They killed the brother and carried Santiago away with them. The boy had been adopted by the tribe and now considered himself a member, playing their games, speaking their language, and avoiding Americans whenever possible.

A few days later the Apaches surrendered to Crook, and Santiago and his adopted people left Los Embudos for Fort Bowie in Arizona. Once there, the boy learned that he was to be sent back to his parents in New Mexico. He burst into tears and proclaimed in Apache that he "wanted always to stay with the Indians." To journalist Charles Lummis, who watched the scene play out, Santiago "acted like a young wild animal in a trap," crying and struggling with the Americans. At length they hoisted him into a wagon and set out for the nearest train station.

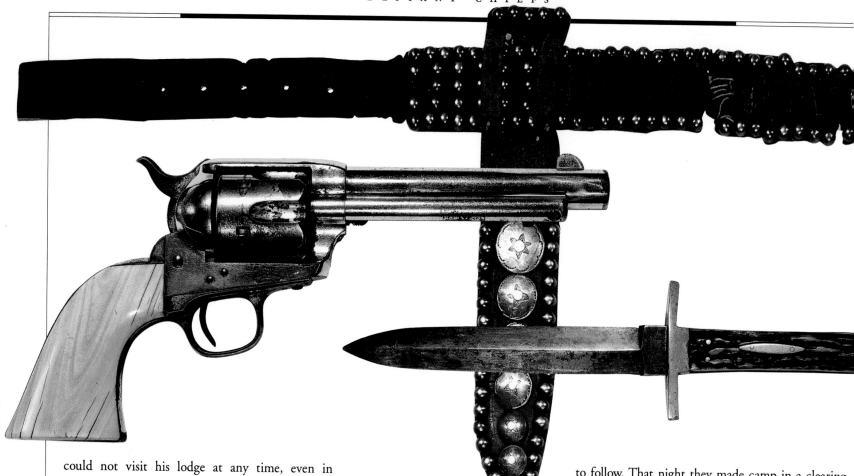

could not visit his lodge at any time, even in wartime. Not if Howard valued his life, the chief replied honestly.

Despite his peculiarities, Howard soon impressed the Apaches as a man of real courage and sincerity. He set out to find Cochise in the fall of 1872 with a small party that included his aide, two Apache scouts from bands that had already reported to reservations, and a former stagecoach driver named Thomas Jeffords, who had won the admiration and trust of Cochise by venturing alone and unarmed into his camp a few years earlier to talk peace. Howard's party rode more than 300 miles from New Mexico into the Dragoon Mountains of southeastern Arizona, where Cochise was believed to be camped. On the western slope of the range, one of the Apache scouts lighted five fires to signal that five riders had come seeking peace.

After a while, two young Apaches on horseback approached and signaled for Howard and the others

WEAPONS AT THE READY

Seen opposite holding a Springfield rifle, Geronimo carried his side arms—an ivory-handled Colt .45 Peacemaker and a factory-made knife for fighting in close quarters—in his glittering weapons belt *(above)*. All of its decorations, including the ringlets on the scabbard and the holster, are made of silver, some of it hammered from Mexican and American coins. Geronimo earned a reputation among Apaches and Americans alike for his superior marksmanship and was still a good shot in old age.

to follow. That night they made camp in a clearing surrounded by granite boulders, where they were met the next morning by Cochise, accompanied by his sister, his wife, and his youngest son, Naiche. In spite of age and illness, Howard noted, Cochise's thick, dark hair was threaded with only a few strands of silver.

The general explained that his government wanted to establish a reservation for the Chiricahuas. The area Howard had in mind was the eastern end of New Mexico's Mogollon Mountains—not a bad place, Cochise acknowledged, but not his people's home, either. The chief countered with a suggestion of his own: If Howard would allow his people to remain on familiar ground around Apache Pass, he would guarantee travelers and settlers in the area against attack. But the notion of living within boundaries was painful to Cochise, and he pleaded with the general: "Why shut me up on a reservation? We will make peace. We will keep it faithfully. But let us go around free as Americans do. Let us go wherever we please."

Howard rejected this plea for freedom, but he agreed to wait for a final answer until Cochise could summon all his subchiefs to make a decision about the proposed reservation, in keeping with the tribal tradition of rule by consensus. Geronimo also came to the parley, and he approved the agreement that Cochise concluded with Howard on behalf of the Chiricahuas after the meeting of the subchiefs. In a major concession, the general abandoned the Mogollon Mountains site in favor of a reservation that would include part of the tribe's homeland, as Cochise had proposed. In return, the chief promised to summon all of his people to take up residence there and to keep peace with the Americans.

Geronimo joined Cochise on the Chiricahua Reservation, along with nearly 1,000 other members of the tribe. Among the other chiefs to report there was Juh, leader of the Nednhi band. He and Geronimo had known each other since adolescence, and Juh's marriage to Geronimo's sister had helped cement their friendship. Over the years Geronimo had often taken refuge in his brother-in-law's mountain stronghold south of the border, and in the years to come the two men would often act in concert.

Geronimo was now in his forties, and bore a deep scar on his right cheek as an emblem of the battles that he had fought. Rather than feeling a defeat at the hands of the Americans, he praised the pact that established the refuge and remembered General Howard in later years with affection. "He always kept his word with us and treated us as brothers," he told Barrett, his chronicler. "We could have lived forever at peace with him."

Indeed, it seemed that Howard had accomplished his goal. Lured by the promise of plentiful rations and protection from lawless whites, more and more Apaches settled on various reservations in Arizona. Those who held out were subject to a merciless military campaign that spanned the winter of 1872 to 1873. So successful was the army in squeezing the holdouts that the following spring, as the army patrols headed back to their garrison, hundreds of Apaches slipped silently into their ranks, by twos and threes. More than 2,000 reported that spring.

True to his word, Cochise made sure that his warriors refrained from attacking travelers and settlers on the American side of the border. He was less successful at halting the Apache raids into Mexico. Fewer than half the Apaches on the Chiricahua Reservation were members of Cochise's band, and many of those who were not—including Geronimo and Juh—saw no reason to obey the chief of the Chokonens. Keeping the peace was supposedly part of the bargain with Howard, but in fact the unruly chiefs, war leaders, and warriors were not willing to surrender their right to raid Mexican villages.

Most Americans in the area wanted the Apaches confined to their reservations at all times and felt that the Chiricahuas in particular should be kept under stricter control. The governor of Arizona, who visited Cochise in 1873, expressed the anxiety of many settlers there: "My impression is that he desires peace, but he and his followers are wild men, and with the best of efforts on our part some real or imaginary cause may at any moment set them on the warpath."

Cochise died in 1874 of the stomach disease that had long plagued him, and within two years the government decided to abolish the Chiricahua Reservation. Henceforth, the tribe would have to reside with other Apaches at San Carlos, a dismal, highly regimented reservation that would prove to be a fine breeding ground for the last feverish outbreaks of Chiricahua resistance.

The heat was terrible," recalled Asa Daklugie of his early years at San Carlos. "The insects were terrible. The water was terrible." Situated in a desolate basin between the Gila and Salt Rivers some 80 miles east of present-day Phoenix, the San Carlos Agency presented a stark contrast to the mountain passes the Chiricahuas loved and longed for. The area was low, hot, and dry, watered only by a sluggish stream that was barely fit for human consumption but perfectly suited for mosquitoes, which bred in stagnant pools along the streambed and spread malaria. Many Apaches there came down with what they called the shaking sickness. Tribal medicine men administered herbs to sufferers to reduce their fever, Daklugie noted, but they could do nothing for the alternating chills that even in hot weather caused people "to shake uncontrollably while covered with blankets."

The government began moving Apaches to San Carlos early in 1875, and before the year was out more than 4,000 people of various tribes were living on the tract. The Chiricahuas were ordered to San Carlos in 1876.

Assigned to escort the tribe to the reservation was its agent, John Clum. An eager young disciplinarian, he had set rigid standards for neatness and cleanliness at San Carlos. He had also outlawed the brewing or drinking of tiswin, the traditional Apache beer, and put reservation dwellers to work building quarters for him and his assistant, an assignment they deeply resented. Among other indignities, they had to wear numbered metal tags around their necks.

In June 1876 Clum arrived at Fort Bowie, near Apache Pass, and called a meeting of the Chiricahua leaders, among them Geronimo and Juh. Geronimo did most of the talking; Juh stuttered badly and preferred being a listener during such discussions. Geronimo knew enough about San Carlos to spurn the place, but he pretended to go along with Clum's proposal. All he asked was permission to assemble his people, who were camped about 20 miles away. Clum gave his assent, and Geronimo and Juh rode off. Back in camp, they picked out their best horses and killed the rest, along with all of their dogs, so they could travel faster, then fled with their respective bands—perhaps 700 people in all.

Juh and his followers headed south to Mexico. Geronimo's band of 100 or so sought refuge with Chihennes living on the Warm Springs Reservation. Although Geronimo was generally a man of his word, he felt that he had every right to deceive Clum. "I do not think that I ever belonged to those soldiers at Apache Pass, or that I should have asked them where I might go," he said later. Clum, on the other hand, took Geronimo's flight as a personal insult and subsequently attributed to him many raids and depredations committed by other Apaches, thus saddling Geronimo prematurely with a reputation as a fierce foe of the Americans.

In fact, he did not yet consider himself at war with all White Eyes. But he did use the Warm Springs Reservation as a base from which to raid surrounding ranches for livestock. In spring 1877 Clum set out from San Carlos with a force of reservation police to arrest Geronimo and his confederates, not just for cattle rustling but on charges of murder as well. After riding for nearly 400 miles, Clum and his men reached Warm Springs on April 20 and sent a message to Geronimo and a few other targeted Apaches, requesting a conference.

The messengers appeared friendly to Geronimo, and he accompanied them to the agency headquarters expecting a parley. Instead, he found Clum and his Indian police ringing the parade grounds and poised to arrest him. Geronimo was tempted to

A DESOLATE COUNTRY

Dust storms choked the air. Insects abounded. Cacti dominated the desert landscape, where temperatures soared past 110 degrees. The San Carlos Reservation in southeastern Arizona "was the worst place in all the great territory stolen from the Apaches," according to one tribesman. But by the late 1870s all the Apaches west of the Rio Grande, numbering some 5,000, had been ordered to move there. It proved a devastating change for people who once roamed the cool meadows and forests of the mountains.

Officials were determined to assimilate the Apaches into the white man's world, with little regard for or understanding of Indian culture. Under army orders, Apache men began digging an irrigation ditch as part of a plan to turn the nomadic hunters into sedentary farmers. But hunting had been not only a traditional means of subsistence but also the basis for Apache social, economic, and military institutions. Although some Apaches had raised crops, the hunter-warriors disdained such work, believing that it would debase them. Not under-

standing the reason behind the men's reluctance, many observers condemned them as lazy. Yet when the army recruited scouts, these same men quickly enlisted for the dangerous job.

Forbidden to hunt and finding desert farming distasteful and difficult, the Apaches had to rely on the government for everything from food to clothing. Some of the agents were unscrupulous and cheated the people out of promised rations by selling them elsewhere for profit. The reservation land itself was being taken from the Indians piece by piece as white settlers, unchallenged by authorities, appropriated promising sections for mining and fields that the Indians had planted.

Though Apaches could earn some money for extra goods by gathering hay *(above)*, hunger was a constant ache. Frequent outbreaks of malaria, antagonism between rival bands, and a fear of soldiers also stirred feelings of despair and desperation. Apaches fled the reservation again and again, the army gave chase, and the spilling of blood that San Carlos was intended to end went on for years to come.

"*Take stones and ashes
and thorns, with some scorpions
and rattlesnakes thrown
in, dump the outfit on
stones, heat the stones red hot,
set the United States Army
after the Apaches, and
you have San Carlos.*"

NOVELIST OWEN WISTER,
VISITOR TO SAN CARLOS IN 1893

Families line up promptly to receive weekly rations, since failing to arrive on time meant no food. People like Jason Betzinez who lived across the river were forced to take extreme measures during high water. "Our method of crossing under such circumstances was to make cottonwood rafts and have swimmers pull these across by tow ropes clenched in their teeth."

Under military supervision, Apaches dig an irrigation ditch in a particularly desolate part of San Carlos. Of all the reservations to which Apaches had been assigned, San Carlos was the least suited to agriculture.

On ration day Apache women shoulder heavy bundles of cottonwood and mesquite to carry home for their fires. For a penny a pound the women would also gather hay for the cavalry's horses. The men at San Carlos did not have a parallel occupation, and though some became scouts, many others fell victim to boredom and hopelessness and drank and gambled to pass the time.

fight, but he saw that he was outnumbered and yielded. Clum himself took Geronimo's rifle and was rewarded with a look of cold hatred that he would never forget.

Geronimo and the others were marched to a blacksmith shop, where shackles were forged for their legs. Then they were penned up in the corral, where they slept on hay like cattle, chained to one another. For Geronimo as for other proud Apache chiefs, such humiliation helped raise the White Eyes to the stature of Mexicans as objects of wrath.

On May 1 the prisoners were transported to San Carlos. At the last moment Clum received orders to conduct everyone at Warm Springs to San Carlos as well. Jason Betzinez, a young cousin of Geronimo's, was among the Apaches forced to relocate. As he and his family traveled westward, they left behind the familiar pine trees and pastures of their homeland. "Our route now ran through arid valleys bordered by jagged, rocky peaks bare of vegetation," Betzinez recalled many years later. "We saw no horses, cattle, or sheep, for the land would scarcely support any living creature."

Geronimo was imprisoned in the guardhouse at San Carlos for two months and then released. Clum would later express regret that Geronimo had not been hanged, but the government never pressed charges against him. Having endured an experience that "might easily have been death for me," as he put it, he found that his influence among the Apaches had increased because he had stood up to Clum.

Geronimo hated life at San Carlos, however, and remained there for less than a year. One day in spring 1878, after drinking too much tiswin, he began scolding a nephew. The young man was so distraught that he committed suicide. Blaming himself, Geronimo fled the reservation and headed for Mexico. San Carlos proved to be no more secure than the reservations it replaced, and Geronimo had little difficulty evading either the reservation police or the federal troops who backed them up. Time and again in years to come, he would slip back to

General George Crook believed that it was his duty to acquaint himself with the culture of the Apaches, and he earned a reputation among them as a forthright, honest man. "Crook was our enemy, but though we hated him, we respected him," stated one Apache.

San Carlos to visit relatives and draw rations, then bolt for Mexico with confederates. For Geronimo, it was an old and familiar pattern. Apaches had never let boundaries stand in their way.

After fleeing the San Carlos Reservation in 1878, Geronimo found sanctuary in the mountain stronghold of his longtime ally Juh amid the peaks of the Sierra Madre in Sonora. The only route to the hideout was a narrow, twisting trail lined with boulders that the fugitives could send crashing down upon intruders. For the next 18 months, the two men were all but lost to history. They may have fought briefly alongside the celebrated Apache war chief Victorio of the Chihenne band, who had fled San Carlos in 1877 and embarked on a long campaign of resistance that ended with his death in battle against Mexican troops in 1880.

By then Geronimo and Juh had returned to San Carlos, where Apaches were thrilling to the words of a visionary Apache prophet named Nochedelklinne. This medicine man promised that one day soon the White Eyes would vanish and the great Apache chiefs who had died would return in triumph. Geronimo and Juh embraced Nochedelklinne's message of hope, and an elderly chief named Nana claimed to have seen the shadowy figures of Cochise, Mangas Coloradas, and Victorio rising in a mist from the earth.

Fearing an uprising on the reservation, officials did all they could to extinguish the fervor Nochedelklinne inspired. In the late summer of 1881, a detachment of more than 100 federal troops arrested the prophet while he was preaching and started on the trip back to agency headquarters with their prisoner. Twenty or so armed Apaches in-

"An Indian in his mode of warfare is more than the equal of the white man, and it would be practically impossible with white soldiers to subdue the Chiricahuas in their own haunts."

GENERAL GEORGE CROOK

censed by the affront to their medicine man stayed close behind them, and when the soldiers stopped to make camp for the night, they moved in closer. Someone fired a shot, and in the barrage of gunfire that followed two soldiers fell dead. At the order of the commanding officer, an American soldier then placed his rifle in the prophet's mouth and fired. A civilian guiding the troops finished the victim off with an ax blow to the forehead.

The execution of Nochedelklinne sparked fitful fighting between troops and angry Apaches, including Juh and Geronimo. In the aftermath, five Apache scouts who had been assigned to guide the troops during the incident were tried and convicted of switching their allegiance to their fellow Indians. Two were sent to Alcatraz; the other three were condemned to death.

Tensions remained at a fever pitch after the fighting ended. A month or so later, Geronimo, Juh, and Cochise's son Naiche fled the reservation in a fury along with 72 men, women, and children. The warriors now regarded every American as their enemy and killed all those they encountered on their way to Mexico.

Ensconced in Juh's stronghold in the Sierra Madre, the fugitive chiefs made an imposing triumvirate. James Kaywaykla, an Apache who fled with them, remembered Naiche as a tall, stately young man. Juh was also tall and of stocky build, whereas Geronimo was shorter, blocky, and muscular. Although Geronimo was not a chief by birth, he emerged as the group's leader. Juh's authority was undercut by his bad stutter, and Naiche, youthful and inexperienced, had only recently inherited leadership of his band when his older brother Taza, whom Cochise had raised to be chief, died. In the view of Jason Betzinez, who would later join the fugitives, Geronimo "seemed to be the most intelligent and resourceful as well as the most vigorous and farsighted. In times of danger he was the man to be relied on." Geronimo also had the advantage of his spirit power. As foretold in his vision many years earlier, he had survived enemy bullets—although more than a few had nicked him—and he had seemingly acquired other supernatural gifts over the years, including the gift of prophecy.

In their mountain haven, Geronimo and the others led a life reminiscent of former days. The warriors hunted and raided; the women dried beef, gathered wild plants, and stitched clothing. While in camp, Geronimo took charge of the training of young boys. He proved a hard taskmaster. In the winter, when ice coated the streams, he commanded the boys to build a fire, warm themselves by it for a few moments, then jump into the frigid water. As the youngsters repeated the ordeal over and over, Geronimo stood by with a switch in hand.

Although the holdouts were in a strong position, they were few in number. Geronimo wanted more warriors and hatched a bold plot to obtain them. Many Warm Springs Apaches still resided at San Carlos. Why should he not call on their services? On April 19, 1882, warriors led by Geronimo and Juh infiltrated the San Carlos Reservation and herded away the startled Warm Springs band before American authorities realized what was happening. One of the Apaches scooped up in the raid, Jason Betzinez, recalled that the audacious strike "threw us all into a tremendous flurry of excitement and fear. We did everything they told us to do. We were given no time to look for our horses and round them up but were driven from our village on foot."

For Apaches who so prized their own freedom and respected that of allied bands, such coercion was extraordinary. Yet Geronimo believed that the White Eyes had already robbed the reservation dwellers of their liberty, and he would stop at nothing to break the stranglehold of his enemies. As his Apaches headed south toward the border, they carried out merciless attacks. At one ranch on the American side, Geronimo seized more than a dozen Mexicans working there and ordered them shot and stabbed, one by one. Later, near the border, he and his warriors attacked another ranch, where

George Crook hired these White Mountain Apache scouts to track Apaches from rival bands. Unlike his colleagues who distrusted Indian scouts, he recognized that their superior tracking skills were essential in hunting holdout like Geronimo. Chief Alchise *(center row, seated at left)* received the Congressional Medal of Honor for valor in Crook's service.

they killed three adults and bashed a child to death.

The Apaches suffered cruel losses of their own. American troops pursuing the runaways killed 17 of them, mainly women and children. And Mexican soldiers pounced on the Apaches south of Janos, where Geronimo's family had been slaughtered many years before, and claimed as many as 75 lives. "It was a dreadful, pitiful sight," Betzinez remembered. "People

were falling and bleeding, and dying on all sides of us."

Despite such losses, when all the Chiricahuas reassembled in Juh's stronghold, they numbered more than 600, the greatest independent Apache force in a decade. Encouraged by their newfound strength, warriors ventured out into the surrounding countryside and sought revenge against the Mexicans, looting and killing at will. These depredations, coupled with the earlier assaults north of the border, led to anxious consultations between Mexican and American authorities, culminating in an extraordinary agreement. With Mexican consent, American forces would probe deep into Mexico to rid that country of Apache renegades.

On May 1, 1883, General George Crook crossed the border with 235 soldiers and scouts in search of Geronimo. A tall man with bushy sideburns and a stern expression, Crook expressed his characteristic disdain for pomp and protocol by wearing a rumpled khaki suit and riding a mule, an animal

Along with their European-style calico skirts and white cotton shirts, members of Geronimo's band wear traditional Apache boots like the pair at right, which one of his relatives made for her toddler daughter. The soft soles allowed warriors to walk with hardly any sound and made tracking the wearer more difficult because they left a faint imprint, or none at all.

that he thought better suited than a horse to the region's rough terrain.

The army could not have found a better candidate to conduct this irregular campaign against Geronimo and his confederates. Possessed of an unusual appreciation of the fighting skills of Indians and of the grievances that fueled their acts of defiance, Crook never took his tribal opponents for granted. Before joining in the campaign against the forces of Sitting Bull and Crazy Horse on the northern plains in 1876, he had served for four years in the Southwest and had made a careful study of the Apaches and their tactics. He admired them for their ability to survive in a harsh land, for their skill at hunting—Crook's greatest passion—and for their elusiveness. He knew what it was like to search tirelessly for holdouts, only to have Apaches introduce themselves to his troops with a hail of arrows.

In this campaign as in his earlier ones, Crook made liberal use of Indian recruits. The only way the army could succeed against the Apaches, he declared, was to use "their own methods, and their own people." Accordingly, the force he brought with him to Mexico included 193 Apache scouts and only 42 soldiers. Most of the scouts belonged to tribes that felt no particular obligation to Geronimo's Chiricahuas. One of the scouts, a White Mountain Apache named Tzoe, was linked to the Chiricahuas by marriage and had visited their hideouts. His guidance proved to be invaluable to Crook.

Dressed in calico shirts and loose trousers, the Apache scouts wore conspicuous red headbands to distinguish them from the enemy. At their waist many of them carried buckskin bags of sacred meal, which they offered to the spirits at dawn and twilight. Unlike the soldiers in their orderly columns, the Apaches marched in little clusters of two or three men. They greatly impressed Crook's aide, John Bourke, who noted that they possessed "vision as keen as a hawk's, tread as untiring and as stealthy as the panther's, and ears so sensitive that nothing escapes them."

In Mexico, Crook and his men saw ample evidence of Apache depredations. "The whole country was a desert," Bourke observed. "On each hand were the ruins of depopulated and abandoned hamlets, destroyed by the Apaches." The men traveled for three days without encountering a single Mexican. In the Sonoran town of Bavispe, which they reached on May 5, a ragged group of townspeople welcomed them with great relief. The villagers had repulsed a recent Chiricahua raid but had been too frightened afterward to venture into their fields.

As Crook's party approached the Sierra Madre, the terrain grew rougher. They would climb one ridge, only to be confronted by another, looming on the far side of a deep canyon. "To look upon the country was a grand sensation," wrote Bourke, "to travel in it, infernal." The men struggled to keep their footing on loose stones and gravel. Sharp rocks pierced their boots, and the rough vegetation tore their clothing. Even some of the surefooted pack mules stumbled on the steep, narrow trails and fell to their death, reminding Crook that the animals were not necessarily infallible as mounts.

Everywhere there were signs of the Chiricahuas, including droppings from the ponies and cattle they had seized on their raids. Before long, Crook's men encountered butchered carcasses and stray animals. To lighten their load the raiders had discarded some of their booty along the trail—clothing, saddles, food, even letters. The scouts boasted that they would kill Geronimo, Juh, and the other troublemakers, but those in the vanguard jostled with one another to avoid being the first to encounter an enemy warrior.

On May 12, guided by Tzoe, the scouts came to a clearing traversed by a stream. There the Chiricahuas had recently camped in large numbers and departed in haste, leaving behind scores of lodges along with animal hides, dried meat, bolts of cotton, and two children's dolls. Over the next few days Crook and his troops passed several more deserted

Apache camps. Then, on May 15, an advance party spotted a small group of Chiricahuas and attacked, killing nine people, mostly old men and women, and capturing five children. Speaking with a captured girl through an interpreter, Crook learned that the Chiricahuas were astonished that the Americans had succeeded in tracking them down, and that many were tired of life on the run. He then released the girl with two companions and told them to assure their people that the Tan Wolf, as they called Crook, had come to lead the fugitives back to San Carlos, not to make war on them.

Crook had little choice but to wait for the Apaches to come to him. As it turned out, most of the Chiricahuas were off raiding in small parties. Geronimo and a few dozen warriors were camped far to the east, in Chihuahua, seeking captives to

trade for Apaches recently taken prisoner by the Mexicans. According to Jason Betzinez, who was with Geronimo at the time, the chief was seated at the campfire with his men feasting on some beef when he had a vision of the children and old people they had left behind in the mountains in the hands of American soldiers. "I cannot explain it to this day," Betzinez remarked years later of Geronimo's insight. "But I was there and saw it."

Geronimo and his warriors hurried back to their kin in the mountains. But the journey took days, and in the meantime Crook obtained the surrender of scores of weary Chiricahuas. Not long after he sent the captured girl off bearing his message, eight Apache women approached him waving white rags. One of them announced that her brother, a chief named Chihuahua, would soon be arriving with his

warriors to make peace. The next morning, Chihuahua appeared as promised, riding his horse straight up to Crook's tent. At first the chief blamed Crook bitterly for the death of his aunt, one of the nine people who had been killed in the recent attack. Then, abruptly, Chihuahua's tone altered. He was tired of fighting, he admitted, and would surrender as soon as he could assemble his followers. Over the next several days some 100 Chiricahuas left their hiding places and gave themselves up to Crook. Geronimo would not be pleased, some among them warned, when he found them in the company of the Americans.

Accounts differ as to how Geronimo and Crook at last came face to face. Crook's aide Bourke reported that Geronimo and his warriors entered the camp peacefully on May 20 to talk. One of Crook's

scouts later insisted that the general was out hunting alone for birds when Geronimo and company surrounded him. In either case, neither the chief nor the general could be certain of prevailing in battle, and the two men began to parley. Crook bargained shrewdly with Geronimo, insisting that he did not really care whether the chief and his warriors surrendered or not: They had plundered and killed so often that he would really prefer to fight it out with them. Mexican troops were moving in on the stronghold, he said, and in a few days the Chiricahuas would be surrounded.

In other circumstances, Geronimo might have put Crook to the test and waged war. But aside from his concern for the Chiricahuas who were already in Crook's hands, he knew that some of his own warriors were tired and demoralized. They had been sur-

A formidable group of Chiricahua Apache warriors, armed with Winchester and Springfield rifles, flank Chief Naiche *(on horseback)* and Geronimo *(in front of Naiche)* in this March 1886 photograph. An admiring army officer observed, "If our little army of 25,000 were composed of such men . . . it would be unconquerable by the best army now existing in Europe."

Geronimo sits opposite General George Crook *(second from right)* at Cañon de los Embudos during surrender negotiations. Captain John Bourke *(third from right)* later wrote that the photographer, C. S. Fly, "coolly asked 'Geronimo' and the warriors . . . to change positions, and turn their heads or faces, to improve the negative."

prised in their hideaway, which they had considered impenetrable, and their supplies were low. As Jason Betzinez recalled, "It was a great relief to give up to superior authority, to have someone take charge. No more worries, no more sleepless nights, fearing attacks by an enemy."

Before giving up the fight, however, Geronimo extracted a significant concession from Crook. The general could lead other Chiricahuas back to San Carlos uncontested, but Geronimo would not accompany them. Instead he would gather up the rest of his band, including women and children who were still in hiding, and proceed with them to San Carlos at his own pace. For Crook the deal was a calculated gamble, but it was one that was worth

taking. Herding the elusive Geronimo and his men back to the reservation would be difficult and might prove disastrous if the chief escaped and decided to avenge the indignity Crook subjected him to. Furthermore, if Geronimo reneged on the deal and shunned the reservation, he would lose influence with other Chiricahuas there who looked to him as a leader.

On May 30 Crook and his men departed, taking with them 384 Chiricahua men, women, and children. Geronimo kept the general waiting at San Carlos for many months. Finally, in February 1884, Lieutenant Britton Davis, whom Crook had sent down to the border to look for Geronimo, spotted the chief and his band of 90 or so followers, bound for the reservation as promised. Geronimo rode a white pony. A huge plume of dust trailed behind the group, stirred up by 350 head of cattle that the resourceful chief and his few warriors had rustled from Mexican ranchers and were bringing north to share with the people on the reservation. This rich haul, reminiscent of Apache raids of old, would have been welcome indeed at San Carlos. But when Geronimo arrived with his booty, Crook, who now had charge of the reservation, felt obliged to confiscate the herd and sell the beef to compensate the Mexican ranchers.

Back on the reservation Geronimo seemed to make an honest effort to settle down and play by the rules. He preferred, he told Crook, to blot out the past and start anew. His old confederate Juh had died the year before, and Geronimo's responsibilities as a leader had increased as a result. His main concern was obtaining a suitable home for his people on the reservation, preferably on high ground with fresh water and an abundance of game. There, he hoped, all the Chiricahuas, including Naiche and his band of Chokonens, could settle together, away from the other Apaches he regarded as strangers, if not enemies.

By May a suitable spot known as Turkey Creek had been found on the White Mountain Reservation, northeast of San Carlos. In late May some 500 Chiricahuas set off for their promising new home at Turkey Creek, where clear waters flowed down from the heights and deer browsed amid the pine trees. That summer they ventured up into the hills to farm and hunt for venison and deer hides. Then, as autumn approached, they departed for lower ground to camp where the winter weather would be milder.

Ensconced in their winter camp they were joined by five Chiricahua women who had been captured by Mexicans several years earlier. The women had slipped away from their masters and traveled hundreds of miles to the border, where army patrols encountered them and took them to the reservation. It seemed that after many years of misfortune, the Chiricahuas at last had reasons to celebrate. Yet even

their festivities were shadowed by government edicts, including the rule against brewing or drinking tiswin that Apaches flouted at the risk of punishment. Moreover, their winter camp was located near Fort Apache, where American troops were garrisoned, and some of the soldiers took callous pleasure in taunting Geronimo and his people. More than once a soldier pretended not to recognize the chief, then turning to a friend, drew a finger across his throat and whispered loudly that Geronimo was slated to be killed.

Geronimo and his followers had good reason to fear condemnation. The previous fall one of their group had been arrested and convicted on charges of planning an insurrection. The man had been sentenced to three years on Alcatraz. Rumors spread through camp that he was chained to a rock "so far from land that no man can swim across that water." He would soon be put to death, people said, and Geronimo and the other chiefs would be next.

When spring came in 1885, the Chiricahuas returned to their summer camp, having kept their agreement with Crook for more than a year. Indeed, since Geronimo came to terms with the general in 1883, not one Apache depredation had been reported in the area. Yet fear and resentment still smoldered, and a seemingly minor incident soon reignited hostilities.

Just before dawn on May 15, 1885, Geronimo, Chihuahua, Nana, and several other Chiricahuas gathered in an angry mood outside the tent of Lieutenant Davis, the officer in charge at Turkey Creek. Many of the men were armed, and they had all drunk tiswin to the point of intoxication. Chihuahua began to berate Davis. The Apaches had agreed to peace, he said, not to being treated like little children who must be told how to act. They had all been drinking tiswin, Chihuahua declared. What was Davis going to do about it?

Davis deferred a decision until he could get a telegram through to Crook and solicit the general's opinion. But through a series of official blunders the lieutenant's plea for help never reached Crook.

Lieutenant Charles Gatewood's distinctive nose earned him the name Chief Long Nose from Geronimo, who had met Gatewood several times before being tracked down by him in August 1886. Gatewood, perhaps the only officer to learn some of their language, won the respect of the Apaches for his courage.

While Davis waited patiently for word to arrive from his superior officer, Geronimo grew increasingly anxious. He feared that the tiswin-fueled protest would be all the excuse that the Americans needed to arrest and execute him, as rumors said they would. Two days after the incident took place he enlisted the support of a few other chiefs, including Chihuahua and Naiche. Together they assembled about 40 men and 100 women and children and broke out of Turkey Creek after first cutting the telegraph wire to prevent Davis from alerting his superiors.

The events that followed were hauntingly familiar to the exasperated Crook. Once more Geronimo and his fellow fugitives crossed into Mexico, pursued closely by American troops who failed to snare the Apaches. Once more Geronimo returned furtively to Arizona. Some of his people, including one of his wives and a daughter, had stayed behind in May. Somehow discovering that they had been moved after the breakout from Turkey Creek to Fort Apache, he boldly scooped them up and doubled back to Mexico, plundering horses and cattle along the way. Once more it fell to the general and his scouts to bring the Apache renegades to bay.

About 20 miles south of the border, in a cottonwood grove in Cañon de los Embudos, Geronimo and Crook met in council for the last time in March 1886. The Apache chief wore a handkerchief around his forehead; the general sported a pith helmet. Both men sat on the ground with a few of their trusted allies. Technically Geronimo was still a free man, but he and his confederates were at the end of their tether. In January forces dispatched by Crook had overrun their encampment in the Sierra Madre, seizing their horses and supplies. Afterward the desperate Apaches had agreed to follow the Amer-

"There were officers who were both honest and truthful, like Crook. . . . And there was Gatewood who was one of the bravest and most modest of men."

Asa Daklugie

icans back to this campground near the border and negotiate the terms of their surrender with Crook.

Geronimo began by reciting his grievances against the army. He had only wanted peace on the reservation, he told Crook, but officials there had plotted against him. Fearing arrest and death, he had slipped away. Now he was prepared to lay down his weapons for good. "There are very few of my men left now," he said sorrowfully. He and his warriors had done some bad things, he conceded, but he was not a bad man. "I never do wrong without a cause," he told Crook. Geronimo deeply resented being branded an outlaw by the Americans, since it was they who had invited conflict by invading his homeland. Nevertheless, if the White Eyes would accord him the respect that was due an old warrior, he would surrender and live out his days in peace.

Crook understood Geronimo's position but feared a repetition of the recent hostilities if the chief was allowed to set the terms of his surrender. "You promised me in the Sierra Madre that *that* peace would last," he said. "When a man has lied to me once, I want some better proof than his own word before I can believe him again." Crook declared that Geronimo and his confederates would have to surrender unconditionally. If they resisted, Crook's troops would fight them to the death. Geronimo sensed that Crook was in earnest. Perspiring profusely, the chief fiddled anxiously with a leather thong he held tightly in one hand.

No one man among the Apaches had the authority to commit the entire group to surrender. But on March 27 first Chihuahua and then Naiche and Geronimo brought their bands to Crook's camp. They learned for the first time the high price of surrender—imprisonment in the East, far from home. Crook softened this great blow somewhat by assuring the Apaches that they would not be imprisoned for more than two years and would be allowed to return home after their release.

But Naiche and Geronimo didn't trust the American's assurance and had scarcely surrendered when they did an about-face. The next evening they went on a drinking spree and, with 18 warriors, 13 women, and six children, eluded the Apache scouts Crook had assigned to keep an eye on them and slipped away.

As it turned out, their suspicions were warranted. Crook learned of their escape shortly after receiving word from Philip Sheridan, the new commanding general of the army in Washington, that his deal with the Apaches limiting their time in prison was unacceptable. Crook, who had made the offer without conferring with his superior, urged Sheridan to reconsider. But after receiving only criticism for allowing Geronimo to get away, Crook offered Sheridan his resignation.

But there was one more duty for Crook to carry out. On April 7 he escorted the Chiricahuas who had surrendered to a railroad station north of the border, where they were put on a train and shipped east for confinement at Fort Marion in St. Augustine, Florida. When they left, they did not yet know that the agreement with Crook limiting their prison terms had been voided by his superior. "He was a hard fighter, a strong enemy when we were hostile," one Apache said of Crook in later years. "But he played fair with us afterwards and did what he could to protect the Indians."

Crook was replaced by General Nelson A. Miles. He had helped to end the long resistance of both Sitting Bull and Chief Joseph and would spare no expense to bring in Geronimo. Miles lacked Crook's appreciation for the ways of the Apaches, and one of his first acts was to fire most of the

Chief Naiche *(center foreground)* and Geronimo *(third from right),* wearing boots purchased at Fort Bowie, take a break with their band en route to exile in Florida. Geronimo's nephew Kanseah later reflected, "When they put us on that train at [Fort] Bowie, nobody thought that we'd get far before they'd stop it and kill us." Expecting the worst, the 11-year-old's mother urged him to "show these White Eyes how an Apache can die."

scouts. He launched the search with 2,000 soldiers, and by summer fully a quarter of the entire U.S. Army—some 5,000 soldiers in all—had been deployed to track down Geronimo, Naiche, and their followers.

Miles cast a large net, but one with many holes in it. Over the next two months, the holdouts struck at points north and south of the border, looting and killing as they went. By July Miles had come up empty-handed. His failure to catch a single Chiricahua forced him to reverse himself and trust in a small party of Apache scouts led by Lieutenant Charles Gatewood to accomplish what thousands of troops could not. Among Gatewood's party were two young Chiricahuas named Martine and Kayitah, who volunteered to help bring an end to a struggle that promised their people

nothing but grief. In late August the scouts spotted Geronimo and his band on a rocky summit above the Bavispe River in Sonora. Raising a white flour sack attached to a pole, Martine and Kayitah climbed toward the peak, where Geronimo and his warriors waited with rifles ready.

Geronimo's 11-year-old nephew, Kanseah, was watching through field glasses as the scouts came into view. He recognized the two Chiricahuas and informed his uncle of their identity. "It does not matter who they are," Geronimo replied. "If they come closer they are to be shot." But Geronimo's warriors were impressed by the bravery of the scouts, Kanseah recalled, and refused to fire on their fellow tribesmen. No chief could compel Apaches to shed blood against their better judgment.

When the scouts reached the summit they assured Geronimo that he had no chance of escaping this time. His enemies, Mexicans and White Eyes

Adorned with war paint to amuse visitors, Geronimo *(left)*, Naiche *(center)*, and Mangus, the son of Mangas Coloradas *(right)*, pose among cannon barrels while confined at Fort Pickens, Florida. The water jug shown at left—constructed of willow twigs and pine pitch—was made by a relative of Geronimo's who used it in Florida, then took it with her to Alabama and finally to Oklahoma.

alike, were arrayed against him everywhere. Reluctantly Geronimo agreed to meet with Gatewood.

The following morning he and his Apaches headed down to the designated spot at a bend in the river. Approaching the lieutenant Geronimo laid down his rifle and offered his hand. Gatewood informed Geronimo that there was no longer any reservation for him to return to: General Miles had decided to relocate all the Chiricahuas from the White Mountain Reservation to Florida. If Geronimo and his band surrendered, Gatewood added, Miles would allow them to join their people in Florida, "there to await the decision of the president as to your final disposition."

Although Gatewood's words left Geronimo's ultimate fate in doubt, the chief yearned to rejoin his people. He had never met Miles, however, and wondered if the general was a man to be believed. "Consider yourself one of us and not a white man," he said to Gatewood. "What would you advise us to do?"

"I would trust General Miles and take him at his word," the lieutenant replied.

Geronimo and his band agreed to accompany Gatewood north to Skeleton Canyon in Arizona, just over the border. There, on September 3, the chief surrendered to Miles, who was deeply impressed with his defeated adversary. "He was one of the brightest, most resolute, determined looking men that I have ever encountered," Miles said of Geronimo. "Every move indicated power, energy, and determination. In everything he did, he had a purpose."

Geronimo's purpose in yielding to Miles was to spare the lives of his followers and rejoin the rest of his people. On September 8, he, Naiche, and the rest of the band that had surrendered were put on an eastbound train. Meanwhile, the 400 or so Chiricahuas at White Mountain were rounded up and packed into sealed railway cars bound for Fort Marion, where those who had surrendered to Crook were already being held. All members of the tribe, even those who had abode by the government's rules, were now to be regarded as prisoners of war.

Contrary to Miles's promises, Geronimo and the other men in his band were not allowed to join their people at Fort Marion. Instead, they were separated from the women and children and confined at Fort Pickens, on a desolate island off the Florida coast near Pensacola.

The ordeal of the tribespeople was far from over. They were moved first from Florida to Alabama, and finally, in 1894, to Fort Sill. In 1898 Geronimo traveled to Omaha from Fort Sill to attend a large exhibition, and there he was surprised and deeply angered to encounter Miles. The old warrior reminded the general of his broken promises and said, "You lied to us, General Miles." Miles responded mockingly, "I did lie to you, Geronimo, but I learned to lie from you, Geronimo, who is the greatest of all liars." It was the last time the two bitter adversaries would see each other.

When the elderly Geronimo related the story of his life to Asa Daklugie and S. M. Barrett in 1905 and 1906, his reminiscences transported Daklugie to the world his father, Juh, knew before the Americans intruded, a world that belonged to Apaches and that remained for elders like Geronimo their inalienable birthright. "It is my land, my home, my fathers' land, to which I now ask to be allowed to return," Geronimo said in one of his last interviews. "I want to spend my last days there, and be buried among those mountains. If this could be I might die in peace, feeling that my people, placed in their native homes, would increase in numbers, rather than diminish as at present, and that our name would not become extinct."

Geronimo was denied that wish. He died in the Fort Sill hospital in February 1909 after falling off his horse. Four years later Chiricahuas were allowed to resettle on the reservation of the Mescalero Apaches in New Mexico. They still could not venture into Arizona because of the hostility harbored by the whites there. After a long and bewildering exile, they were back in familiar country not far east of the land that Geronimo and so many others had cherished and defended—and that had cared for them in return. "The acorns and piñon nuts, the quail and the wild turkey, the giant cactus and the palo verdes—they all miss me," Geronimo said late in his life. "I miss them, too. I want to go back to them." ◆

THE INDIAN TERRITORY'S FATE

Despite the unseasonable heat, scores of Kiowas and Comanches, wrapped in their customary blankets, crowded into a room near the Fort Sill Agency in the Indian Territory on September 28, 1892, to meet with federal commissioners from Washington. Many standing near the back as the white men spoke could not hear the interpreter translating their remarks and drifted away after a while. But the Kiowa chief Lone Wolf remained in the stifling room, listening intently. He was determined to have his say before the meeting ended.

At stake was the right of his people to retain their reservation in its entirety and keep the government from carving it up. Lone Wolf had long defended Kiowas and Comanches against white intrusions. In 1874, as a young warrior, he had followed Quanah Parker and other leaders into battle against the hide men at Adobe Walls who were slaughtering the buffalo. He fought so bravely there that he was later awarded the name Lone Wolf by the celebrated elder war chief of the same name. When the younger Lone Wolf learned what the government now had in mind, he knew that he would once again have to fight hard in defense of his people.

The three-member commission visiting Fort Sill—headed by former governor of Michigan David Howell Jerome—was one of 15 traveling throughout the Indian Territory to arrange for the allotment and sale of tribal lands in accordance with an act of Congress passed in 1887. A number of tribes elsewhere, including the Lakota Sioux, had already been subjected to this allotment process, which assigned each Indian family a parcel of land and sold what re-

mained of the tribe's territory to whites. The impact on the Indians had been devastating. Yet Jerome and his fellow commissioners painted a glowing picture of what allotment would mean for the Kiowas and Comanches: no more hunger or dependency, and a chance to share in the privileges and prosperity of the larger American society.

When Lone Wolf at last had a chance to speak, he challenged that rosy prediction. His people had made progress toward a new way of life, he said, but the government should not "push us ahead too fast on the road we are to take." The allotment program would thrust the tribes abruptly into unknown territory and lead to their downfall, he predicted. Lone Wolf was not the only chief to warn against hasty action. Present at the meeting was Quanah Parker, who had dealt amicably with white officials in recent years. He too saw danger in imposing sweeping changes on reservation dwellers. "Do not go at this thing like you were riding a swift horse, but hold up a little," Quanah advised the commissioners.

Particularly worrisome to the Indians present was the prospect of having to sell their territory. Time and again, tribes had been induced to exchange the land they cherished for cash or annuities that failed to meet their needs. Many felt that the land left to them was too precious to part with. "Mother earth is something that we Indians love," declared a Kiowa named Isseo at the meeting. "The Great Father at Washington told us that this reservation was ours; that we would not be disturbed; that this place was for our use." He and his people dreaded the thought of "selling our mother to the government."

Such eloquent protests failed to sway the commissioners. What did concern them was a legal objection that Lone Wolf and others raised. The Medicine Lodge Treaty of 1867 that established their reservation had guaranteed them "absolute and undisturbed use and occupation." Under the treaty's terms, any modifications to its provisions had to be approved by three-quarters of the adult males on the reservation. Officials in Washington had instructed the commissioners to obtain the required signatures by any means. And, given the strong opposition the Indians at the meeting were voicing about allotment, the commissioners could see that obtaining the signatures in a legal and aboveboard manner might well be impossible.

This opposition had taken the commissioners by surprise, and to quash it they resorted to deceit, telling their listeners that if they failed to approve the offer of 160 acres per family, under the General Allotment Act that figure would be reduced to 80 acres. Their claim was false, but it succeeded. Lone Wolf and other chiefs felt that they could not subject families to so steep a penalty; reluctantly they signed the document the commissioners placed before them. Many others then fell into line behind their chiefs and added their signatures.

When Lone Wolf discovered that the commissioners had deceived the Kiowas and Comanches, he, along with many others, asked to have their signatures erased. That request was denied, and the commissioners counted their names when they informed Washington that the deal had been approved by more than three-quarters of those eligible to sign. In fact, they had fallen short of that goal, but the reservation agent—who stood to profit personally by approval of the plan—had deliberately understated the number eligible. Furthermore, some of those who signed were whites, and other signatures had been forged.

For the next eight years Lone Wolf tried to overturn the fraudulent deal. He lobbied against congressional approval of the so-called Jerome Agreement with the help of Quanah Parker and white ranchers who had grazing leases with the Indians and did not want to see the area opened to new settlers. Despite their efforts, in 1900 Congress ratified the agreement.

Fighting on, Lone Wolf filed suit against Secretary of the Interior Ethan Allen Hitchcock to block him from upholding the deal because it violated "solemn treaty provisions." The case reached the Supreme Court in 1902. The following year, more than a decade after the meeting with the Jerome commission, he sat in the gallery of the Supreme Court as the decision was announced. Congress had absolute power over Indian affairs, the Court ruled, even when its acts defied prior treaty agreements. The deception Lone Wolf had documented was inconsequential because the consent of the Indians in disposing of their lands was unnecessary. Who, then, would protect tribes from official abuse if not the nation's chief magistrates? The Court presumed that "the United States would be governed by such considerations of justice as would control a Christian people in their treatment of an ignorant and dependent race."

For Lone Wolf, the Court's dismissive judgment was as cruel as any defeat he ever suffered in battle. As he feared, the allotment program proved to be yet another setback for his people. Few families were able to get by on their small holdings, and most sold them out of necessity and went to live near the agencies. They had lost their greatest asset—the land they loved.

Meanwhile, whites in the territory were lobbying for statehood. Among the tribes who struggled to retain their identity amid this onslaught were the Cherokees. Now they joined with the other so-called Civilized Tribes—the Creeks, Seminoles, Choctaws, and Chickasaws—and proposed the creation of the state of Sequoya, encompassing the eastern part of the Indian Territory, where these tribes had presided capably over their own affairs for nearly 70 years.

Congress ignored their appeals, and the land that the Medicine Lodge Treaty had set apart for Indians was folded into the new state admitted to the Union in 1907. The name chosen for it was Oklahoma, from a Choctaw word meaning "home of the red people." The name would stand as a bitter and ironic reminder of what had been but was no more. The Indian Territory had vanished.

✦ **Jason Betzinez** The young Chiricahua Apache was transported to Florida in 1886 with Geronimo and his followers. He escaped the malaria that ravaged the prisoners and was sent to Carlisle Indian Industrial School in Pennsylvania along with the other children and youths aged 12 to 22, against the strenuous protests of their parents. Years later he wrote an account of the Chiricahua struggle called *I Fought with Geronimo*.

✦ **Davy Crockett** Defeated for reelection to Congress after opposing the Indian Removal Act, Crockett headed west in 1835 to explore a new frontier in Texas. He joined up with Texans fighting for independence from Mexico and was killed in the Mexican attack on the Alamo on March 6, 1836. His exploits as a frontiersman and Indian fighter were related in *The Crockett Almanacs*, beginning in 1835, as well as in his fanciful autobiography, *A Narrative of the Life of David Crockett*, published in 1834.

✦ **George Crook** Promoted to the rank of major general in 1888, Crook was put in command of the Division of the Missouri, comprising most of the Great Plains. Although he campaigned hard against Indians, Crook believed that many tribes had legitimate grievances and recommended that authorities pursue diplomatic solutions before resorting to force. He argued for Indian rights, including citizenship, and for strict adherence by the federal government to its treaty obligations. Trusted by many Indians, he was called Grey Fox. He died in 1890 at Division Headquarters in Chicago.

✦ **Sam Houston** The adopted son of Cherokee chief John Jolly, Houston supported the rights of Cherokees throughout his life and sympathized with other hard-pressed tribal groups. In 1833 President Andrew Jackson appointed him to negotiate with Indians in the vicinity of Texas. He soon became involved with the Texas independence movement and was elected president of the Republic of Texas upon its formation in 1836. In that position, and later as governor of the state of Texas, Houston held talks with Comanche leaders and tried unsuccessfully to resolve their bitter differences with encroaching white settlers.

✦ **Oliver Otis Howard** Like George Crook, Howard rose to the rank of major general and used his influence to advocate fair treatment for Indians. Their joint efforts led to the transfer of Geronimo and other Apaches from detention in Florida as prisoners of war to a less restrictive confinement at the Fort Sill Agency in Oklahoma. Howard was awarded the Congressional Medal of Honor for his actions in battle during the Civil War. He related his experiences with the native peoples of the West

in three books, *Nez Perce Joseph* (1881), *My Life and Experiences among Our Hostile Indians* (1907), and *Famous Indian Chiefs I Have Known* (1908).

✦ **Ishatai** The Comanche prophet and holy man who inspired the attack at Adobe Walls continued to exert considerable influence among his people after they were confined to the reservation. As a chief there, he was second in importance only to Quanah Parker.

✦ **Kicking Bear** After the massacre at Wounded Knee, the Lakota ghost dance leader Kicking Bear led a large party of warriors against the 7th U.S. Cavalry in the Badlands north of the Pine Ridge Agency. Their planned attack was thwarted, however, by the arrival of black troopers, or buffalo soldiers, of the 9th U.S. Cavalry. Finding himself surrounded, Kicking Bear negotiated a bloodless  surrender with General Nelson Miles, in charge of the operations against the ghost dancers. He gave up his rifle to Miles on January 15, 1891.

✦ **Ranald Slidell Mackenzie** After subduing the Comanches and supervising them on the reservation, Mackenzie and his regiment took part in the army's offensive against the Lakotas and their allies after the Battle of the Little Bighorn. In late 1876 he used Cheyenne auxiliaries in an attack on Cheyenne holdouts camped in the Bighorn Mountains of Wyoming. He was eventually promoted to brigadier general but suffered a nervous breakdown in 1882 and was committed to a mental institution in New York City. He died seven years later.

✦ **Nelson Appleton Miles** Despite the disastrous events at Wounded Knee, Miles remained in military service and rose in the chain of command. In 1894 he led federal troops in Chicago assigned to quell disturbances during the 1894 Pullman strike. In 1895 he was appointed commander in chief of the army, and in 1898 he took to the field with troops again during the Spanish-American War. He retired from the army in 1903 with the rank of lieutenant general.

✦ **Naiche** The son of Cochise was imprisoned in Florida along with Geronimo and the other Apache leaders. In 1894 he was relocated to Fort Sill. Not until 1913 was he allowed to return to Arizona. He died of influenza in 1921.

✦ **John Parker** Ransomed in 1842 at about the age of 12, John was too attached to Comanche ways to remain in white society.

He soon ran away to look for his sister, Cynthia Ann. Using his Comanche name, Nermernuh, he journeyed unmolested through the Comanchería. After a long and fruitless search, he settled in the desert in Mexico, taking as a wife a Mexican girl who, like himself, had been captured by Comanches.

✦ **RACHEL PLUMMER** After 18 months as a Comanche captive, Rachel was ransomed by her Parker relatives and returned to Texas. In an account of her ordeal, she related how she had scored a coup as a prisoner by clubbing to death an old Comanche woman who had constantly tormented her. Upon her return to white society, however, Plummer faced abuse of a different kind from settlers who considered her tainted by her contact with Comanches. She died less than a year after her return.

✦ **RED CLOUD** Committed to peace after he agreed to the Treaty of Fort Laramie in 1868, Red Cloud did not participate in the struggles of Sitting Bull and Crazy Horse against the U.S. Army in 1876. Afterward he met with Crazy Horse off the reservation and persuaded him to surrender for the good of his followers. Late in his life, in failing health, Red Cloud was baptized as a Roman Catholic. He died in 1909.

✦ **JOHN ROLLIN RIDGE** The son of John Ridge and the grandson of Major Ridge, John Rollin Ridge became embroiled after their executions in the bitter feud between the Ridge and Ross parties. After killing an opponent in self-defense, he fled the Cherokee Nation, fearing an unfair trial. He ended up in California, where he made a name for himself as a poet, writer, and editor, glamorizing the exploits of his relative Stand Watie, a noted Confederate commander during the Civil War. After the war Ridge returned to the Cherokee Nation and took up politics again, backing an effort to establish a separate nation for the so-called Southern Cherokees—former Ridge party enthusiasts who had sided with the Confederacy.

✦ **SUSANNA RIDGE (SEHOYA)** Following the execution of her husband, Major Ridge, in 1839, Susanna fled to Arkansas and sold off her husband's goods from the Ridge store in the Cherokee Nation. She died in 1849 at nearly 80 years of age.

✦ **JOHN ROSS** In his final act of leadership, Ross, at the age of 75, was part of a delegation to Washington aiming to block efforts to partition the Cherokee Nation into Northern and Southern sectors, along lines that had formed during the Civil War. Ross died during the trip, on August 1, 1866, but the mission went forward. The remaining delegates in his party signed a treaty with the United States guaranteeing one unified Cherokee Nation. Ross was honored posthumously as its chief.

✦ **SEQUOYA** In 1842 Sequoya embarked on a quixotic quest for a lost band of Cherokees that was said to have left the eastern woodlands during the American Revolution and migrated to the Southwest. Travel in the searing heat of the desert caused his health, which was already poor, to deteriorate, and he  died in Mexico in 1843. Among those who honored him for inventing a Cherokee script and helping his people to stand tall was Hungarian botanist Stephan Endlicher, who named the towering redwoods of coastal California *Sequoia gigantea* in his memory.

✦ **PHILIP HENRY SHERIDAN** In his capacity as commander of the Division of the Missouri, Sheridan directed devastating campaigns against the Comanches, Kiowas, Arapahos, Northern and Southern Cheyennes, Lakotas, and Apaches, effectively winning the West for Anglo-Americans. However, his harsh policy of "total war," entailing year-round attacks on women and children as well as on warriors, embittered the defeated tribes and left them deeply suspicious of white authorities. Sheridan replaced William Tecumseh Sherman as commander in chief of the army in 1883 and was promoted to the army's highest rank, general of the army, in 1888. He died that same year.

✦ **SAMUEL AUSTIN WORCESTER** The Congregational missionary, present at the death of Elias Boudinot, lived out his remaining years in the Indian Territory. There he headed the Park Hill Mission and established schools and a publishing house that produced works in Cherokee, as well as materials for the Choctaws and the Creeks. He abhorred alcohol and was active in the Cherokee Temperance Society. He died in 1859.

✦ **WOVOKA** After his prophecies of a great new world for Indians went unfulfilled and the ghost dance movement faded, the Paiute holy man lived for many years on a tribal reserve in Nevada and visited reservations in Nevada, Montana, Wyoming, Oklahoma, and Kansas. At the behest of silent-film cowboy Tim McCoy, Wovoka even visited a California film set, where he explained his philosophy to McCoy and nine Arapaho actors. Some Indians continued to regard him as a genuine visionary and medicine man and offered him cash and gifts of hats, beaded vests, and moccasins in return for his services as a healer and rainmaker. He died in Nevada in 1932.

MAKAH COWICHIN
QUILEUTE OKANAGAN
QUINAULT CHEMAKUM SANPOIL
CHEHALIS TWANA KALISPEL
CHINOOK COLUMBIA
COWLITZ SPOKANE
CLATSKANIE KLICKITAT COEUR BLACKFEET GROS VENTRE ASSINBOIN
TILLAMOOK YAKIMA D'ALENE
TENINO PALOUSE FLATHEAD
ALSEA CAYUSE NEZ PERCE
SIUSLAW

HIDATSA

OJIBWA
(CHIPPEWA) OTTAWA

MALISEET
PASSAMAQUODDY

EASTERN
ABENAKI

WESTERN
ABENAKI

TUTUTNI TAKELMA
KLAMATH NORTHERN Little MANDAN
TOLOWA KAROK MODOC PAIUTE NORTHERN Bighorn YANKTONAI MENOMINEE POTAWATOMI
YUROK SHASTAN SHOSHONE River
WIYOT HUPA WINTU ACHUMAWI CROW LAKOTA DAKOTA WINNEBAGO
CALIFORNIA YANA Snake River BANNOCK MASCOUTEN SAUK
ATHAPASKAN YUKI MAIDU CHEYENNE DAKOTA FOX
POMOAN WESTERN KICKAPOO
WAPPO NISENAN WASHOE SHOSHONE EASTERN PONCA IOWA
PATWIN SHOSHONE OMAHA MIAMI
COAST MIWOK MIWOK UTE River ARAPAHO PAWNEE MISSOURI
COSTANOAN YOKUTS OWENS VALLEY OTO
ESSELEN MONACHE PAIUTE SOUTHERN KANSA
SALINAN TUBATULABAL PAIUTE

SENECA
CAYUGA ONONDAGA
ONEIDA
MOHAWK
MAHICAN

MASSACHUSETT
WAMPANOAG
POCUM-
TUCK NARRAGANSETT,
NIANTIC,
MOHEGAN
PEQUOT

SUSQUE-
HANNOCK DELAWARE

PISCATAWAY

SHAWNEE POWHATAN NANTICOKE

SAPONI
MONACAN
TUTELO

CHUMASH KAWAIISU
KITANEMUK CHEMEHUEVI HOPI NAVAJO JICARILLA
TATAVIAM WALAPAI ZUNI RIO GRANDE KIOWA MEHERRIN NORTH CAROLINA
SERRANO ACOMA KERESANS TEWA NORTHERN ENO ALGONQUIANS
CAHUILLA MOHAVE LAGUNA JEMEZ TIWA OSAGE YUCHI SUGEREE VIRGINIA & NORTH CAROLINA
HALCHIDHOMA WESTERN SOUTHERN TANO UNKNOWN CHEROKEE IROQUOIANS
MISSION INDIANS YAVAPAI APACHE TIWA KIOWA- QUAPAW WOCCON
CHIRICAHUA PECOS APACHE CHICKASAW CHERAW
QUECHAN MARICOPA APACHE TOMPIRO WICHITA KOASATI CATAWBA
COCOPA PIRO COMANCHE CHAKCHIUMA MUSKOGEE WATEREE
PAPAGO OSAGE (CREEK) PEDEE
JOCOME & CADDO CUSABO
UPPER PIMA JANO Red River TUNICA GUALE
MESCALERO APACHE KITSAI OFO
WACO NATCHEZ CHOCTAW ALABAMA
TOHOME CHATOT HITCHITI
LIPAN APACHE HOUMA NANIABA
TONKAWA ATAKAPA MOBILE APALACHEE
KARANKAWA BILOXI PENSACOLA
Rio Grande CHITIMACHA TIMUCUA
COAHUILTECAN
TRIBES TOCOBAGA
MOCOCO AIS
OCITA GUACATA
CALUSA TEKESTA

PACIFIC OCEAN

ATLANTIC OCEAN

GULF OF MEXICO

LEGEND

NAMES INDICATE LOCATION OF TRIBES AT
FIRST CONTACT WITH EUROPEANS BETWEEN
1500 AND 1800.

☐ LANDS CEDED TO WHITES BEFORE 1775

— BOUNDARY LINE OF 1763

Miles

0   200   400

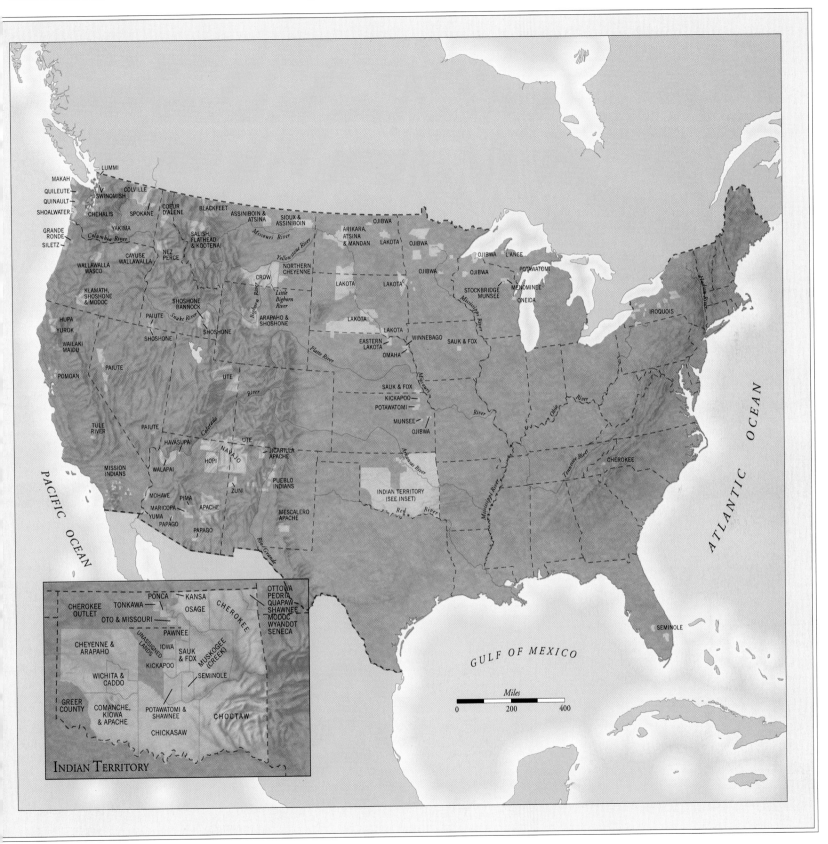

Reservation Lands in 1890

LUMMI
MAKAH
QUILEUTE
QUINAULT
SHOALWATER
SWINOMISH
COLVILLE
CHEHALIS
SPOKANE
COEUR D'ALENE
BLACKFEET
ASSINIBOIN & ATSINA
SIOUX & ASSINIBOIN
OJIBWA
GRANDE RONDE
SILETZ
YAKIMA
Columbia River
SALISH-FLATHEAD & KOOTENAI
Missouri River
ARIKARA, ATSINA & MANDAN
OJIBWA
OJIBWA
L'ANSE
WALLAWALLA WASCO
CAYUSE WALLAWALLA
NEZ PERCE
Yellowstone River
NORTHERN CHEYENNE
LAKOTA
LAKOTA
OJIBWA
OJIBWA
POTAWATOMI
KLAMATH, SHOSHONE & MODOC
SHOSHONE BANNOCK
CROW
Bighorn River
Little Bighorn River
LAKOTA
STOCKBRIDGE MUNSEE
MENOMINEE
ONEIDA
HUPA
YUROK
PAIUTE
Snake River
SHOSHONE
ARAPAHO & SHOSHONE
LAKOTA
LAKOTA
IROQUOIS
WAILAKI MAIDU
SHOSHONE
EASTERN LAKOTA
WINNEBAGO
SAUK & FOX
POMOAN
PAIUTE
OMAHA
UTE
River
Platte River
SAUK & FOX
KICKAPOO
POTAWATOMI
TULE RIVER
PAIUTE
Colorado River
MUNSEE
OJIBWA
HAVASUPAI
UTE
River
Gila River
MISSION INDIANS
NAVAJO
JICARILLA APACHE
WALAPAI
HOPI
ZUNI
PUEBLO INDIANS
INDIAN TERRITORY (SEE INSET)
CHEROKEE
MOHAVE
PIMA
MARICOPA
YUMA
PAPAGO
APACHE
MESCALERO APACHE
Red River
PAPAGO
Rio Grande
Tennessee River
Ohio River
Mississippi River
Arkansas River

PACIFIC OCEAN

ATLANTIC OCEAN

GULF OF MEXICO

SEMINOLE

Indian Territory

CHEROKEE OUTLET
PONCA
KANSA
TONKAWA
OSAGE
CHEROKEE
OTTOWA
PEORIA
QUAPAW
SHAWNEE
MODOC
WYANDOT
SENECA
OTO & MISSOURI
PAWNEE
CHEYENNE & ARAPAHO
UNASSIGNED LANDS
IOWA
SAUK & FOX
MUSKOGEE (CREEK)
KICKAPOO
WICHITA & CADDO
SEMINOLE
GREER COUNTY
COMANCHE, KIOWA & APACHE
POTAWATOMI & SHAWNEE
CHOCTAW
CHICKASAW

Miles
0   200   400

181

CHRONOLOGY OF GOVERNMENT-INDIAN RELATIONS

PRE-1800

1763 King George III establishes a boundary line in the Appalachian Mountains between the colonies and the Indian lands west of the mountains. The practice of treating Indian nations as sovereign entities is established.

1775 The Revolutionary War begins. The colonies, united under the Articles of Confederation, assign responsibility for managing Indian affairs to the federal government. Many tribes fight alongside the British in expectation of fair treatment and retention of their lands.

1783 The Treaty of Paris formally ends the war. The United States pursues a pacification policy with Indian nations on its northern, southern, and western frontiers, but white encroachment into Indian lands continues.

1785 In South Carolina, the Treaty of Hopewell, between the U.S. and the Cherokees, Choctaws, and Chickasaws, fixes boundaries for Indian lands, withdraws federal protection from anyone encroaching on those lands, and establishes a basis for prosecuting anyone committing a crime there.

1787 Congress adopts the Northwest Ordinance covering the area from present-day Ohio to Wisconsin. The ordinance declares that lands will never be taken without the consent of the inhabitants, that just compensation will be provided for ceded lands, and that no whites will invade Indian lands except in wars authorized by Congress.

1795 After their attempt to drive out white settlers and rout U.S. troops from present-day Ohio fails, the Shawnees, Miamis, Potawatomis, and Chippewas are forced to sign the Treaty of Greenville, ceding lands that will eventually compose the lower two-thirds of Ohio.

1800-1809

1803 The United States and France sign the Louisiana Purchase treaty. President Jefferson recommends that the eastern Indian tribes abandon their homelands and migrate to the newly acquired territory west of the Mississippi.

CREEK HEADMAN WILLIAM MCINTOSH FOUGHT WITH ANDREW JACKSON IN THE CREEK WAR.

1810-1819

1810 John Marshall, chief justice of the United States, declares Indian lands west of the Appalachian Mountains to be vacant, invalidating King George's 1763 boundary line and upholding states' claims to the lands.

1812-1813 Shawnee leader Tecumseh and the Northwest tribes he united to oppose American encroachment on their homelands join forces with the British during the War of 1812. Upon Tecumseh's death at the Battle of the Thames in Ontario, resolve among the Indians weakens, and the alliance disintegrates.

1814 Upper and Lower Creek, Cherokee, and American forces defeat the Red Stick Creeks, ending the Creek War. General Andrew Jackson forces Creek allies to sign a treaty forfeiting all Creek land in Alabama and Georgia to the United States.

1817-1818 Violating territorial boundaries, Andrew Jackson leads U.S. forces against the Seminoles in Spanish Florida, precipitating the First Seminole War.

1850-1859

1851 Ten thousand Plains Indians from nine different tribes meet with government negotiators at Fort Laramie, Wyoming. They sign the 1851 Fort Laramie Treaty, which provides for fixed territories for each tribe, the installation of military posts, and safe passage for whites traveling the Oregon Trail.

1855 The Blackfeet Nation signs a treaty with the United States allowing whites to settle in and travel through their land in Washington Territory in return for goods and annuities. Tribes are granted continued use of the land but may not establish their own permanent settlements.

BANNER OF CHEROKEE VOLUNTEER UNIT THAT FOUGHT FOR THE CONFEDERACY

1860-1869

1865 As punishment for aligning themselves with the Confederacy in the Civil War, the Cherokees, Chickasaws, Choctaws, Creeks, and Seminoles are forced to vacate the western half of the Indian Territory. Arapahos, Shawnees, Potawatomis, and other tribes are moved in by the U.S. government to occupy the vacated land.

1867 A congressional committee headed by Senator James Doolittle of Wisconsin concludes that Indian nations are so weak that the best way to protect them from whites is to intern them on reservations and expand the reservation system enough to accommodate the entire Indian population.

1867 The Indian Peace Commission and the Comanches, Kiowas, and other tribes of the southern plains sign the Medicine Lodge Treaty, which establishes reservations for them. The Indians agree to move onto the reservations.

1868 The Indian Peace Commission and representatives of the Lakotas and other tribes of the northern plains sign the 1868 Fort Laramie Treaty, with provisions modeled on the Medicine Lodge Treaty.

1869 Seneca Ely Samuel Parker becomes the first Indian to be appointed commissioner of the Bureau of Indian Affairs.

1870-1879

1871 Congress decrees that it will no longer make treaties with any Indian tribes as independent nations. However, it affirms the validity of the 371 existing treaties between the U.S. government and various tribes.

1872 General Philip Sheridan, as commander of the Division of the Missouri, issues the order that no reservation Indian may leave the reservation without permission of the agent.

1874 The Black Hills, reserved for the Lakotas under the 1868 Fort Laramie Treaty, are appropriated by the U.S. government after gold is discovered in the area.

1824 Secretary of War John C. Calhoun reorganizes the Indian Department, established in 1789 as an arm of the War Department, into the Bureau of Indian Affairs.

1827 Cherokees living in Georgia assert that they are a sovereign nation with sole jurisdiction over their lands. They adopt a constitution patterned on the U.S. Constitution. The state legislature votes to nullify it.

COOKING POT ISSUED TO CHEROKEE FAMILY FOR USE ON THE JOURNEY TO THE INDIAN TERRITORY

1830 The Indian Removal Act paves the way for the mass relocation of the Cherokees, Choctaws, Chickasaws, Creeks, and Seminoles from their homelands in the Southeast to the newly created Indian Territory, in present-day Oklahoma.

1831-1832 After reviewing court cases concerning the rights of the Cherokees in Georgia, Chief Justice Marshall rules that Indian nations are domestic rather than foreign and have only limited sovereignty. They may sign land cession treaties but lack the power to control any other internal matters.

1834 Congress makes the Bureau of Indian Affairs an independent agency operating under a commission and reporting directly to Congress.

1837 A smallpox epidemic ravages the Mandans, Hidatsas, and Arikaras of the upper Missouri River as a result of their contact with whites.

1838 Members of the Cherokee, Choctaw, Chickasaw, and Creek tribes begin their journey on the so-called Trail of Tears, a forced migration from their homelands in the Southeast to the Indian Territory. Thousands succumb to exposure, disease, and starvation in the course of the migration.

1846 The United States annexes the Oregon Territory from Great Britain. Occupied by at least 20 tribes, including the Salish, Nez Perces, Chinooks, and Flatheads, the land will become the states of Oregon, Washington, Idaho, and Montana.

1848 The Mexican War ends in American victory, and Mexico cedes the territory from which Arizona, California, Colorado, Nevada, New Mexico, Utah, and Wyoming will be carved. The mass migration of Americans into the ceded territory increases pressure on the indigenous tribes.

1849 In the first year of the gold rush some 85,000 emigrants join the 15,000 whites already in California. The state government makes payments to civilian Indian fighters, and the tribal population plummets in a decade from an estimated 150,000 to as few as 30,000.

CALIFORNIAN.

SAN FRANCISCO, WEDNESDAY, MARCH 15, 1913.

GOLD MINE FOUND.—In the newly made raceway of the Saw Mill recently erected by Captain Sutter, on the American Fork, gold has been found in considerable quantities. One person brought thirty dollars worth to New Helvetia, gathered there in a short time. California, no doubt, is rich in mineral wealth; great chances here for scientific capitalists. Gold has been found in almost every part of the country.

1883 The U.S. Supreme Court rules that the United States does not have jurisdiction over crimes committed by one Indian against another on reservations.

1885 Congress overrides the Supreme Court's 1883 ruling by passing the Major Crimes Act, which grants federal courts jurisdiction over reservation Indians who commit crimes against each other.

1886 A Supreme Court ruling sustains the validity of the Major Crimes Act, consolidating federal power over Indians.

1887 The General Allotment Act, or Dawes Act, attacks the traditional practice of holding tribal lands in common by partitioning reservations into 160-acre parcels and assigning them to individuals. All unassigned lands will be given or sold to whites for settlement or corporate use or set aside for federal use. To keep property in Indian hands, the act prohibits the sale of individually owned parcels to whites for 25 years. However, the land held by Indians will fall from 138 million acres to 48 million acres over the next 47 years.

1889 The U.S. government buys two million acres of Indian land in the Oklahoma District for distribution to white homesteaders under the provisions of the Homestead Act, setting off the first of several land rushes.

1890 In an effort to rout out the ghost dancers, members of a messianic religious cult, the 7th Cavalry kills more than 200 Lakotas at Wounded Knee, South Dakota.

1891 Congress suspends the Dawes Act prohibition against whites leasing allotted lands from Indians.

1898 The Curtis Act forces land allotment on the Cherokees, Chickasaws, Creeks, Choctaws, and Seminoles living in the Indian Territory. They had previously escaped allotment because of treaties signed prior to the Dawes Act.

ALLOTMENT CERTIFICATE IDENTIFYING LAND PARCEL OF A MEMBER OF THE CHICKASAW NATION

1901 The U.S. Census Bureau records a national population of fewer than 250,000 Indians.

1902 For the first time the federal government offers gas and oil leases on the Indian lands in Oklahoma Territory, established in 1890. Whites as well as Indians are eligible for the leases.

1902 The passage of the Federal Reclamation Act encourages further settlement and agricultural development in the West by paying subsidies to whites who develop water resources.

1903 The U.S. Supreme Court rules that portions of treaties with the native nations can be abrogated without altering the force of the treaty. The United States can thereby retain title to lands ceded by the Indians in those treaties but avoid providing further annuities or protections required by other provisions of the document.

1907 Oklahoma becomes a state, incorporating the Indian Territory.

1910 The Bureau of Indian Affairs establishes the Indian Medical Service to provide healthcare on reservations.

The editors wish to thank the following individuals and institutions for their valuable assistance in the preparation of this volume:

Giuliana Bullard, National Archives, Washington, D.C.; Betty L. Bustos, Panhandle Plains Historical Museum, Canyon, Tex.; Mario Einaudi, Arizona Historical Society, Tucson;

ACKNOWLEDGMENTS

Joanne Green, Museum of the Cherokee Indian, Cherokee, N.C.; Ben Kracht, Northeastern State University, Tahlequah, Okla.; John R. Lovett, University of Oklahoma Libraries,

Norman; Tom McKinney, Bacone College, Muskogee, Okla.; John Powell, Newberry Library, Chicago; Victoria Sheffler, University Archives, Northeastern State University, Tahlequah, Okla.; Sandy White, Department of Archives and History, Atlanta.

PICTURE CREDITS

The sources for the illustrations that appear in this volume are listed below. Credits from left to right are separated by semicolons; credits from top to bottom are separated by dashes.

Cover: National Anthropological Archives, Smithsonian Institution, Washington, D.C., neg. no. 1426-A. 8: National Anthropological Archives, Smithsonian Institution, Washington, D.C., neg. no. 52811. 9: Library of Congress, neg. no. 04-33751. 10, 11: Library of Congress. 12: State Historical Society of North Dakota, Bismarck. 13: Richard Erdoes, Santa Fe, N.Mex. 14: National Anthropological Archives, Smithsonian Institution, Washington, D.C., neg. no. 1010. 15: Library of Congress, neg. no. 614816. 16: Courtesy American Antiquarian Society, Worcester, Mass. 18: Library of Congress. 19: Map by Maryland CartoGraphics, Inc. 20: Library of Congress, USZ-62-4678. 23: The Granger Collection, New York, no. AE758.09. 26: William L. Clements Library, University of Michigan, Ann Arbor. 29: Western History Collection, University of Oklahoma Libraries, Norman, Phillips no. 1474, inset, Library of Congress. 30: Library of Congress. 31: Rare Book and Manuscripts Division, New York Public Library, Astor, Lenox and Tilden Foundations. 32: National Portrait Gallery, Smithsonian Institution, Washington, D.C./Art Resource, New York. 33: Thomas Gilcrease Institute of American History and Art, Tulsa. 34: Archives and Manuscript Division of the Oklahoma Historical Society, Oklahoma City, neg. no. 19615.43. 36: William L. Clements Library, University of Michigan, Ann Arbor. 39: National Museum of American Art, Smithsonian Institution, Washington, D.C./Art Resource, New York—Florida State Archives. 40: Courtesy Georgia Department of Archives and History. 43: National Anthropological Archives, Smithsonian Institution, Washington, D.C., neg. nos. 1063-V; 1044-B. 44: National Archives Ratified Indian Treaty No. 199, Record Group 11, photograph by Evan H. Sheppard. 46: Archives and Manuscripts Division of the Oklahoma Historical Society, Oklahoma City, neg. no. 20911.2. 47: Archives and Manuscripts Division of the Oklahoma His-

torical Society, Oklahoma City, neg. nos. 19615.77A; 15798. 48: Archives and Manuscripts Division of the Oklahoma Historical Society, Oklahoma City, neg. no. 1046.B. 50: Courtesy Chattanooga-Hamilton County Bicentennial Library, Chattanooga. 51: D'Arcy McNickle Center for the History of the American Indian, Newberry Library, Chicago. 52, 53: Western History Collection, University of Oklahoma Libraries, Ballenger Collection, photograph no. 6; Western History Collection, University of Oklahoma Libraries, Faux Collection, photograph no. 44; Western History Collection, University of Oklahoma Libraries, Faux Collection, photograph no. 66. 54: University Archives, John Vaughan Library, Northeastern State University, Tahlequah, Okla., photograph by Don Wheeler. 55: Western History Collection, University of Oklahoma Libraries, Ballenger Collection, photograph no. 8; University Archives, John Vaughan Library, Northeastern State University, Tahlequah, Okla., photograph by Don Wheeler. 56, 57: Western History Collection, University of Oklahoma Libraries, Ballenger Collection, photograph no. 29; University Archives, John Vaughan Library, Northeastern State University, Tahlequah, Okla., photograph by Don Wheeler; Western History Collection, University of Oklahoma Libraries, Ballenger Collection, photograph no. 7; University Archives, John Vaughan Library, Northeastern State University, Tahlequah, Okla., photograph by Don Wheeler. 58: Western History Collection, University of Oklahoma Libraries, Rose Collection, photograph no. 935. 61: Map by Maryland CartoGraphics, Inc. 63: National Museum of American Art, Smithsonian Institution, Washington, D.C., no. 1985.66.487/ Art Resource, New York; Panhandle Plains Historical Museum, Research Center, Canyon, Tex. 64: National Museum of American Art, Smithsonian Institution, Washington, D.C., no. 1985.66.51/Art Resource, New York. 65: Heard Museum, Phoenix. 66, 67: Library of Congress. 69: Courtesy Depart-

ment of Anthropology, Smithsonian Institution, Washington, D.C., cat. no. 360233A, photograph by Larry Sherer. 70: National Museum of American Art, Smithsonian Institution, Washington, D.C./Art Resource, New York. 72: Texas Collection, Baylor University, Waco, Tex. 74, 75: National Museum of American Art, Smithsonian Institution, Washington, D.C./Art Resource, New York. 77: Panhandle Plains Historical Museum, Research Center, Canyon, Tex. 78: The Granger Collection, New York. 79: Kansas State Historical Society, Topeka. 81: Panhandle Plains Historical Museum, Research Center, Canyon, Tex. 82: National Anthropological Archives, Smithsonian Institution, Washington, D.C., neg. no. 1746-a-2. 84: Kansas Collection, University of Kansas Libraries, Lawrence. 85: Photograph by Ruth Gartland. 86: Western History Collection, University of Oklahoma Libraries, Norman, neg. no. 1177. 87: National Anthropological Archives, Smithsonian Institution, Washington, D.C., neg. no. 1782-Q. 88, 89: National Anthropological Archives, Smithsonian Institution, Washington, D.C., no. 94-12013; Fort Sill Museum, Fort Sill, Okla., neg. no. P3115. 90: Fort Sill Museum, Fort Sill, Okla., neg. no. P7637—National Anthropological Archives, Smithsonian Institution, Washington, D.C., neg. no. 1747-a-1. 92: Library of Congress. 93: Courtesy National Park Service, Nez Perce National Historical Park Collection. 94: National Anthropological Archives, Smithsonian Institution, Washington, D.C., neg. no. 1386-c. 95: Panhandle Plains Historical Museum, Research Center, Canyon, Tex. 96: National Anthropological Archives, Smithsonian Institution, Washington, D.C., neg. no. 42-021. 97: Courtesy American Numismatic Society, New York, photographed by Frank Lerner. 98: National Anthropological Archives, Smithsonian Institution, Washington, D.C., neg. no. 3052. 99: Phoebe A. Hearst Museum of Anthropology, University of California at Berkeley, cat. no. 1-27204. 100: Library of Congress, neg. no. USZ-62-98534. 101: Courtesy Chief Plenty Coups State Park Museum, Pryor, Mont., photographed by Michael Crummett. 102: Denver Public Library, Western History Department,

BOOKS

Andrist, Ralph K. *The Long Death: The Last Days of the Plains Indians.* New York: Macmillan, 1964.

Axelrod, Alan. *Chronicle of the Indian Wars: From Colonial Times to Wounded Knee.* New York: Prentice-Hall, 1993.

Baker, T. Lindsay, and Billy R. Harrison. *Adobe Walls: The History and Archeology of the 1874 Trading Post.* College Station: Texas A&M University Press, 1986.

Ball, Eve, Nora Henn, and Lynda A. Sánchez. *Indeh: An Apache Odyssey.* Norman: University of Oklahoma Press, 1988.

BIBLIOGRAPHY

Barrett, S. M. (ed.) *Geronimo's Story of His Life.* New York: Duffield, 1907.

Bass, Althea. *Cherokee Messenger.* Norman: University of Oklahoma Press, 1936.

Benner, Judith Ann. *Sul Ross: Soldier, Statesman, Educator.* College Station: Texas A&M University Press, 1983.

Bernotas, Bob. *Sitting Bull: Chief of the Sioux* (North American Indians of Achievement series). New York: Chelsea House, 1992.

Blish, Helen H. *A Pictographic History of the Oglala Sioux.* Lincoln: University of Nebraska Press, 1967.

Bourke, John G.:
An Apache Campaign in the Sierra Madre. Lincoln: University of Nebraska Press, 1987.
On the Border with Crook. New York: Charles Scribner's Sons, 1891.

Brown, Dee. *Bury My Heart at Wounded Knee: An Indian History of the American West.* New York: Holt, Rinehart & Winston, 1970.

Carter, R. G. *On the Border with Mackenzie, or Win-*

ning West Texas from the Comanches. Mattituck, N.Y.: J. M. Carroll, 1935.

Carter, Samuel, III. *Cherokee Sunset: A Nation Betrayed.* Garden City, N.Y.: Doubleday, 1976.

Chalmers, Harvey, II. *The Last Stand of the Nez Perce: Destruction of a People.* New York: Twayne Publishers, 1962.

Clark, Blue. *Lone Wolf v. Hitchcock: Treaty Rights and Indian Law at the End of the Nineteenth Century.* Lincoln: University of Nebraska Press, 1994.

Connell, Evan S. *Son of the Morning Star.* San Francisco: North Point Press, 1984.

Crook, George. *General George Crook: His Autobiography.* Edited by Martin F. Schmitt. Norman: University of Oklahoma Press, 1960.

Dale, Edward Everett, and Gaston Litton. *Cherokee Cavaliers.* Norman: University of Oklahoma Press, 1940.

Debo, Angie. *Geronimo: The Man, His Time, His Place.* Norman: University of Oklahoma Press, 1976.

Dillon, Richard H. *Burnt-Out Fires.* Englewood Cliffs, N.J.: Prentice-Hall, 1973.

Estin, Ann Laquer. "Lone Wolf v. Hitchcock: The Long Shadow." In *The Aggressions of Civilization: Federal Indian Policy Since the 1880s.* Edited by Sandra L. Cadwalader and Vine Deloria Jr. Philadelphia: Temple University Press, 1984.

Fehrenbach, T. R. *Comanches: The Destruction of a People.* New York: Da Capo Press, 1994.

Finger, John R. *The Eastern Band of Cherokees, 1819-1900.* Knoxville: University of Tennessee Press, 1984.

Fleming, Paula Richardson, and Judith Luskey. *The North American Indians in Early Photographs.* New York: Dorset Press, 1986.

Foreman, Grant. *Indian: The Emigration of the Five Civi-lized Tribes of Indians.* Norman: University of Oklahoma Press, 1989.

Freedman, Russell. *Indian Chiefs.* New York: Holiday House, 1987.

Godbold, E. Stanly, Jr., and Mattie U. Russell. *Confederate Colonel and Cherokee Chief: The Life of William Holland Thomas.* Knoxville: University of Tennessee Press, 1990.

Hagan, William T. *United States-Comanche Relations: The Reservation Years.* New Haven, Conn.: Yale University Press, 1976.

Haley, James L.:

Apaches: A History and Culture Portrait. Garden City, N.Y.: Doubleday, 1981.

The Buffalo War: The History of the Red River Indian Uprising of 1874. Garden City, N.Y.: Doubleday, 1976.

Harcey, Dennis W., Brian R. Croone, and Joe Medicine Crow. *White-Man-Runs-Him.* Evanston, Ill.: Evanston Publishing, 1993.

Hittman, Michael. *Wovoka and the Ghost Dance.* Edited by Don Lynch. Carson City, Nev.: Grace Dangberg Founda-tion, 1990.

Hudson, Charles. *The Southeastern Indians.* Knoxville: University of Tennessee Press, 1976.

Jaimes, M. Annette (ed.). *The State of Native America: Genocide, Colonization, and Resistance.* Boston: South End Press, 1992.

Josephy, Alvin M., Jr. *The Patriot Chiefs: A Chronicle of American Indian Resistance.* New York: Viking Press, 1958.

Kelly, Lawrence C. *Federal Indian Policy* (Indians of North America series). New York: Chelsea House, 1990.

King, Duane H. (ed.) *The Cherokee Indian Nation: A Troubled History.* Knoxville: University of Tennessee Press, 1979.

McLoughlin, William G. *Cherokees and Missionaries, 1789-1839.* New Haven, Conn.: Yale University Press, 1984.

McReynolds, Edwin C. *The Seminoles.* Norman: University of Oklahoma Press, 1972.

Mihesuah, Devon A. *Cultivating the Rosebuds: The Education of Women at the Cherokee Female Seminary, 1851-1909.* Chicago: University of Illinois Press, 1993.

Miller, Lee (ed.). *From the Heart: Voices of the American Indian.* New York: Alfred A. Knopf, 1995.

Mooney, James. *The Ghost-Dance Religion and Wounded Knee.* New York: Dover Publications, 1973.

Moulton, Gary E. (ed.) *The Papers of Chief John Ross, 1807-1839* (Vol. 1). Norman: University of Oklahoma Press, 1985.

Moquin, Wayne, and Charles Van Doren (eds.). *Great Documents in American Indian History.* New York: Praeger Publishers, 1973.

Neeley, Bill. *The Last Comanche Chief: The Life and Times of Quanah Parker.* New York: John Wiley & Sons, 1995.

Noyes, Stanley. *Los Comanches: The Horse People, 1751-1845.* Albuquerque: University of New Mexico Press, 1993.

Opler, Morris Edward. *An Apache Life-Way: The Economic, Social, and Religious Institutions of the Chiricahua Indians.*

New York: Cooper Square Publishers, 1965.

Perdue, Theda:

The Cherokee (Indians of North America series). New York: Chelsea House, 1989.

Slavery and the Evolution of Cherokee Society, 1540-1866. Knoxville: University of Tennessee Press, 1979.

Perdue, Theda (ed.). *Cherokee Editor: The Writings of Elias Boudinot.* Knoxville: University of Tennessee Press, 1983.

Perdue, Theda, and Michael D. Green (eds.). *The Cherokee Removal: A Brief History with Documents* (The Bedford Series in History and Culture). Boston: St. Martin's Press, 1995.

Prucha, Francis Paul. *The Great Father: The United States Government and the American Indians.* Lincoln: University of Nebraska Press, 1984.

Ramsay, Jack C., Jr. *The Story of Cynthia Ann Parker: Sunshine on the Prairie.* Austin, Tex.: Eakin Press, 1990.

Rausch, David A., and Blair Schlepp. *Native American Voices.* Grand Rapids: Baker Books, 1994.

Roberts, David. *Once They Moved Like the Wind: Cochise, Geronimo, and the Apache Wars.* New York: Simon & Schuster, 1993.

Shadburn, Don L. *Cherokee Planters in Georgia, 1832-1838: Historical Essays on Eleven Counties in the Cherokee Nation of Georgia* (Vol. 2 of Pioneer-Cherokee Heritage series). Roswell, Ga.: W. H. Wolfe Associates, 1990.

Skelton, Robert H. *A History of the Educational System of the Cherokee Nation, 1801-1910.* Fayetteville: University of Arkansas, 1970.

Stanley, F. *Satanta and the Kiowas.* Borger, Tex.: Jim Hess Printers, 1968.

Tillett, Leslie (ed.). *Wind on the Buffalo Grass: The Indians' Own Account of the Battle at the Little Big Horn River & the Death of Their Life on the Plains.* New York: Thomas Y. Crowell, 1976.

Utley, Robert M. *The Lance and the Shield: The Life and Times of Sitting Bull.* New York: Henry Holt, 1993.

Viola, Herman J. *Diplomats in Buckskins: A History of Indian Delegations in Washington City.* Washington, D.C.: Smithsonian Institution Press, 1981.

Waldman, Carl. *Who Was Who in Native American History: Indians and Non-Indians from Early Contacts through 1900.* New York: Facts On File, 1990.

Walker, Robert Sparks. *Torchlights to the Cherokees: The*

Brainerd Mission. New York: Macmillan, 1931.

War for the Plains (The American Indians series). Alexandria, Va.: Time-Life Books, 1994.

Washburn, Wilcomb E. (ed.) *History of Indian-White Relations* (Vol. 4 of Handbook of North American Indians series). Washington, D.C.: Smithsonian Institution, 1988.

Waters, Frank. *Brave Are My People: Indian Heroes Not Forgotten.* Santa Fe, N.Mex.: Clear Light Publishers, 1993.

Wheeler, Keith, and the Editors of Time-Life Books. *The Scouts* (The Old West series). Alexandria, Va.: Time-Life Books, 1978.

Wilkins, Thurman. *Cherokee Tragedy: The Story of the Ridge Family and the Decimation of a People.* New York: Macmillan, 1970.

Wissler, Clark. *Indians of the United States.* Garden City, N.Y.: Doubleday, 1966.

PERIODICALS

Barnard, Henry (ed.). "Public Education among the Cherokee Indians." *American Journal of Education,* Vol. 1, 1856.

Davis, John Benjamin. "Public Education among the Cherokee Indians." *Peabody Journal of Education,* Vol. 7, July 1929-May 1930.

Mihesuah, Devon A.:

"Commendable Progress": Acculturation at the Cherokee Female Seminary. *American Indian Quarterly,* Summer 1987.

"Out of the 'Graves of the Polluted Debauches': The Boys of the Cherokee Male Seminary." *American Indian Quarterly,* Fall 1991.

Perdue, Theda. "Letters from Brainerd." *Journal of Cherokee Studies,* Winter 1979.

Rogers, J. Daniel. "Bloody Knife's Last Stand." *Natural History,* June 1992.

Satz, Ronald N.:

"Cherokee Traditionalism, Protestant Evangelism, and the Trail of Tears, Part I." *Tennessee Historical Quarterly,* Fall 1985.

"Cherokee Traditionalism, Protestant Evangelism, and the Trail of Tears, Part II." *Tennessee Historical Quarterly,* Winter 1985.

Van Orden, Jay. "C. S. Fly at Cañon de los Embudos: American Indians as Enemy in the Field, A Photographic First." *Journal of Arizona History,* Autumn 1989.

OTHER SOURCES

"The Last Years of Sitting Bull." State Historical Society of North Dakota, June 1-September 30, 1984.

"Letter from the Secretary of the Interior to the Committee on Indian Affairs in Response to Resolution of the Senate of January 13, 1899, Relative to Condition and Character of the Kiowa, Comanche, and Apache Indian Reservation, and the Assent of the Indians to the Agreement for the Allotment of Lands and the Ceding of Unallotted Lands." Senate Document No. 77, *Jerome Agreement with Kiowa, Comanche, Apache Indians,* 55th Cong., 3d Sess., January 26, 1899, Serial No. 3731, Vol. 7.

Numerals in italics indicate an illustration of the subject mentioned.

INDEX

TIME® Time-Life Books is a
division of Time Life Inc.

TIME LIFE INC.

PRESIDENT and CEO: George Artandi

TIME-LIFE BOOKS

PRESIDENT: John D. Hall
PUBLISHER/MANAGING EDITOR: Neil Kagan

THE AMERICAN STORY

DEFIANT CHIEFS

EDITOR: Sarah Brash
DIRECTOR, NEW PRODUCT DEVELOPMENT:
Curtis Kopf
MARKETING DIRECTOR: Pamela R. Farrell

Editor, Special Projects: Roxie France-Nuriddin
Text Editors: Stephen G. Hyslop (principal), James Lynch
Design Director: Dale Pollekoff
Art Directors: Ellen L. Pattisall, Alan Pitts
Associate Editors/Research and Writing: Annette Scarpitta,
Jarelle S. Stein
Copyeditor: Judith Klein
Picture Coordinators: Catherine Parrott, Betty Weatherley
Editorial Assistant: Patricia D. Whiteford
Picture Associate: Anne Whittle

Special Contributors: Amy Aldrich, Ronald H. Bailey,
Patricia Daniels, Thomas A. Lewis (text); Roberta Conlan
(editing); Jane Coughran (picture editing); Vilasini
Balakrishnan, Arlene L. Borden, April Jones, Daniel
Kulpinski, Mary H. McCarthy, Maureen McHugh,
Elizabeth Schleichert, Myrna Traylor-Herndon (research
and writing); Barbara L. Klein (research); Maggie
Debelius (writing); Magdalena Anders (pictures); Jennifer
Rushing-Schurr (index).

Correspondents: Christine Hinze (London), Christina
Lieberman (New York), Maria Vincenza Aloisi (Paris).

Vice President, Director of Finance: Christopher Hearing
Vice President, Book Production: Marjann Caldwell
Director of Operations: Eileen Bradley
Director of Photography and Research: John Conrad Weiser
Director of Editorial Administration (Acting): Barbara Levitt
Production Manager: Marlene Zack
Quality Assurance Manager: James King
Library: Louise D. Forstall

The Consultant
Frederick E. Hoxie is vice president for research and
education at the Newberry Library in Chicago and
former director of its D'Arcy McNickle Center for the
History of the American Indian. The series consultant for
Time-Life Books' The American Indians, Dr. Hoxie is the
author of *A Final Promise: The Campaign to Assimilate the
Indians,* 1880-1920 (1984) and *Parading through History: The
Making of the Crow Nation in America,* 1805-1935 (1995), and
editor of *Indians in American History* (1988) and *Discovering
America* (1994). He has served as a history consultant to
the Cheyenne River Sioux tribe, the Little Big Horn
College Archives, and the Select Committee on Indian
Affairs of the U.S. Senate. He is a founding trustee of
the Smithsonian Institution's National Museum of the
American Indian in Washington, D.C.

Library of Congress Cataloging-in-Publication Data
Defiant chiefs / by the editors of Time-Life Books.
    p.   cm.—(American story)
    Includes bibliographical references and index.
    ISBN 0-7835-6254-3
    1. Indians of North America—Government relations.
2. Indians of North America—Wars. 3. Indians of North
America—Biography. I. Time-Life Books. II. Series.
E93.D344 1997
973'.0497—dc21   96-50105
                                                      CIP

On the cover: Photographed in 1898, Kiowa chief
Two Hatchet fought a U.S. government program
that violated the tribal tradition of owning land
communally, which was continued after the Kiowas
settled on a reservation. Despite the vigorous opposition of Two Hatchet and other leaders, the government forced the division of the reservation into
small parcels, some of which were sold to whites.